To Lillie, Follow your Dreams, wherever they take you, Mandie x

CHASING THE ECLIP...

& OTHER AD...

Memories ...

By Mand...

"Wow, loving it so far… what an adventure, the descriptions are fantastic, I can almost imagine you there!"
   Laura McMaster, Hostel Manager, New Zealand.

"Really enjoyed reading about your exploits, and your self confessed failures with food, navigation, packing and so forth"
   Phil Suter, Director & Business Owner, UK

"A thoroughly entertaining laugh out loud delight as Mandie and her faithful Dinky Doo shimmy their way around the globe on the trail of the perfect spots for the eclipse. An essential companion to any newbie backpacker's travel guide'
   Pollyanna, Seasoned Traveller, UK

"Excellent book, really well written,
   Nicola Savidge, Poet, UK

"A very down to earth, and hilariously honest account of an Essex girl's adventures chasing the sun"
   Hellen Riebold, Author, UK

CHASING THE ECLIPSE & OTHER ADVENTURES
Memories of World Travels
By Mandie Adams

Dedicated to my family & friends,
my motivational guides,
Come wander with me through the changing moons,
and the turning of the tides....

Mandie

1st Edition 2021 Mandie Adams   All Rights Reserved.

Copyright: This is NOT a Public Domain Work, and I hold the necessary Publishing Rights. No part of this book may be reproduced or utilised in any form or by any means, electronic or mechanical, including photocopy, recording, or by any information storage and retrieval system, without permission in writing from the author.

Some photographs may be the copyrighted property of others; acknowledgement of those copyrights is hereby given.

Cover photo created by Darren Hopkins and Mandie Adams

ASIN: B097YZWX6T

ISBN: 9798526819930

Author Contact Details:
Email: chasingeclipses@gmail.com
Facebook Page: Eclipse Chasing & Adventures @eclipseadventurer
Instagram: chasingeclipses.adventurer
Twitter: Eclipse Chaser @eclipsemandie
Website: travellingtoeclipses.wordpress.com

CONTENTS:-

		Page
1.	INTRODUCTION	5
2.	PROLOGUE - THE START OF MY JOURNEY	8
3.	AFRICA 2001	12
4.	VENEZUELA 2005	34
5.	TURKEY 2006	63
6.	ARGENTINA & BRAZIL 2007	74
7.	MOUNT EVEREST BASE CAMP 2008	102
8.	CHINA 2009	130
9.	EASTER ISLAND 2010	158
10.	POLAND 2011	178
11.	AUSTRALIA 2012, VIA:-	187
	ISTANBUL 2012	190
	DUBAI 2012	194
	BANGKOK 2012	197
	MALAYSIA 2012	202
	AUSTRALIA 2012	208
	NEW ZEALAND 2013	239
	INDIA 2013	250
	AMSTERDAM 2013	272
THE END?		278
APPENDIX I & II		279

~ ~ ~

ACKNOWLEDGEMENTS

I am grateful to many people who have had input into this book, whether it be on a practical level, or the motivation to proceed and to actually get round to writing this book.

Thank you to those who kindly read through my ramblings, and help make sense of them. I subjected Dale Thomas (who gave me the kick up the arse to get this book written!) to this operation, and the established author Hellen Riebold who offered lots of practical advice, and insight into the book-writing process.

A big 'Thank You' too, to all those who agreed to keep their own names. I wanted to honour them in this book, but they too felt honoured to be in here, a win-win!

I must credit two main sources for the underpinnings of my hand-drawn maps - both Rudolph Woolf, Phillips Atlas and good old Google Maps which I used to reconstruct the routes I took. You may discover that your home town has been knocked off a coastline, or your country has changed shape - that is the beauty of my hand-drawn maps.

I am very grateful to my cousin Darren Hopkins, who surprised me every time with his technology skills, and must take credit for the cover and back photos of this book.

I will thank in advance, all you readers, I expect there to be many of you, and for you to pass on the word of what an inspiring eclipse chasing, travelling book you have read! I wish you all well on your journey, wherever that may take you.

~ ~ ~

INTRODUCTION

For several years now, after hearing about my misadventures travelling around the world to chase eclipses, my family and friends have been encouraging me to write a book, and here it is. I have finally sat down to relay my tales of bumbling my way around the world, getting lost, last-minute packing, complaining about the weight of my luggage and generally finding myself in all kinds of escapades!

People have often commented that I am courageous travelling on my own However, I have never felt like a solo traveller, mainly because I have met so many people, and I was always accompanied by my little teddy bear Dinky Doo (named after my first pet). Dinky Doo not only provided great company because he never argued about where we were going or what we were doing but was also very useful for when I wanted to block people out of my photos. Yes, strategically placing a paw or his head made it appear that every place I visited was devoid of people and that I was the only person there.

I did not expect when I started out travelling, meeting so many interesting and amicable people, many of whom turned out to be lifelong friends. I have contacted all relevant people to ask their consent for their name to be in this book. I wanted to honour them, and the times we shared so that we can look back and laugh together. All other names I have changed, or they are fictional.

I am often asked 'why eclipses?' and I hope this book will explain. But first, for those of you not so au fait with total solar eclipses (as I was not before I became addicted), here is a brief description of the workings of these phenomena. You will also find a list of eclipse terminology for easy reference at the bottom of this introduction. You can use this to refer to whilst reading through the book.

A total solar eclipse happens when all three planets, the sun, moon and earth, are directly aligned. This movement causes a circular shadow over our planet, and because the moon is much smaller than the earth, its shadow only covers a small part of the earth's surface - this is the path of totality, and is where you can see the darkest part of the shadow (it's umbra). Those people not in the path of totality are in areas covered by partial shade (its penumbra) and will witness a partial eclipse. First contact occurs when the moon starts to move onto the sun's disc. It will look like the moon is taking a bite out of the sun, and the sun takes on a crescent shape as the bite gets larger. This is the partial phase, and as the sun becomes smaller behind the moon, the sky slowly darkens. On average this phase lasts as hour to an hour and half. An eerie twilight descends as we move into 2nd Contact and the moon completely covers the sun. This can be confusing for animals and birds who may show unusual behaviours. Shadow bands may be visible just before totality, with shadows rushing in waves rapidly from horizon to horizon.

In the final moments before totality the 'Baily's Beads' appear. The Baily's Beads occur as the light shining through valleys on the moon's surface appear as beads on the periphery of the moon. They are followed by the "Diamond Ring Effect", where the final flash of light from the sun's surface portrays the outline of a diamond ring as it disappears from view. These can be seen as long as there is not cloud cover. Totality occurs for only a few minutes, where the moon-crossed sun appears as a black disc with a white circle around it (the Corona). Totality ends when the moon's movement begins to uncover the sun's surface. The diamond ring may appear again, before the eclipse proceeds through its final partial phase (3rd Contact) for approximately an hour. When the sun is once again wholly exposed, we have reached 4th Contact, as the moon has completely moved away from the sun.

It is perilous to look directly at the sun at any point leading up to, or after, absolute totality, and one should wear special solar glasses. The only time to view the eclipse with the naked eye is when the moon is fully covering the sun in totality. It is worth noting that sunglasses are not adequate protection. This is the end of your session on how to enjoy a total eclipse safely!

These memories of my world travels are written from the heart, and partly from my travel journals. That therefore is how they will read, not necessarily in a narrative format you may expect - well, I always like to be different! At the start of each relevant chapter, you will find brief information about where the total eclipse was due to appear, the date and time, length of totality, and where I chose to view it. Also, at the beginning of each chapter, there will be some fascinating facts about each country. At the end of each chapter there are overall trip costs (relative to that time); and you will find some insights should you be inspired to travel to these places, in the form of 'Top Tips". Who knows, you could be the next eclipse chaser by the end of this book!

~ ~ ~

Eclipse Terminology for Easy Reference

1st Contact - the moon begins its journey across the sun. Also referred to as the 'Partial Phase'.
2nd Contact - the moon is now covering the whole of the sun's disc, and is just before 'Totality'. The 'Total Phase' is when totality occurs, and the mid-point of that is maximum eclipse. Totality lasts a few minutes.
3rd Contact - the Sun begins to reappear as the moon slowly moves away, and we are back in a partial phase again.
4th Contact - this is the end of the eclipse, and end of the partial phase, the moon has completely left the face of the sun.
Baily's Beads - these occur a few seconds before totality during 2nd Contact. Little beads of sunlight shining through openings of chasms/valleys/mountains on the edge of the moon's surface.
Corona - a ring of the sun's rays on the periphery of the moon. Occurs at totality.
Diamond Ring effect - along with the light from the sun's corona, a sole glowing jewel adjoins it giving the visual effect of a diamond ring. This usually occurs appx 10-15 seconds before and after totality (but not always fully visible, e.g. if cloud cover).
Shadow Bands - ripples of light appear across Earth's ground/walls.

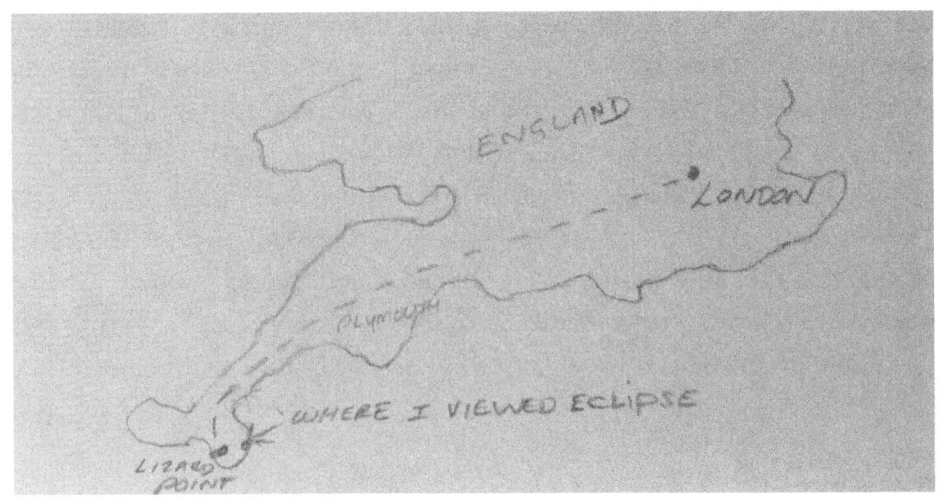

PROLOGUE

The Start of My Journey

My fascination with solar eclipses arose from the first eclipse I travelled to see here in the UK in 1999. I was drawn in by the beauty of the total solar eclipse, I was amazed by the phenomena of the various stages, and I wanted to learn more about this spectacular and rare event. I found myself affected by my feelings of awe during this eclipse and aware of the crowd's ecstatic reactions.
Although in my own country and a relatively quick jaunt, this trip still turned out to be a mini-adventure of its own. I had been on the overnight bus from London to Plymouth, and it was a long journey. To travel onwards to Lizard Rock, I needed to get a local bus, and so having found said bus, I bounded aboard. However, what I hadn't accounted for was my bladder! It was brimming, and I desperately needed to find a toilet. The journey to Lizard Point was not supposed to take very long, so I thought I could make it. Then we hit the droves of

traffic that were coming to a standstill, all heading out to view the eclipse.

By now, I was desperate, and thinking I was being clever, having spotted a bush lined lane opposite, I went to the driver blurting out my predicament. He agreed the best thing to do was to get off the bus, head down the lane, and relieve myself behind a bush. He helpfully suggested that if I could make it to the end of the road, I would find a car park with a small building that was a toilet block. I alighted the bus and headed down the lane.... but what I had not accounted for was the sheer amount of vehicles starting to use it too (had they followed me?) and the low height of the shrubbery. I vowed to try and make it to the car park at the end of the lane and then realised I had no idea where I was, whilst I watched my bus slowly drive away.

Nearing the end of the lane, I spotted a building, and although it did not look like a toilet block, there were quite a few water board vans there which I guessed were in the car park. I sprinted toward the building, only to be stopped by a guy I refer to as the Professor. I named him that since he was a University Lecturer, and it, therefore, seemed apt. The building turned out to be a private bungalow, so I was now trespassing, and the Professor was a guest at a party there. He explained that I would have been able to use their bathroom, except that they had no water, and that was why all the water company vans were there. He very kindly directed me to the toilet block, which I only just made, whilst he retreated to the bungalow.

Having settled myself on a hillside near the beach somewhere, which was, of course, nowhere near Lizard Point, I was surprised to see the Professor coming towards me from the opposite direction in which I had left him. Planting himself a short distance away on a cliffside, he waved over to me and judging by the look of anticipation on his face, I guessed it was his first eclipse too. Perhaps he also wanted that solitude for this unique experience.

The eclipse itself, in my memory, was spectacular. It was my first one and was kind of like a first love. I felt privileged to be at the first total eclipse in England since 1927 and the last solar eclipse of the century here. I did not know what to look for, I was a novice, and all I knew was that it would be daylight, then it would turn dark, and the moon would cross the sun.

At 09:57, first contact occurred, although I did not know that was the term for it at the time, and I could see a little nibble taken out of the sun by the moon. Gradually, over the next hour or so, the bite got more prominent. The disc of the sun was covered more and more by the moon, resulting in a smaller and smaller crescent shape of the sun. Clouds were wafting past intermittently, and the air was gradually cooling. Occasionally, they would drift in front of the partial eclipse, but nothing could dampen my spirit!

It was 11:11, and an eerie silence descended upon the crowds as the sun became fully covered by the moon - it was totality! I was so excited I could barely breathe. The sky had darkened, clouds parted, people were silhouetted, birds were flying to their nests to roost for the night, there were shades of orange above the sea in the distance just above the horizon. I took this all in silently, wanting to savour every moment. For a full 2 minutes and 23 seconds of totality, I was transfixed to the spot, absolutely lost in my world of thoughts. But then, as totality ended and the moon began to shy away from the sun, the silence was shattered by loud cheering and clapping. I joined in the applause and felt suddenly overwhelmed due to the sheer magnitude of what I had experienced, and so I shed my first total eclipse tear. I was captivated and wanted to see more!

The Professor approached me, and we exchanged excited insights into each of our experiences of the eclipse. We both agreed that we had been fortunate to see as much of the eclipse as we did, without cloud cover. Unlike many areas in Cornwall where the eclipse had been covered in cloud. For once, my bladder had done me a favour as I believe it was fate that day that made me need the toilet and leave the bus to inadvertently find a spot without cloud and subsequently see such a beautiful eclipse. To my surprise, a few weeks later, a brown envelope addressed to me arrived at my University, and inside was a photocopy of the total eclipse sent by the Professor. Yes, I decided I had some lovely memories of the eclipse and started to research when I would see the next one. Little did I know back then that this eclipse was going to help shape the future changes in my life. This would not come to light until thirteen years later when I began to follow my life plan of travelling more. Eclipse chasing had a definite influence on that, taking me to places I may well never have thought of visiting. But would any of these journeys lead me onto my spiritual path? Would the total eclipse have any impact on emotional and spiritual being?

I find it difficult to explain to friends and people I meet about travelling to eclipses when they ask - Why do I travel to see them? How do they work? What is so special about them? For me, all I can say is that every total solar eclipse I have seen has been unique in its own right, cloud or no cloud. Each set of travels have been individual experiences, tailor-made from the people I meet, the friends I make, the activities I undertake, and the sights I see. Through all the discoveries, mishaps and challenges, every single one of these trips has been an adventure!

~ ~ ~

Total Solar Eclipse, England 1999

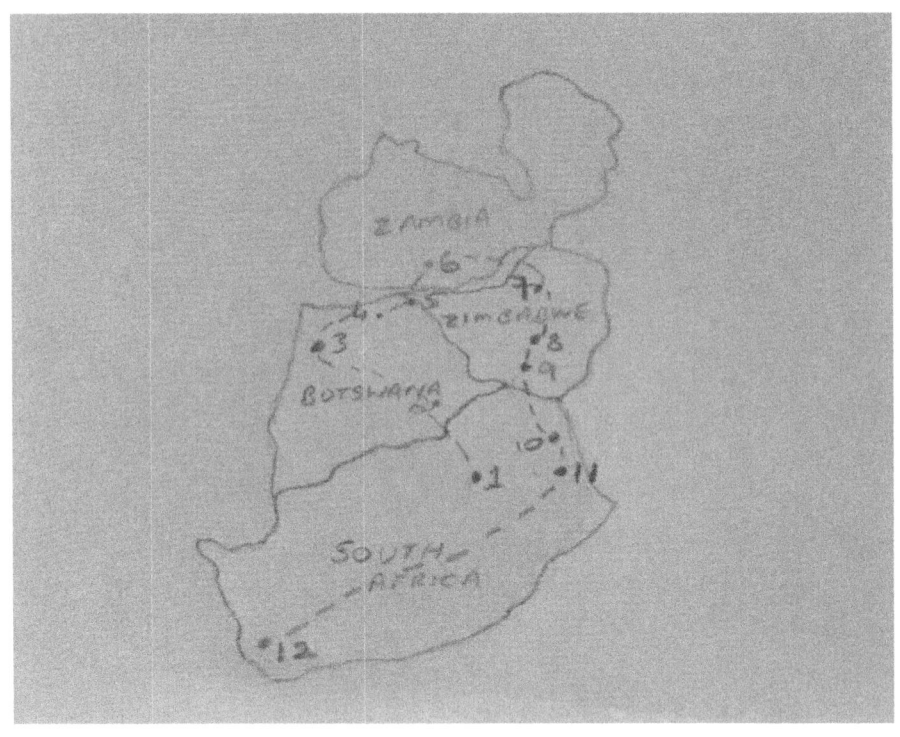

AFRICA ROUTE - 23 DAYS

1. SOUTH AFRICA - JOHANNESBURG
2. BOTSWANA - BUSHLAND
3. BOTSWANA - OKAVANGO DELTA
4. BOTSWANA - CHOBE NATIONAL PARK
5. ZIMBABWE - VICTORIA FALLS
6. ZAMBIA - VICTORIA FALLS
7. ZIMBABWE - LAKE KARIBA *TOTAL ECLIPSE*
8. ZIMBABWE - ANTELOPE PARK, GWERU
9. ZIMBABWE - MATAPO NATIONAL PARK
10. SOUTH AFRICA - KRUGER NATIONAL PARK
11. SOUTH AFRICA - GRASKOP
12. SOUTH AFRICA - CAPE TOWN

AFRICA 2001

It's Not Fair!

Eclipse path: Atlantic - Africa - Madagascar.
I viewed it at: Lake Kariba, Zimbabwe.
Date/Time of Maximum Totality: 21.06.2001 at 13:11 Local Time
Length of Totality: 4m 57secs.

AFRICA is the second largest continent, consisting of 54 countries, with 1500-2000 different languages. It is the source of the world's longest river, the Nile that is 4,258 miles; and has the largest hot desert, all 3.6 million square miles of the Sahara. Let's look at the countries I visited on this African trip.

Botswana - has the capital city of Gabarone, but nearly 40% of the country is made up of national parks and nature reserves, providing plenty of space for wildlife to roam. Just as well, as they have the world's largest concentration of African Elephants! Other world records include: the world's largest inland delta, the Okavango Delta, a wonder in itself, as who would expect so much water in the middle of a desert (the Kalahari); and the world's shortest border, a mere 150-metre strip of land touching Zambia.

The relatively large country of landlocked Zambia is the habitat of the Ansell Mole-Rat, a near-blind species, yet they can sense magnetic fields with their eyes. They live alongside a comparatively small human population in relation to the size of the country (about three times the size of the UK). Zambia is home to one of the world's seven natural wonders but cannot claim sole ownership of Victoria Falls (the world's largest curtain of falling water) and Lake Kariba, both of which are shared with Zimbabwe.

Zimbabwe is a multi-currency nation, as it abandoned its currency of the Zimbabwean Dollar and replaced it with the likes of the US dollar, Euro, and South African Rand. There are random power outages lasting

1 to 3 days, so check your change before the lights go out! Zimbabwe's capital city is Harare which is about five times the size of Liverpool, ironic really, as it is very likely that the locals will be supporting Liverpool FC, Chelsea, Manchester United or Arsenal football clubs. And who knew that men with large stomachs are considered wealthy? Apparently, it shows they can afford to eat meat each day. Perhaps that is why they prefer to support a football team rather than play themselves?

South Africa is unusual in that it has three capital cities, those being: Cape Town (Legislative),Pretoria (Administrative), and Bloemfontein (Judicial). You may well be aware that South Africa has been host to the 2010 Football, the 2003 Cricket and the 1995 Rugby World Cups, but it also hosts the world's largest bicycle race. The Cape Town Cycle Tour covers a 109 km distance over its south peninsular with 35,000 willing peddling participants.

This was my first trip abroad to see a total eclipse and my first trip to Africa. I hadn't researched or planned too much because I had opted for an adventure tour where all that work would be done for me, and I would see an eclipse en route. I just needed to rock up with my necessities and enough money to see me through. Was I well prepared? Aside from packing the usual useful items such as extra passport photos, sewing kit, padlocks for locker (e.g. in hostel dorm rooms), travel washing line, and a small but powerful pair of binoculars (essential on safari), I had packed a head-torch. I figured this would be a valuable multi-purpose item for camping, night toilet trips, and reading in my tent. I believed I was intrepid with such preparedness and useful items, ready for anything on my 3-week escapade with my faithful teddy bear Dinky Doo beside me.

I was off, and I could tell I was onto an adventure because no sooner had my two friends, June and Sarah, waved me off after check-in at Stansted Airport, I was on my way back. I had duly followed the directions I had been given and proceeded to the correct terminal, only to hear my name called over the loudspeaker system. At first, I was in disbelief, was that my name announced? This had never happened to me before in an airport. In mild panic, I went over to the nearest customer help desk. I was advised that my flight to Amsterdam had been delayed, and they had to do something with me because I had a connecting flight with their airline. That something involved the customer service representative rushing me back through Customs and Arrivals at Stansted and somehow locating my luggage on the way. We made a loop back to the check-in desk, where I was processed again and advised that I would have to run (with my luggage as it could not be transferred) through Amsterdam Schiphol airport. If you have ever visited this airport, you will have some clue as to the sheer vastness of it, but at the time, I had not had that pleasure and so was blissfully unaware of the marathon I had ahead.

Upon reaching Amsterdam airport, it soon became apparent that I would have to sprint, but which way? Whilst running, I enlisted the assistance of one of the staff, who very kindly and adeptly sped along with me (and had the bonus of carrying my backpack!). With their assistance, I made it onto my flight, but only by the skin of my teeth! I settled into my seat whilst the other passengers looked on at this crazy woman having palpitations and trying to get her breath back. I pretended not to notice and plugged in my music, drifting off into a pleasant little doze. All that action had tired me out, and I had only just started my trip.

Having had enough time on the flight to recover from my marathon, I reached Johannesburg, somewhat refreshed and full of the joys of spring. I waited for my luggage, and finally, my backpack came through - with no sleeping bag attached! This was not good as I had borrowed it, and so it wasn't mine to lose. I waited and waited, watching the same final few items of luggage revolving round and round until I could wait no more. There was a minibus waiting (hopefully) to transport me to my accommodation. Bewildered, I contacted a member of the airline staff and was given a claim form to buy a new one. I explained that it was needed urgently due to camping within two days and was assured all would be fine, and I would be refunded. This did little to ease my fear of telling my friend June that her sleeping bag was somewhere in the ether between Amsterdam and Africa.

One of the first people I met from my forthcoming tour was Christine, who became a lifelong friend. Christine very kindly offered to come with me to buy a new sleeping bag. She may have regretted that decision when, having only just left the hostel, we crossed a road and nearly got killed mowed down by the speeding traffic. Of all the ways to be killed on a journey in a renowned dangerous city (there was a reported abundance of robberies and muggings), being hit by a car was not one I envisaged. To be fair, though, it taught me that it is best to learn the direction of the traffic and look the right way. At least I managed to get a decent sleeping bag, and after this purchase, Christine and I made our way back safely to the hostel. No exciting sightseeing for us, just the essentials in life, like sleeping bag shopping.

I spent the evening in the garden under the dark starry night drinking the little bottle of bubbly I had brought with me from England, and eating cheese puffs. I was gazing at the stars when I heard a noise somewhere in the vicinity. I decided to call it an early night due to my early start on tour in the morning and the possibility of a wild animal lurking in the bushes. Where was Dinky Doo when I needed his protection? He was wise and was waiting back in the room. Safely back in my room and fumbling around in the dark, I managed to break my new alarm clock. I would be reliant on Christine now, and at that point, I was unaware of her ability to faff around unnecessarily even at unworldly hours of the day.

The following morning I met the rest of my tour compadres for the next couple of weeks; they hailed from various parts of the world, from Europe to America to Australia. With the addition of the two crew who had the joyous task of looking after us, Trixie and Matt, there was a total of thirteen of us (fourteen including Dinky Doo). We would be making our merry way across delta, field and rivers in Africa in the hope of seeing the total solar eclipse. Why would we all travel so far to see an eclipse? For some people viewing the total eclipse, it would be due to their deep interest in astronomy. For others, it would simply be the beauty of the eclipse through its various stages. I fell into the latter category, with the addition of enjoying the whole 3-week experience where I would meet new people in a country I had not visited before. For all of us, we visited the total eclipse in the knowledge that it was a rare event, and would be something we felt privileged to see.

The first day was a long day of travelling, as there was a fair old distance to travel. We happily spent that time getting to know each other in the truck, playing music and learning card games which varied in rules from country to country. Of course, there was time for enjoying the varying scenery too. We departed from a sprawling city metropolis out into rolling grasslands and tree-dotted plains. During our first day, we were introduced to the rota system and were put into small teams. Each team would be responsible for shopping, cooking meals and washing up on their allocated day. On the positive side, it made it fair so that everybody took their turn, and we all tended to help each other out anyway. On the downside, it meant getting up an hour early to start breakfast.

We crossed into Botswana Bushland and set up camp, and this first experience of staying in the bush was a real eye-opener for me. It was tranquil that evening, sitting around the campfire just as the sun was setting, laughing, chatting, exchanging stories from around the world - that was until I got my penny whistle out! Yes, I was determined to learn how to play a musical instrument, having never been that way inclined before. I believed this to be the perfect time and setting. Not sure how the others felt about it - even Dinky Doo held his paws to his ears!

~ ~ ~

The next day my team were on meal duty, meaning we had to get up at 05:00 to cook and prepare breakfast. I am the first to say that I am not a morning person, so my breakfast creations must have left a lot to be desired! It felt like it would be a long day, but having muddled our way through, we did then have plenty of time for relaxing on the truck due to the several hundred kilometres we were travelling to the Okavango

Delta. I could only hope that we didn't miss too much beautiful scenery while we had our eyes shut.

After stopping off briefly for supplies in Maun, we arrived at our campsite in the Okavango Delta late afternoon. We cooked burgers on a 'Braai' (meaning 'to grill') that evening, and the crew, deciding I was not safe cooking near an open flame, taught me how to make potato salad and coleslaw. I could see my culinary skills were going to improve by the end of this trip! It was another sociable night round the fire, and we spent our time chatting, laughing and joking. Our creative crew also started up a murder mystery game which was to take place over several nights. Would we solve the mystery and find out how, why and who the murderer was?

After all that excitement and a hard day's work of cooking, I slouched off to bed in preparation for another early start, waking up what seemed to be only a few hours later, at 06:00. We had an exciting day to look forward to as we would be making our way along the Okavango Delta. We floated along in dug-out canoes through the vast ecosystem of the Okavango Delta. The scenery was lush with bushy trees and green swamp grasses reflecting in the deep blue calm water. All was tranquil, a perfect time I thought to continue my penny whistle practice. This time I concentrated on 'Twinkle Twinkle Little Star' and was determined to get it right. That was until my beloved penny whistle was snatched from right under my nose!

I decided to turn my attention to the surrounding nature, using my new binoculars to spot hippopotamus and my first ever sighting of a woodpecker. It was just as well that I spotted something, as we did not get to see even one animal on the 3-hour bushwalk we subsequently went on that afternoon. It was a disappointed group that sat down to dinner that night around the campfire. However, we all cheered up when the singing and dancing began with our African guide and porters. We learnt their traditional cultural dance, whilst they also jigged around to our music- mostly the disco shuffle, where (primarily British people) step from side to side on the spot. To jazz it up a bit, we might throw in a clap or finger click or bob up and down; the great thing is that it fits most music beats.

It was a fun evening, but faced with an early start, I decided to head off to the tent just about an hour before midnight, after our next saga in the murder mystery had taken place. Once settled down, I suddenly remembered the rule about not having food in the tent due to the temptation for wild animals to want to come in and eat it. I realised I had cough sweets in my first aid kit and decided it would be good to put these into the metal chest outside containing our food that would be padlocked overnight.

I did not take a torch out with me for some bizarre reason and consequently fell over the metal trunk, which unbeknown to me had been moved near my tent. Due to the box size, it was not so much of a fall as a dive into mid-air, landing the other side of it, not far from those remaining around the campfire. It was pretty clear that all had witnessed my mishap; so aside from having two cut knees and scrapes down my legs, my pride was also damaged. I was further startled by our guide shouting out at me for not carrying my torch. There was no touch of sympathy or asking if I was alright. I hobbled off dejectedly back to my tent with a newly sore ankle. There was little sympathy either from my tent companion Christine who was still chuckling about it!

~ ~ ~

Our early morning bushwalk the following day, with an 05.30 start, was much more fruitful than the previous day. We were guided by Slug (that being our guide's nickname), who we were assured was an expert in his field. He was carrying on the family tradition and had been out guiding with his father since he was a little boy. So happy in the knowledge we were in safe hands, we wandered out into the remote Bush, trying to spot as many animals as possible. Our first reward was an excellent view of three giraffes; it was all the more remarkable because they were wild giraffes in their natural habitat. Things went downhill from there.

Slug got very excited when we spotted an elephant nearby amidst some trees. This elephant was initially oblivious to our presence while merrily munching away on leaves, so we were safe. That was until Slug made the rest of the group stay back behind some trees and picked me out to get closer to take some photographs. He explained to me that he did not have a camera and would like some close-up pictures. Slug had been monitoring our cameras, and mine apparently had the quietest zoom lens, so I was to walk very slowly with him towards the elephant. Apprehensively, I followed his instructions and edged forward with him towards the munching elephant, camera at the ready, zoom lens in position. However, the elephant spotted us and started to stride towards us from among the trees. I have no shame in admitting that fear took over me, and I wanted to run. I was somewhat surprised, though, to feel that Slug also had the same fear! This man who had tracking in his blood was following tradition and living his life in the remote bush of the Delta. How could this be?

These thoughts were distracting me from the real issue right in front of us, but I could still hear Slug repeatedly telling me not to run but to crouch and back off slowly. I followed instructions but was getting a pain in my left arm where Slug was digging his fingers in, gripping my arm like there was no tomorrow. That was how I knew he was not happy in this situation. It did not instil much confidence in me, but somehow we made it back to the group at what seemed a decade later, without the elephant.

As there were so many of us, it was decided we would all walk backwards very slowly so as not to gain any more attention from the elephant. Once we were at a safe distance, I got a lot of pampering from the group. They all said I had been courageous and sensible under the circumstances, but they then also found the look of sheer terror on my face amusing - I had looked like a scared rabbit in car headlights!

Needless to say, there were lots of elephant jokes around the campfire at lunchtime, and I was to continue to be the butt of all elephant jokes thereafter. It was a treat to get back into our Mokoros (dug-out canoes) and relax while floating along the Delta to our campsite (out came the penny whistle!). I left promising to send Slug the photos of our elephant encounter. How on earth they were going to reach him out in the remoteness of the Delta I did not know, but a promise is a promise.

That afternoon, we were treated to a scenic flight over the Okavango Delta. It was fantastic - not just to admire the incredible scenery but also to view the animals from a much safer distance. It was truly amazing to be able to see zebras, antelope and elephants in their groups running through the water and living their lives, ignoring us in the man-made machine hovering over them.

We finished the day off with a fun evening in the bar, carrying on our murder mystery and some of the group having a competition to climb the ceiling-high pole in the middle of the bar. Of course, our guide won; after all, she was there every few weeks to get practice. I found it much more fun and less energetic to watch - I would save my energy for the movement of my hand and arm getting my drink to my mouth!

Fortunately, for those of us who had overdone it in the drinking stakes that night, the following day was a day of driving due to the distance to cover to arrive at Chobe National Park. Therefore there was the opportunity to sleep off hangovers! Whilst the others napped, the driver put on my dance tape, and I was merrily singing and dancing, getting Dinky Doo out to 'Jump Around' (by House of Pain) with me. The long journey was also an opportunity to put the world to rights, and while the time away pondering the meaning of life while enjoying the passing scenery. We passed through vast desert plains and grasslands, sometimes on tracks rather than roads, which just added to the genuine feel of the remoteness we were traversing.

Due to the length of time on the truck, it also meant that I got to master the art of the toilet system; this involved ringing a bell to notify the driver to stop, taking the required amount of toilet paper, and finding a discreet spot. Needless to say, with my bladder system, our truck would make several toilet stops each day, and this newfound activity initiated my thrill at marking my territory out in the wild in various countries.

~ ~ ~

The following morning breakfast duty called again. I managed to churn out, along with my team, a few scrambled eggs, some bread, muesli, and cereals. After the torture was over for us all (including those eating breakfast), we drove off on the final stretch of our journey to Chobe National Park. I was interested to see how hardened their stomachs were to our breakfast offerings and just how many toilet stops would be required.

No sooner had we arrived at our destination than we were greeted by a hyena that ran right alongside our truck. It was a real treat for my first safari as we drove along, seeing impala, buffalo, elephants, baboons, fish eagles, and a bird protecting its eggs. A highpoint was stopping for coffee, where a couple of warthogs came up to be fussed and petted. Naturally, we all obliged.

After a rest at our camp for the night, we visited the local crocodile farm, where there were crocodiles of all shapes and sizes. I didn't mind the whole experience too much, as the crocodiles were in large enclosures, and were not made to perform for us. I was content until informed that the resident donkeys were chopped up as meat for the crocodiles to eat! Was this true or a cruel joke? It would be all the more brutal as I had just had my photo taken with Silver the donkey. I left the crocodile farm upset, wanting to ride off into the sunset with Silver to save his life! It took a while for the others to placate me that afternoon. However, my spirits rose at the prospect of our sunset cruise on the Chobe River. It was a beautiful sunset, with more viewings of elephants, hippos, kingfishers, and lizards, all topped off with a lovely buffet meal on board. We finished off the evening around the campfire for the final episode of murder mystery, with scintillating conversation and lots of laughs. We had genuinely bonded as a group, just as well the amount of time we spent cooped up in the truck. Who was the murderer? It turned out to be Christine; I would sleep with one eye open that night in the tent!

We headed out of Botswana and made our way into Zimbabwe. It was not too stressful at the border, I think, primarily because our guide and driver had the experience of crossing this border often, so we were smoothly guided. We headed to Victoria Falls, where we would stay for a few days to get our breath back and organise our optional trips. We were also given the option of a chalet upgrade instead of staying in tents; most of us decided to take that offer up. What luxury, a thatched roof over our heads, mosquito nets, and a bed, for just around a dollar more per night. It was also the last night of the trip for some of the group, and we went out for a meal together, saying our rather emotional goodbyes. However, it was out with the old and in with the new, as they say, when the next day, we welcomed our new members of the group, some of whom had come specifically to see the total solar eclipse.

We were now only a week away from seeing the total eclipse, and an issue reared its ugly head on our truck. Although the company knew this was what most of us had come to see, it was not advertised or priced as being a solar eclipse tour. Therefore the route could change. There was unrest brewing in Zimbabwe (as well as on our truck), so our course would have to be the safest possible. We were on tenterhooks as to whether we would get to see our solar eclipse.

Before moving on, we had one day of sightseeing, visiting one of the natural Seven Wonders of the World, Victoria Falls (known as 'Mosi-oa-Tunya' or 'The Smoke that Thunders'). We were warned to wear our raincoats as we were about to get incredibly wet, and they were not kidding. Out on the boardwalk, the spray coming from the Falls soaked us to the skin! Afterwards, we wandered up to the top of the Falls to the Zambezi River, where what surprised me most was that it was like a nice tranquil stream at the top of the falls, almost as if you could wade through it and meditate at the same time. Yet, once at the brink of the falls, it was a ravaging gushing rush of water that could easily take your life! Facing Victoria Falls is another sheer wall of basalt, and this contributes to the tremendous spray of water trapped between the cliffs and the series of gorges that thunders up into the air. The various lookout points dotted along the wooden walkway vouched for this effect, not only due to the spectacular views of the falls through the watery mist, but also the spray that had showered down upon us.

Once we were suitably dried off back at camp, a few of us visited the Victoria Hotel. It was very plush and conjured up images of the elite back in the day in their Victorian dress having afternoon tea and sitting in the armchairs smoking pipes. No, I would certainly not have been able to upgrade to this place to stay in, and, truth be told, I was happy enough with my thatched-roof hut rather than a tent.

~ ~ ~

It was a relief that we were not on breakfast duty the next day. However, it made no difference, as for some bizarre reason, it was still dark when I arose, indicating it was still early hours. Christine's alarm had buzzed loudly, and so I had got up, had a shower that turned out to be cold, dressed, brushed my teeth, and was ready for breakfast. I was getting some strange looks from the security guys who were lazing by the pool, so before re-entering my tent, I asked them the time; maybe I was a bit early for breakfast? I was very early for breakfast - it was only 01:30! I was cursing Christine and her clock. Amazingly having slept through it all, she found it very amusing five hours later when I informed her of what had happened.

Luckily I managed to get some more sleep on the truck on the return to Zimbabwe, where we were heading to Lake Kariba. It was not so lucky that we were headed to Lake Kariba as it turned out to be outside the eclipse totality path. The crew had been advised that it was dangerous to head to our original destination, the North East of Harare, in the safari areas and had felt it was unnecessary to tell us this. In my naivety, I believed them when they promised us a brilliant partial eclipse and did not see what other option I had other than to stay with the group.

We stopped off to buy some African-style waxed cloth, ate lunch, and located our campsite 'The Warthog'. Ironically, it was so named due to several pet warthogs living there. However, it was not them we were to be worried about; it would be the hyenas that stalked the camp at night, making it very dangerous to go to the toilet block. Not that my bladder would acknowledge this potential danger. Hence I did not get the deepest sleep whilst listening to the noises outside during the night and wondering if I could make it to the toilet hut! Thankfully, after the one night, we were taken down to our houseboat at Lake Kariba for the next two days and nights. Finally, we were close to the day of viewing the solar eclipse, hopefully. I had concerns about us being too far out from the central line of totality, which would mean we would only get to see a partial eclipse. Furthermore, the weather reports indicated there could well be cloud cover, leaving little chance for us of a clear eclipse.

However, that was the least of my worries in that immediate moment. There was a debate about whether there were crocodiles in the lake. Well, I was not going to take any chances. We were allowed to swim in the lake, but I took the safer route and swam in the large cage lowered into the water. That was until I saw all the others who were swimming next to the houseboat were safe. Their arms and legs were still intact - so being unusually brave, I jumped in to join them. I made sure many photos were taken, and I was straight back out again.

~ ~ ~

ECLIPSE DAY - 21ˢᵗ June 2001

Making sure all body parts were still intact after swimming the day before, I got ready for the main event of the trip - the total solar eclipse viewing. Of course, there was also the toga party for which we had bought our lovely African material. We looked a flamboyant lot with our togas, turbans, and fake hair extensions. We were excited, but sensibly ate a hearty lunch, as the party and eclipse viewing turned out to be a very raucous affair.

The start of the partial eclipse phase was around 11:43, leading to totality at 13:11 that would last for just under one minute. Yes, you read that right, under one minute, and I had travelled all that! If I had been in the totality path of the eclipse and not in an area where only a partial eclipse could be seen, I would have been treated to almost four minutes and a clear blue cloudless sky. Those fortunate enough to be in the right place of totality were treated to Jupiter in the sky, the crescent sun, and the diamond ring. I, like the rest of our group, had been deprived of them all!

Having drunk many alcoholic beverages, all I could see of totality was a clouded partial eclipse in a hazy sky. I could see the shape of a sun and a moon wound together in the distance. All was quiet, and I was talking to a monkey on the riverbank. I was sure that the monkey would talk back; after all, the eclipse is a special moment for all of us, and monkeys are known for being human-like and able to communicate with us, aren't they? Then the toga adorned group at the front of the boat gave out a cheer at the end of the totality period, and I rejoined them. I was crestfallen, but the monkey conversation and more alcohol numbed the pain. I still had the feeling that something mystical had occurred, and no matter what, it had still been worth venturing this far.

We watched over the next thirty minutes or so as the sun and moon untangled themselves from each other, drifting apart slowly but surely amongst the wafting clouds until the sun shone brightly on its own once more. We were going to make the most of what was left of it, and as a group we shared our thoughts, gazing out to the sky from our remote location. We spent the rest of the day partying on the houseboat in our togas, singing and dancing, with another highlight being a rare passing boat with some hunky men stopping off to chat. They had been enticed by the flashing of boobs at them (not mine I must add).

~ ~ ~

I learned a valuable lesson the next night - pay the extra dollar for upgraded accommodation when staying somewhere that you are warned becomes freezing at night. I will never know why Christine and I did not upgrade; after all, we had already experienced the comfort it had brought. We had reached our campsite at the Antelope Park near Gweru, a private conservation game reserve. We had eaten dinner and were sitting around the campfire, wanting to stay warm for as long as possible in the chill night air around us. We had all been chatting about our partial eclipse experience. Several others on the tour were not happy as they had specifically booked this tour with the total eclipse as the main event. I decided to put this one down to experience and not to get caught out again. Finally, around 23:00, Christine and I plucked up the courage to go to our shared tent. As was usual, we got into our nightwear (which this time consisted of our day clothes and extra layers), turned our torches off and snuggled into our cosy sleeping bags on opposite sides of the tent. By the morning, we were practically entwined in each others' arms due to the increasing coldness. It must have been survival instinct, as we tried to radiate off of each other's body heat.

The day did become warmer, and after a hearty breakfast all was well with the world. We trotted off on a horseback safari which I thoroughly loved, and I am sure I would have loved so much more had I been able to control the horse. It seemed to go a bit fast at times, bearing in mind this was probably only my second time on one ever. I managed to escape with only one cut arm and an enquiry as to whether I had a tetanus shot! None of that mattered as I had been up close and personal with several animals such as zebras and wildebeest, purely through being on the horse.

It transpired that the horseback safari was a more dangerous affair for me than the afternoon activity of walking with orphaned baby lions. We walked with two baby lion cubs called 'Cass' and 'Bandit'. We were provided with long sticks that we could use for walking. Only in extreme necessity should we use them to hold across the cub's mouth if either of them went to bite us. This turned out to be one of my most memorable experiences to date. We walked for a few miles with the cubs through fields and across streams and were given the opportunity to stroke them. I was a tad nervous about this but after seeing all the others still had their arms and hands intact, I gave it a go. With the perfect day behind us and a lovely dinner, you will not be surprised to learn that both Christine and I upgraded to a chalet that night!

The following day we visited the Chipangali Orphanage that looks after several species of animals including, cheetah, leopard, rhino, and hyenas. The orphanage is a haven for animals with little or no hope of living in the wild, including those rescued from illegal trades and owners. Our guide had just paid our entry fees for us, and we had assembled inside the entrance to receive our tickets and instructions when suddenly we heard a voice shouting out, "get out of the way, get out of the way". We turned to where the voice was coming from, and hurtling towards us at full speed along the path was a rhinoceros! Within that split second, most of the group had jumped into the hedgerow, except for me and one other. The rhino, wanting to be petted, had us both pinned up against a wall! Yet again, I was on the receiving end of the animal jokes that night around the campfire.

Our rhino experiences did not end there. The next day we went on a game drive and hike out into the Matobo National park. We met our guide there, and he duly walked us out into the Bush to track rhino. It was not too long before we spotted two wild rhinos, and the guide believed they might have spotted us. He explained that their poor eyesight meant they had a restricted field of vision. We were close, and they could smell us, something that prompted them to start walking towards us. Our guide told us all to walk backwards really slowly, and every so often, we would all have to crouch down (I had a distinct case of deja vu from the elephant saga at this point). It was fascinating because as we edged our way back for several hundred metres, the rhinos followed us, stopping when we crouched down and continuing as soon as we walked again. It was an unnerving yet surreal experience, as the rhinos seemed curious about us rather than wanting to attack.

The rhinos followed us back to our truck and stood watching us from just behind the vehicle as we all clambered in, but thankfully they didn't charge at it as we drove off! We laughed and joked about our experience as we walked up one of the Matapos Hills, and our guide tried to fathom out what had happened as he had never seen that before. According to him, the rhinos would usually have ignored us or would have charged at us; he had never seen them simply follow anyone. The subsequent beautiful views over green fields interspersed between the shades of granite and forested hills were wasted on us, and we were not as immersed in the San Paintings on the rock walls of the Nswatugi cave as we could have been. I suppose we were just glad the rhinos couldn't follow us up the 1,500 metres we climbed to the summit. I think it would have looked quite funny in our group photo with us all smiling at the camera, having reached our goal, and being photobombed from behind by two rhinos with devouring grins on their faces!

We were all tired that night, and so it was a quick beer around the campfire and back to our tents, ready for an early start in the morning and another long drive. We were about to leave Zimbabwe and head into South Africa. It turned out to be a relaxing day as we stopped off at a small town called Messina and had lunch there. I was particularly pleased as I purchased my favourite food - chips, and it was a significant portion at that! I was pretty much in heaven, and that was before we even arrived at our accommodation with hot springs. I spent at least two hours in the hot pool and did not want to get out, but my sleeping bag was calling me.

The next day we had a very successful safari through the Kruger National park. We spotted lions, zebras, rhinos, elephants, water buffalo, and a family of hyenas. We only needed to see a leopard to complete our sighting of the "big five". Later I was thrilled having spotted a leopard's bum as it sped off in the distance, thinking even just that might count. By the end of our day, we had also seen plenty of giraffes and even three distant cheetahs. The wild animal life meant we had the luxury of using toilets (for safety reasons) at various camps along the way, as opposed to our usual marking of territory in the wild.

After spending another safari day in Kruger but not seeing very much more animal life, we left our camp, making our way to a town called Graskop. It did not matter that we had not seen so many animals on the last day on safari, as we seemed to turn into a pack of animals ourselves in Graskop. This was because there was some money left over in the kitty that we had all chipped in to. Our guide Trixie suggested to us that we could use our money in a pub called the House of Beer. Well, we were not going to argue with that, and our subsequent animal like behaviour left a lot to be desired!

I recall little more from that night, other than a lot of mixing with the locals, drinking, and dancing (including on tables and the bar). I started to notice late in the night, or early morning, that all the single girls from our group were kissing men. But not me, I was too busy chatting and dancing with a young local guy named Rob. He could not believe I was 36 years old, mainly because I was, in his words 'jamming' just like him and his friends. Meanwhile, the music seemed to be on a loop with the same songs playing repeatedly; I still have flashbacks today when I hear the song 'Teenage Dirtbag'! Nobody cared, certainly not those snogging away to their heart's content. Rob and I just carried on dancing.

At some point, Rob offered to walk me back to our hotel, which I was ready to accept as I did not feel like my legs would make it (we had been upgraded from tent to hotel for the last night). However, Trixie, ever the killjoy, with some difficulty, rounded up our group and marched us down the road to our hotel. I was sharing a room with Christine, Kathy, and Gina, and eventually, after some excited chatter, we all drifted off to sleep. After about an hour, I awoke with a start, realising that I was the only single female who had not been kissed. That was it; I had to wake Christine because if I could not sleep, then she could not either and had to share my pain! She awoke to me repeating, "it's not fair, it's not fair, everyone got a kiss except me" Christine thought this hysterical and could not stop laughing. Eventually, as they had been woken too, Gina and Kathy walked me back to the pub to see if we could find Rob so I could have my kiss, and they could have their sleep. Alas, the pub was shut.

On our final day, we were taken back to Johannesburg, all with severe hangovers, and after saying our emotional goodbyes, I flew from there to Cape Town. I was to stay at the St. John's Waterfront Lodge for the next few days on my own, which was kind of bittersweet. I wanted some time to myself after travelling around as a group cooped up in the truck, let out every so often for sightseeing, toilet stops and copious amounts of drinking, but I did miss the new friends I had made too. I liked the mix of nationalities and the range of conversations we had, really putting the world to rights between us. We had shared a solar eclipse, it may have only been partial, but it was still a memorable experience for us all in its own right.

But onwards and upwards, literally, as the next day, I was making my way up to the top of Table Mountain by cable car. I felt this to be very brave, considering I don't even like to go in lifts, but it beat walking up there. Either way, there were some stunning views over Cape Town from the top of the mountain on such a lovely clear sunny day.

Continuing in tourist mode, I subsequently visited the Kirstenbosch Gardens. I strolled around amongst the grandeur of the manicured bushes, lawns, exotic trees, and bright flowers, vaguely aware that the path was going gently uphill. I had followed a track amongst the trees, with a flowing river and a slightly distant Table Mountain visible before me. The trail got steeper and rockier. I became unsteady on my feet and I stumbled over a small rock, falling to the ground. I rolled down into the trees, which thankfully barred my way into the river. I got to my feet, with one leg and one elbow grazed and cut, but worse than that, my pride was tarnished. Why on earth had I felt so embarrassed when there was nobody within the immediate vicinity? I had wandered off-piste, and it was only upon my return to my hostel that I was to learn after describing my track and the surroundings that I had been walking up Table Mountain!

I had an early start the next day as I was going on a day trip to Cape Point. Or was I? The day started well as we had a great fun guide and an enthusiastic driver who took us as far as the ferry for Seal Island. We bobbed around on the boat looking at seals laying on rocks, seals sleeping, and seals looking over at us with disdain. We returned to our minibus only to be told it was not in good enough condition to continue the journey. We would have to return to their base instead of going to Cape Point. I pointed out to the guide, this was a once in a lifetime trip, and I was disappointed that I might never get to see Cape Point. All was not lost though, as I got a full refund and we were taken to a pub for a free drink.

It was my final day in Cape Town and a day to make my last memories there; for me, this usually included photographs (back then, cameras with film were the norm). I wanted to visit Robben Island, famous for its former Maximum Security Prison. Most inmates had been black men incarcerated for Political Offences, including Nelson Mandela. He was imprisoned there from 1964 to 1982 for crimes of sabotage, treason, and violent tyranny. I was keen to learn more about this man, who was later to become President of South Africa.

The ferry to the island was initially cancelled due to stormy waters, and I began to despair, for my flight was that evening, and I could potentially miss the ferry or the flight. Thankfully, the ferry was able to depart when the waters had calmed down. I did not realise upon reaching the island that we were supposed to be on an organised minibus. I missed this as, to my despair, my camera was not working properly. Was it the battery, was it the film?

I went to the little shop nearby for help, but the shopkeeper shepherded me out knowing I should be on the minibus. Too late, it had gone! However, I might have struck gold because I got a lift to the first stop, the prison, by an off-duty guide who had been an inmate there. Hence I got lots of inside (pardon the pun!) information and a private ride. I wandered off again from the group and found a couple of penguins with their babies behind a large rock. I was disappointed when I remembered I had no camera to record this incredible spectacle. I enjoyed the rest of the tour around the prison and the island. One primary impression for me on that trip was the stunning view over to Cape Town.

I was mulling it all over on the ferry on the way back, which was a very choppy ride, and involved getting very wet. I had been noticed by the three teenage schoolgirls sitting on a bench opposite where it was drier. They held out their hands to me to help me over to them while the boat bobbed up and down, and we sat chatting for the rest of the journey.

But I was cutting it fine for getting my flight, so no time for long goodbyes. It was a swift trot from the waterfront to my hostel to collect my bags, jump into my airport transfer, and check-in. The guy behind the counter was accommodating. After recounting to him the tale of my lost sleeping bag on the outward journey, he wanted to make sure this sleeping bag was secure. To do this, he found a roll of wide brown tape and wound it around the stuff bag containing said sleeping bag. At the same time, he was taping his tie underneath it too! I did not like to seem impolite, so I did not say anything, but then my laughing was probably not the response he would have liked either. I had a cheery last memory of South Africa. I spent my long journey back to England reflecting on all the fun times I had, the friends I had met and made, and the first Solar eclipse I had seen abroad, albeit through a haze of cloud and alcohol! Okay, so I hadn't seen a total eclipse as I was too far away, and there was a lot of cloud cover; however, I was still only learning about eclipses. This experience would not deter me from venturing abroad again to see them, this was just the start of my quest.

~ ~ ~

Overall Trip Cost: £1800 (Flight £540, Tour £725 and £535 All Other Costs/Spending)
Top Tip: If it is your first solo trip and you do not feel confident to backpack/travel around on your own, try an adventure tour (usually slightly cheaper than touristy tours) for the first part of your journey. Then if you feel confident, leave enough time at the end of the tour that you are comfortable with to explore on your own, perhaps a few days, a week, two weeks, or even a month or more, depending on what you are comfortable with.

Zimbabwe, Horseback Safari

Zimbabwe/Zambia, Victoria Falls

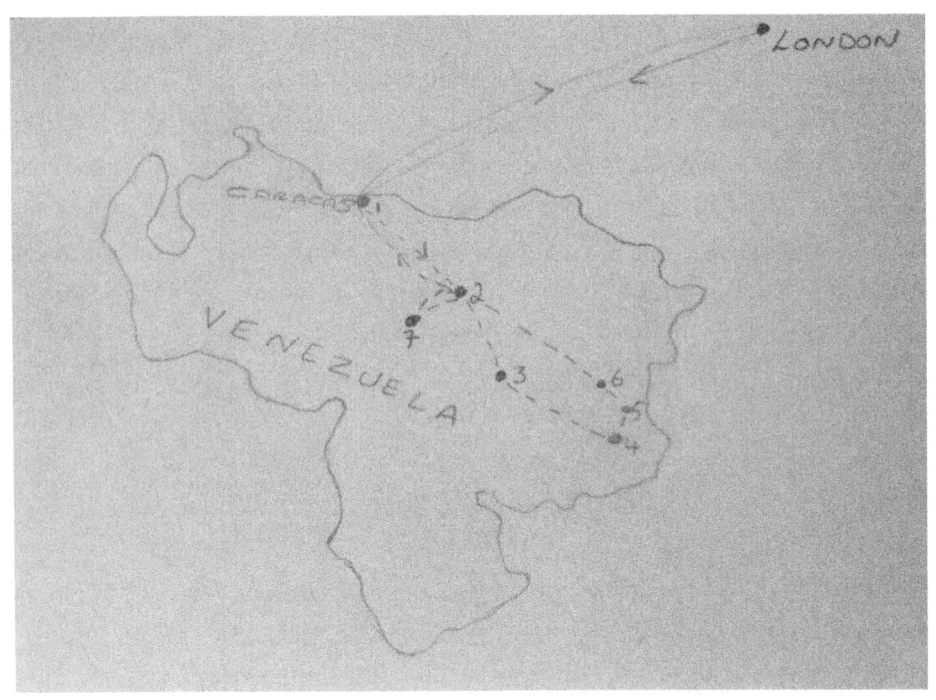

VENEZUELA ROUTE - 21 DAYS

1. CARACAS
2. CIUDAD BOLIVA
3. CANAIMA NATIONAL PARK
4. SANTA ELENA DE UAIREN
5. MOUNT RORAIMA
6. GRAN SABANA
7. RIO CAURA

VENEZUELA 2005

From the Lost World to the Lost Island

The Bolivarian Republic of Venezuela, more commonly referred to as Venezuela, is located in northern South America, with Spanish being the official language. A large portion of the population lives in the north of Venezuela near their capital city of Caracas. Venezuela is home to one of the world's largest national parks, the Canaima National Park. This incidentally is home to the world's largest waterfall, Angel Falls (over 3,000 ft high). It has only two weather seasons, hot and dry or hot and wet, explaining the mighty waterfalls. But, who would have known that baseball is the most popular sport to be both played and watched? Or there is a Christmas tradition involving roller skating to church with family, after which a big feast is eaten. Whilst heartedly munching, you would not be able to watch an episode from the tv show "The Simpsons", as it is considered inappropriate and banned from public viewing.

I was approaching my 40th birthday, and unlike those excited by this seeing it as "life begins at 40", I was traumatised by the thought of this impending birthday looming over me! I was with a sizeable group of colleagues in the pub one lunchtime One of them was celebrating her 40th birthday. She was one of those very thrilled by it, passionately harping on about all the things she was going to do! The next thing we all knew, I burst into tears, in public and in front of all my colleagues! And all they could get out of me in between my wails was that I did not want to be 40... So what was I going to do?

I decided I would go to the 'Lost World' of Mount Roraima, the inspiration of the 1912 novel by Sir Arthur Conan Doyle. I would follow in the footsteps of his character Professor Challenger, facing adventure in an exotic location where danger and crisis abound! Would

I follow the storyline, running the gauntlet between ancient prehistoric warring tribes and prehistoric creatures. I doubt that part of it, but would we discover any of the rare plants or creatures thought to be extinct as Challenger did? I had heard of the tiny black frog that lives only on the Lost World, would I see it? At that point, my naivety did not account for how akin to the story my journey would be up to Lost World.

I would fly to Venezuela and start my adventure in one of the most dangerous cities in the world, Caracas. Yes, surely that would take my mind off being 40? And better still, why take the easy route and book through a tour agency back home in England, known to me and local. No, I would book with a Venezuelan company, unknown to me; but they would know all the remote places and look after me. Boy, I didn't realise it then, but I was right, and some. Dinky Doo was safely packed, as were my usual useful items, my head torch, and washing powder. I would take a small amount enough to wash my smalls on the go and keep my backpack smelling fresh - I just hoped it would not be mistaken at customs for a certain kind of drug! I would content myself with another type of substance, and with a few red wines under my belt, the travels began. I was on my way to Caracas airport.

I had been warned not to take a taxi from the airport as there was every likelihood I would never be seen again. Once in the cab, I would be kidnapped and shot, and my valuables would disappear, as would I. The Venezuelan tour company thoughtfully sent a Representative to meet me based on my concerns. Once reaching the airport, it dawned on me, how would I know what he looked like, how would he recognise me, what if someone pretended to be from the tour company? And so it went on, until I reached Caracas airport and saw a tall, handsome young man holding my name up, now that was more like it.

After a day of chilling out and being pandered to by the tour company, I decided to brave it and go into Caracas city centre on my own. However, I was armed with advice from the tour company and other travellers to be careful and stay in the central area. I wandered around for a while, getting my bearings in the main square (Plaza Bolivar) and then decided to have a quick sit down on a bench. Sit down, yes, but quick it was not.

A mother decided to plop her little boy down next to me and walk off, leaving him there gazing at me! Next to me, the least maternal person I know, what would be the odds. I did not speak, I could not, he would not understand m. So I sat there and sat there whilst he swung his legs backwards and forwards and looked over at me now and again. I pretended I couldn't see him. This went on for nearly an hour until I could bear it no more. I tried to speak to a couple of passers-by, but they couldn't understand me. Eventually, I walked over to a Museum Attendant and explained the situation. He found it quite amusing but decided he would have to take me seriously and went to look for the mother. He duly found her nearby, and there was a lot of shouting and gesticulating. At that point, I decided I should disappear in case the attention turned to me. Incidentally, the little boy remained unfazed by the commotion and seemed quite disappointed at my doing a runner.

I took a stroll around the Plaza Bolivar, filled with fountains, children drinking lemonade and feeding black squirrels. There were African tulip trees and groups of friends engaging in conversation and laughter, all watched over by the central statue of Simon Bolivar. Born in 1783, Bolivar became known as 'El Libertador' (The Liberator) due to leading many revolutions against the Spanish, most of which he won on behalf of several countries, including Venezuela. Bolivar's dying wish in 1830 was to have his whole archive of life writings destroyed, his wish was disobeyed, and his famous writings survive to this day.

I crossed through the Plaza to the Cathedral located on the eastern side of Bolivar Square. It had begun life as a mud-walled chapel in the mid-16th century. Over time it evolved into a church and then into the Cathedral it is today, a long way away from its original mud wall concept. Now packed with stunning gilded altars with ornate side chapels. Pleased with my find, I moved onto the smaller but no less elaborate, Museo Sacro de Caracas, a stunning colonial building. It was a former prison but now holds the remains of early church leaders lying in sealed niches and a collection of religious art.

On the southern side of the plaza stands the City Hall 'Palacio Municipal. This stunning and impressive building was declared a

National Historic Landmark in 1979. It was initially built in 1696 to house the Colegio Seminario de Santa Rosa de Lima. It was subsequently turned into the Real y Pontificia Universidad de Caracas in 1725. It was renamed Universidad Central de Venezuela by Simon Bolivar, and although having retained that name, it is now used to seat the Municipal Council with some areas open to the public. I took advantage of those parts that can be viewed - including the Museo Santana on the ground floor housing a miniature version of the city of Caracas. Dinky Doo, who would have fitted nicely into the little city, seemed nonplussed, but I was enjoying the culture.

There was much more to see, and after viewing more colonial buildings from outside, it was time to return to my accommodation. I hoped my research in getting my bearings had paid off so I would be headed in the right direction home. I was not going to be aided by the craziness of the street signage, which had some kind of weird system of its own. It could have been one of those 'all roads lead to nowhere' situations where I ended up right back where I started! To be fair, though, the metro system itself was clean, easy to use, and so it was I found my home.

After my full day of sightseeing, I had just enough time to ready myself for the next part of my journey. I was going off on a deluxe overnight bus taking me to the city of Ciudad Bolivar, the capital city of Venezuela's southeastern Bolivar State. It initially seemed pleasant on the overnight bus; I could lay my seat right back and relax - and then the air con came on! At that point, I had my first lesson on how cold it could be on a coach. Why had I not taken notice of the other passengers so knowingly clutching jackets and blankets? Note to self: always take a sleeping bag onboard transport with me in future.

~ ~ ~

After a reasonably good nights sleep, I arrived in Ciudad Bolivar at about 09:00. A lovely porter, a bus driver friend, helped me with my luggage and telephoned my accommodation to confirm I had arrived. He also kept me company until Cedric, the tour company manager, appeared to escort me to the hostel. My porter would accept no money for his help and gave me a big hug goodbye. Cedric was a friendly chap also, chatting with me as we were driving along. All was well until the car broke down at the side of the road. Cedric tried his best to restart it, but nothing. Luckily, or not so luckily, a jeep pulled up. It turned out to be a neighbour, quite random, as we had left the built-up areas and were heading into the fields. I hesitantly got into the jeep, not because I was going out into the wilds with a toothless stranger, but because the jeep in no shape or form could say it had passed its MOT. Was it that, or was it more to do with the bullet holes in the window? Who knows, but I got in anyway, and we trundled off across the dirt tracks.

Upon my eventual arrival at the Posada La Casita hostel, I was promptly told they were full. How could this be? I had been booked through the tour company, and the porter at the bus station had called to advise them I had arrived. I was given options, now that's more like it. Option 1) Sleep in a hammock; Option 2) Occupy a bunk bed in an open hut; Option 3) Go to a hotel in town. Well, I didn't fancy being in an open hut as there could be all kinds of animals out there in the wild, and I might get cold in the night. Having travelled all night and all morning, I didn't fancy the thought of more traipsing about back into town. So the hammock it was. This hammock became one of the first of many, to the point where I considered hanging one up in my bedroom at home and disposing of my comfortable double bed!

I had a lovely afternoon relaxing by the pool and spent the evening being sociable with the other guests, three of whom were going to be on my Lost World tour. One was an adorable Japanese girl called Maiko, who, lovely as she was, posed some competition in the drinking stakes. The other two were, a couple from Spain called Michael and Marina (who turned out to be competition in the fitness stakes on the trek!).

~ ~ ~

The next day, we hit the road, well actually, the air. I hadn't realised it was small six-seater planes that would take us to Canaima. No fear of flying for me. I was going to make sure I got a seat with good views! During the flight, we passed over a vast metal ore mining area, where metal is mined from an Asteroid that hit Venezuela millions of years ago. We were also shown the Guri Impounding Dam, from which 60% of the whole energy of the country originates.

Once we landed in Canaima National Park, we were taken by boat via the Caniama Laguna to our indigenous camp. The Canaima National Park is 30,000km squared (approximately the size of Belgium) and is a UNESCO Heritage site. No wonder, too, with stunning waterfalls, grassy savannahs, and dramatic tepuis (flat tabletop mountains), it was no surprise that this stunning landscape would hold such a prestigious title. Luckily, for me but not for them, I was placed into a group with two Spanish guys. They promptly became my guinea pigs for testing out the Spanish I had attempted to learn. How long would they last? There was no escape for them; we would be in dugout canoes for three days, so they were my captive audience, and had nowhere to run or hide. Shame I had not taken my penny whistle!

Day one, and we were already boating out into the wilderness of the National Park. We would be travelling along the Carrao River to the El Sapo (Frog), and the smaller El Sapito (Toad) Falls. I managed to bagsy a seat at the back of the boat with the German girl Monika, which turned out to be the most comfortable because we got to use all the bags as cushions! The only thing missing was my two Spanish friends who had managed to manoeuvre, whilst I wasn't looking, to the front of the boat. Never mind, I could practice my German on Monika instead. The only problem being that my most fluent German occurs after a good few drinks when suddenly I become a native speaker. But all was well with the world as we set off downstream through the lagoon and along the Carrao River, arriving at El Sapo Falls first. Whilst a curtain of water thunders down, you can look across the Carrao river to three more Tepuis. All set in green prairies, you can view the Zamuro (vulture), Venado (deer) and Cerbatana (blowpipe) tepuis. El Sapito being a smaller set of waterfalls, but nonetheless magnificent due to the red tinge in the water, was on the same hiking loop as El Sapo. Here we were treated with the opportunity to take a refreshing swim around. Better still, at El Sapo Falls, not only could you hike the trail to look over the top of the Falls, but you could walk behind the veil of Falls. I liked this; I wanted to get a photo.... yes, I got it. However, now I am somehow on my bottom, on a wet ledge, just a few feet away from where the water was plummeting into the river. Was I more aware of the fact that I had fallen embarrassingly on my arse in front of the group, or was I more concerned at what could have been my fate a few feet away? Not sure which was worse, but I had learned a lesson, at the first of what was going to be many waterfalls visited during my trip in Venezuela.

After all that excitement, it was time to head back through the lush landscape in our dugout canoe. In light of the early start in the morning for tour day two, I snuck off to my hammock to get at least some rest. Not being a morning person, the 05:30 alarm call did not go down well with me! Still, it was exciting as this was the tour's highlight, a river trip to Angel Falls. I couldn't eat much at that unforsaken hour, but breakfast was served, and then we were divvied up into our canoe groups again. The scenery was once again superb as we drifted along the colourful Rio Carrao leisurely for seven hours through the virgin rainforest and rich savannah. Monika and I lazed against the backpacks at the back of the boat, taking it all in. This was bliss.

Little did I know that upon arrival at Mayupa Pier, there would be no time for food, now I wished I had eaten breakfast. But no, it was straight off on a 45-minute hike where we traversed through the savannah. This was followed by a boat trip along the river Churun to the Island of the Mouse. Subsequently, we had a 90-minute walk through the jungle to El Mirador. But it was so worth it because here we got our first panoramic views of the spectacular Angel Falls, the highest waterfalls on earth. The water leapt from the top of a Tepuis, plunging down its sheer rock face. After taking our snaps, we were taken around to the base of the falls and got to splash around in Lover's Pool. Typical, that yet again I was single!

Day three, and it was back to the boat taking us on our return journey to the indigenous village and the Canaima Laguna. Why on earth we had to get up at 05:00 to start this trek, I do not know. But at least it was relaxing. That was until we had to alight the boat for a 45-minute hike because of the strength of the rapids (or did they just want us off the canoe for a while!). Either way, we went past stunning scenery during our walk, and so all was well with the world again.

My positivity and sleepiness must have paid off. Reaching the airport for the return to Ciudad Bolivar, whilst slouching against some bags and plants, I was picked out by one of the Captains to go on one of the small six-seater planes. This would take us back over the Angel Falls instead of the usual straight flight back; what a result! This would typically cost extra, but they needed my weight in the plane to even it up. It wasn't long into the flight, and after the 'oohing' and 'aahing' above the falls, I came back down to earth (or could have done). We were flying through blinding white puffy clouds, and this was my first experience of being so close to them. Should I protect my eyes from this snowy whiteness? I was sitting in the front seat next to the pilot; he would know what to do, I would follow his example. I looked across to him.... his eyes were shut. He was having a snooze! None of the others were aware as they could not see from behind with the white glaring at us. What could I do? I had to save our lives. All I could think to do was to start exclaiming loudly with the oohs and aahs again, pointing out as if I had seen some spectacular landscape below. It worked. He woke up and carried on driving.

It was such a pleasant relief to see Cedric's smiling face greeting us as we landed at Ciudad Bolivar. He took us back to the Posada, where we chilled out for a while, and then it was time for me to prepare for my next de luxe bus trip. This time my sleeping bag was going inside the bus with me, and as there was not enough room for it in my day pack, I stuffed it into my old faithful Lidls carrier bag. This was it. I was heading towards the primary purpose of my trip to Venezuela - Mount Roraima, Sir Arthur Conan Doyles 'Lost World', and I was still only 39 years old.

At the bus station, I talked with an Austrian guy. He turned out to be one of only two English speaking people on the overnight bus to Santa Elena. The bus arrived at 19:00, and, like everybody else, I threw my luggage underneath in the lockers. The driver crammed it all in like there was no tomorrow until you would think that no more could fit in - but magically, it did. In addition to our luggage, the driver managed to pack in at least a years worth of crated medical supplies into the lockers. We all herded onto the bus, staking our claim to a seat and settling into it, ready for the long journey ahead. The layers of clothing and hats and gloves were gradually being put on as the air con started to work its magic, turning the bus into a moving fridge. It was almost a relief to get out into the heat of the night air at the first checkpoint. It was not so much relief having to get every single object out of my bag at some unworldly hour to show the guards. But after that trauma, I returned to my seat and promptly fell into a deep sleep.

It was some hours later that I felt a weird sensation. As I was still half asleep, I couldn't reason as to what it could be, but it felt like the bus was going backwards. Then there was a jolt. Worse still, hysteria broke out in Spanish. I couldn't understand what was happening. People from the back of the bus started screaming, crying and running to the front of the bus. I couldn't help noticing, although I thought I was dreaming, that they were running upwards. Two or three of them grabbed at me, yelling at me in Spanish, and I realised they were trying to tell me to get out of the bus.

Two thoughts went through my head: I know you are told not to do it, you shouldn't spend time collecting bags, but there was no way I was leaving my day pack on the bus (it had documents and valuables in it), so my bag was going with Dinky Doo and me. Secondly, whatever was happening, if this was it, then I wouldn't be able to say goodbye to my family and friends. I huddled with the others trying to get to the front of the bus, where the driver sat in a zombie-like state (although I take my hat off to him, as he did not desert his vehicle). We jumped off several feet down to the ground, as the front of the bus happened to be pointing up into the air!

Outside of the bus, it became clear what had happened. The bus had been laden too heavy and had rolled backwards down this steep mountain and over the edge. It had gone through the crash barrier and into the trees (it was the trees that had saved our lives). The scene reminded me very much of the film 'The Italian Job' with the bus hanging over the mountain's edge. A Spanish girl came over to see if I was okay; she was the only other person who spoke English. It turns out she was from Spain (as opposed to being a native Venezuelan). Her name was Isabella, and she too was going on the trek up Mount Roraima. How random was that?

There was one young soldier on board, and I did feel for him because it became his duty to round us all up (all 52 people) and march us all up the hill around the bend into a parking area out of danger. It was dark, and there would be the occasional vehicles veering in either direction. Well, I thought we were out of harm's way until I asked him if Isabella and I could go to the toilet in the bushes. Yes, I can be discreet, but also, I like to mark my territory. He replied that we could not go into the bushes as there were, amongst other animals, snakes out there. So it was with some embarrassment that Isabella and I walked about a hundred feet uphill and squatted down, really not that far from the remaining bus passengers!

Sometime later, whilst I was standing with the Austrian guy and Isabella, a Spanish lady approached me holding out a gift. It was my sleeping bag which I had left on the bus, in my good old faithful Lidls carrier bag. This was one of those moments that made me laugh but also bought a tear to my eye because this kind lady had bought a little piece of England to me amid all this chaos. The Austrian guy and Isabella watched, bemused. It struck me that I almost hadn't made it to my 40th birthday, and yet I had come away to escape it. What would be the odds!

Women and children were being loaded into any spare seats on passing buses and trucks, which were not that frequent. So it was a few hours later, in the early morning, that Isabella and I were bundled onto the third unsuspecting bus that trundled up the mountain. I had my reservations about getting on another bus, but what was the other option, wasting away at the roadside until dawn or hiking hundreds of kilometres to my destination. That was not a viable option; off on the bus I went.

I was met at Santa Elena de Uairen by a pleasant German guy called Hanz from our tour company. He had already heard about our bus plight on the National news! He, therefore, also knew we would be late and would not have our trekking gear with us. What we did not know at that point was that our trekking gear in our backpacks that had been stored in the bus lockers, was not going to turn up before we set off. For some strange reason, I had separated the only two credit cards I possessed, from my cash (which I was carrying on me) and had hidden them away in my backpack. I was left with minimal funds on me. I, therefore, spent the afternoon buying a few essential clothes and necessary items for the trek, and Hanz kindly loaned the rest to me (a tent, equipment etc.). Amazingly, I had my sleeping bag; the coldness of my first air-con bus had done me a favour after all.

The following day, twelve happy campers (13 with Dinky Doo) set off from Santa Elena in a jeep to a small village near the base of Mount Roraima to meet our porters. The age-old debate about using other people for carrying our heavy gear was raised, but it was validly pointed out by our guide that having them would assist with our safety. In addition, the tour company paid for this assistance to support the local economy and people. I was more concerned that we may end up stranded on the mountain plateau as in the book of the Lost World, although I doubted we would be attacked by dinosaurs. Would our intrepid team reach the summit and then emerge back into civilisation unscathed?

We took our first sprightly steps into the unknown after getting ourselves sorted out with bags, cameras, food, water, etc. Me, with my first ever pedometer proudly attached to my belt. We started at the trailhead of the Paratepui and took the time, as we began to meander through the foothills of the Gran Sabana, to get to know each other. Our motley crew consisted of those I had already met - Isabella, Maiko, Marina and Michael. The newbies were: Greta from Braunschweig,

Germany (a place close to my heart that I had visited many times), Tim from Denmark; Lucie from Croatia; Carolyn from Germany (who I think was an Olympic athlete in her bid to get to the top first!); Leah and Jose from Ibiza; Monty from California; and me! All led by our very experienced, friendly and informative local guide Benito.

A few hours later, we took a break for lunch. It had not been too hard going so far; I recalled only one steep part, which seemed all the more relentless in the 36-degree heat. No, so far, the hike had been like a walk in the park, and so we continued until we reached our base camp for the evening at Rio Tek. Little did I know that evening, whilst we relaxed around the campfire eating, drinking, chatting, how challenging the hike was about to become in the next few days. I clearly hadn't thought this through. I would be climbing a mountain, for goodness sake. What part of that did I not understand? In fairness to me, I had never climbed a mountain before and so was oblivious to the amount of effort required. This naivety and ignorance would save me (I believe) in several incidents further into this trip and many more trips to come.

The next day I set off on my meander through the park, through the meadows with buttercups and soft grass underfoot... then I woke up! Hiking yes, meandering no! The pace was set, and we marched off, over valley and hill and stream, until we came to what looked like an innocent bubbling stream- which wasn't! It was a river where I could be facing my second near-death experience, and I still had not reached the age of 40. Our guide Benito had called us together and explained that there was only one local man in his small canoe to help us across this river. He would have to make several crossings to take all our luggage. Although women were given the option of taking a turn in the canoe, as many people as possible were encouraged to swim across the river. Now, although I am by no means a strong swimmer (I can manage to get a few laps around my bath, but that's about it), I didn't think it could be that hard and wanted to save the canoe man another trip.

So I watched as most of the women were taken across in the boat except the Olympic athlete Carolyn. She swam across, making it look easy enough to attempt. I plunged into the water confidently, flapping frantically away until it suddenly dawned on me that I wasn't going in a straight line over towards the rest of the group who were waving and calling to me. No, I was being swept away by the strong, very strong, current downriver! What was I to do? I didn't know what to do except try not to panic. What saved my life that day was the look of sheer fear on Benito's face, he was just about to leap in to save me. I saw that look and knew I was in deep trouble. In fact, I still recall to this day the thought going through my head 'shit, this is it'. I didn't want to drown, so I took what must have been my last ounce of energy and lunged through the water to a big rock.

I clung onto that rock as if my life depended on it (well, it did, really) until I managed to get enough breath back to edge towards the others at the side of the river. When I reached them, everyone cheered and clapped. They threw a blanket around me as I was trembling all over and gave me sweets. Indulging in this pampering, I thought, 'at least while I am sitting here, I don't have to be hiking elsewhere'. Jose approached me, not to make a fuss of me like the others, it turned out, but to proudly announce that he had captured the whole event on video! I didn't know whether to laugh or shout at him. Of course, I chose to laugh; I would have to if the whole trip was going to be like this. I still hadn't reached the age of 40, and at this rate, there was every chance I wouldn't! The rest of the day, although it was a challenging uphill hike, was nothing compared to crossing that river, and I used my music on my mp3 player to keep me motivated. That was amid conversations with those making a fuss of me and the swapping of life histories. Yes, it only takes one hike to get to know each other intimately and come away with stories you could use for blackmailing purposes if you so wished!

The following day we left our second base camp and set off on what was to be the most challenging part of our journey yet. Naturally, it was here my pedometer broke, and a couple of men decided at our pit stop to fix it. They tried bringing it back to life by taking it apart and putting it back together. Unsurprisingly, it would not work again. I kept my own pace, as did others, as we continued upwards, practically vertically.

There were a few streams, various types of terrain, which mainly consisted of rock. These were sometimes rocks that were slipping underneath your feet, and so you took one step up and fell back three. We had a waterfall pointed out to us. Perhaps I should have listened more intently to the potential dangers, or was I lucky my naivety came into play? Either way, when I reached the waterfall, I had to manoeuvre behind it along the ledge. I found myself clinging on for dear life to the rock wall and trying to push my way through against cascades of a waterfall! A few minutes later, out the other side, I was soaking wet (as was my backpack). I looked back, seeing the sheer force of it and wondered how I had got through it, only to see a few of the men also struggling their way through, clutching on for dear life while edging sideways.

On the last stretch, I scrambled up the sliding rocks beneath my feet until I realised I had made it to the top. Not only that, but I was the fourth one out of the twelve of us to do so! I was greeted by Carolyn (who had made it first, of course) and Michael and marina. I was rewarded by holding one of the little black frogs in my hand that are native to and can only be found on Mount Roraima. Life was good- I had made it to the Lost World! We waited until the guide and rest of the group arrived and then set off across the eerie landscape of Mount Roraima towards our camp for the night. The landscape was not so much a landscape as what I imagined a moonscape to look like. I guess the easiest way to describe it would be as a large grey/black flat rocks of varying sizes and formations set in a blanket of mist. We found our camp and scrambled for the least rainy places to pitch our tents.

The following morning the girls appeared outside my tent to sing Happy Birthday to me. I promptly surprised them all by bursting into tears. Not long after, the guide appeared, bringing a flower as a gift to cheer me up. I liked the flower and decided I would keep it by me at all times. I spent the rest of the day exploring with the others and attempting to overcome the trauma of reaching the age of 40! I soon cheered up late morning when we were taken for a walk around the tabletop mountain. It was a strange otherworldly yet beautiful place, and we were in for a special treat when we reached the 'Jaccuzis'. These were one of nature's wonders, a series of natural shallow pools where we could float around to our heart's content. It seemed a nice enough way to spend a birthday, even if it was a 40th. Even Dinky Doo indulged in a dip in the pools.

Benito had to drag us away to take us to the Valley of Crystals, but we were amazed at the sight before us once there. In the heart of the plateau, here was this valley containing white or transparent quartz crystals in varying shapes and sizes of stone. We walked amongst the crystals whilst being warned that no taking of souvenirs was allowed. There would be three reasons not to: firstly, it would be morally wrong; secondly, it would be bad luck according to Indian beliefs, and you could be injured on your descent of this Tepuis; and thirdly, there would be a penalty if caught with a crystal with the threat of Venezuelan jail as a final deterrent. I think it is safe to say we left with just our memories of the crystals.

At dinner that evening around the campfire, the group all sang Happy Birthday to me in their native languages - German, Danish, Spanish, Japanese, etc. It was one of those birthday moments you do not forget and was followed by a kind of makeshift birthday cake (all the more delicious because of the thought that had been put into it). That evening was also the first time I had been on top of a mountain, seeing the moon and sun out together, in different directions, but both visible.

The next day, it was sadly time to leave the top of the Lost World. We packed up and set off after devouring breakfast and taking our last mountain top view down to the savannah. Of course, we all knew what was coming in terms of terrain! And, of course, there was the waterfall to look forward to. As it turned out, due to the lack of rain, the waterfall had dried out somewhat, so it was a lot easier on the return.

Well, the hike down would have been more leisurely if it had not been for poor old Greta, who got seriously ill with diarrhoea. Greta was very weak and could hardly walk, and of course, needed to go to the toilet quite often. The decision was made that the porters and the rest of the group would go ahead to base camp to not slow down the whole group (it would not be safe), and the guide and I would stay with Greta. She was not eating and was barely drinking enough water, and at one point, she laid down on the ground and told us to go on ahead and leave her there.

The guide was needed, not only as it was his duty, but for his first aid skills, and knowledge of return route etc., all of which I did not have. But what I did have, to make up for that lack of skills, was encouragement for her to try and keep going. And so it was, all the way back down, for hours and hours, I was singing and telling stories, just to keep her motivated to make it back down. It worked, not maybe for the reasons I thought, but perhaps because she just couldn't stand any more of my voice!

It was dark as we started towards the home stretch, and only Benito had a torch; it was getting a bit spooky. Then suddenly, we saw the glow of half a dozen torches; thankfully, some of the men and porters had come to find us as they were getting worried. The guide subsequently informed me that he had never been back that late in all his years of guiding. I felt the need for a nice cold beer, no dinner, just a beer and then bed; I was exhausted. Greta had made it back to base and thanked me for saving her life (but not for my singing!).

It was our final day trekking back to the base, and Greta was feeling slightly better. The terrain was a lot easier through the foothills, and so our hike passed without event. That was until we got to the security post at the exit. Everyone had bags searched in case of theft of Roraima crystals; these had been illegally mined in the past. I sat innocently waiting in the jeep with the others when we heard a commotion.

What on earth was going on? There was a lot of stamping and loud voices! I was called into the security office, and there was my bag sitting on the table! I couldn't understand; I hadn't stolen any crystals? Benito quietly explained that there was a rare flower in my bag and that he had admitted giving it to me. I was dumbstruck, but not for long, I was ordered to talk, and I would have lied if it had not been for the fact Benito had already made an admission. I would have made up some kind of story, I tried to twist the truth a bit, but it wasn't going to work. I asked Benito if I should offer them money? No, he exclaimed, that would only make things worse. I was ordered back out of the building by the security, back to the jeep. I had to admit to the rest of the group what had happened, and bless them, they tried making me feel less guilty by saying he should know better and not pick the flower. I just felt so awful that I had forgotten about it in my bag since my birthday and had not left it behind.

Worse still, when we got back to Santa Elena, I had to tell Hanz what had happened. That one of his most reliant and knowledgeable guides had been suspended from guiding on Mount Roraima for six months. I could see Hanz's face on which it was clearly written that he believed me to be a one-woman walking disaster zone! First the bus accident, near drowning and now this. However, Hanz later became an absolute star, providing me with food and accommodation that was not included in my tour. Why? Because when my backpack eventually arrived in Santa Elena into his care, half the items in it, including my good camera, credit cards and other valuables, had been stolen.

I can honestly say I have had better days than that one, but still, I decided to carry on with the tour. The tour company had given me the option of returning to Ciudad Bolivar to stay near one of the directors for a few days. I think by this point, they wanted me out of their country and off their tour, but I wasn't finished just yet. The trip had been challenging so far, but there had been positive times - I had survived the Lost World, and I had a lot more exploring to do.

~ ~ ~

Yes, for some reason, I felt the need to risk life and limb and carry on. So I embarked upon their Gran Sabana tour, which I had prepaid anyway. I suspected my new guide, Emilio, had already been warned about me. Either that or he just took an instant dislike to me, well, the feeling was mutual. Our first morning was, however, quite pleasant all in all, visiting the Jasper Falls. Although the falls themselves are minor compared to others, the landscape is truly stunning. The water flows over rock formations of red jasper (a type of silica used as a gemstone), almost resembling a scarlet river. On our return, we stopped at the Mirador observation point to enjoy immense views across the landscapes of the whole Savannah to Brazil and back over to Mount Roraima. Yes, very pleasant indeed and an excellent prelude to my long-winded, tedious afternoon jaunt at the local police station reporting to the Chief of Police about my stolen items. Hanz was there to assist me, especially with translation. Still, I cannot say any of the police officers were excited about my being there, judging by their laid back approach and listless looks on their faces. I can still see it now, the officer hunched over a typewriter, tapping away, one digit at a time.

There were just three people on the Gran Sabana tour: Suzie and Jodie (both from the USA), and myself, with our guide Emilio. So on day two, we all merrily left the Santa Elena area and headed off through various locations - all involving water. We viewed waterfalls from the top, the bottom, the front, the back; we climbed over rocks through to waterfalls and viewed them from afar. By the third day, I was waterfalled out. So was pleased when I got to spend one morning wandering around an indigenous village, entering a class containing a teacher and several small children. They all looked surprised, but I held out a bundle of pens to the teacher, who took them smiling, instructing the children to sing to me. There was not much conversation, just a lot of smiling and gesturing and gales of laughter when I took Dinky Doo out of my bag to show them.

That afternoon we set off to a natural rock plateau, where we engaged in water sliding across the rock. Now, this I could enjoy, and I even braved it later and jumped off the top of a rock race into the water several metres below. The Piscean in me was being unleashed. My newfound confidence in water did not last long, though, when we visited the 'Curtain Falls'. It was nice to view them from the pathway, not so nice to find we were heading into the depths of a cave behind them. We had to leave all our clothes, towels and belongings behind in the jeep (except our swimwear). We were going to be climbing rocks and swimming behind the falls! Dinky Doo sensibly decided to stay on dry land.

We were joined by a young local lad, who could not speak English, and randomly appeared from nowhere. He clambered over the large wet slippery rocks with us, behind the thundering water gorging into the river. Everything was okay until two-thirds of the way across. I realised that the following (and final) sector involved swimming under the lower part of the rock face through a cave and out to the other side. I realised this because I could see Jodie, Suzie and Emilio doing that very thing - with only their heads showing above the waterline. I froze, panic set in, and I mean, it truly set in! What could I do, and where could I go?

I looked to the right- I could not go that way; that was where they were swimming under the cave. I could not go behind - it was a rock face; I couldn't go out to the front as the raging waters were plummeting down! At that point, in my state of panic, I noticed the cascades of water were creating some kind of vacuum of air in which I felt I couldn't breathe. This had a knock-on effect as once I realised I was struggling to inhale, my panic state made me question whether I was still indeed breathing. I had to go left, the way we had come but had forgotten what a mission it was. I was aided by the young local lad, slipping and sliding over the rocks. With his help, I reached land with just a few scrapes and bruises. I was pleased I could breathe again; but felt that the guide Emilio had won this one. His tour had worn me down, and I had had to retreat!

With another tour successfully (or not so successfully) finished, I returned to Santa Elena. The tour company ensured I had somewhere to stay and fed and watered me before my return bus journey to Ciudad Bolivar the next day. On that bus, I was sat next to a young female called 'Angel' who told me that she travels around for six months each year..... this was similar to my life plan. I believe it was fate for me to sit next to Angel that day.

I was met at the bus station by my good old faithful friend Cedric, and I could not quite tell if he was as pleased to see me as I was to see him, but he made a good show of it. Cedric had already heard of my near-death disasters and all the rest of the chaos I had caused. However, he still offered me the opportunity to squeeze in one more tour before my departure in a few days that I already had credit for. I figured that going somewhere would probably be better than just lazing around in

Ciudad Bolivar for four days (what was I thinking!). Either way, I would need to get on my pre-booked flight to Caracas in five days, ready for my flight back to the UK. The remote Rio Caura river beckoned me, and with little money to my name and a misplaced sense of adventure, that was where I headed.

~ ~ ~

The tour jeep arrived to pick me up escort me to the office at Las Trincheras, a small village at the start of the Rio Caura, into what became my next nightmare adventure. The other passengers for the Rio Caura tour were three young French couples: Juliet and Pierre; Claudine and Anton; Adele and Gerard. We didn't get to know each other very well while going through the checking-in process. This was partly because, in my mind, we had a few days to do that, tied in with them not speaking much English (or pretending not to). But also partially as I had taken a shining to our guide Edwin and was quite happy getting to know him. So without much more ado, we all set off with our crew- Edwin, the canoe driver Junior, and the cook Dario. We cruised along the river, through the lush terrain of the jungle, with Dinky Doo's head poking out of my bag, just relishing the ride. Although I was savouring the serenity, I was beginning to wish I had bought along my pennywhistle, even just to annoy the others.

Our first evening was very chilled out and bordered on the romantic for me, as I spent the late evening with Edwin on the beach looking up to the stars. The moment was spoiled by Edwin informing me of all the different kinds of reptiles and fish that could be in the water, including piranha and sea snakes. The following day, I woke up with only one regret: I had not put more mosquito repellent on. All I could do now was smother myself in antihistamine cream and hope for the best. Sporting my new mosquito-bitten look, I joined the others for breakfast before our next venture in the boat, along the Rio Caura again. It was more beautiful scenery, with the sun shining and the trees reflecting in the water. When we stopped off for lunch, Edwin got us all into the water for a swim. I was slightly apprehensive due to the thought of piranha, but I was assured all would be okay.

It was well worth the immersion into the unknown of the waters, because it was not long before the sweet-water dolphins 'Tornina's' surrounded us. Edwin showed us how to splash our legs to attract them nearer to us. Contrary to belief, the splashing would not frighten them away, and the dolphins gaily swam around us, coming over to us, as opposed to us going over to them. This was truly amazing to be with wild dolphins and not paying to go in an enclosed area to see them.…, this was much more natural. Not long after, my joy was short-lived when Pierre and Dario appeared with a piranha they had fished for - from the very same river we had just been swimming in!

Late afternoon we arrived at our base camp, 'El Playon', a small beach paradise in the heart of the rainforest. I spent most of the evening alone because my group did not feel much need to talk to me (or I to them). Edwin had disappeared to mingle with other tour groups. Still, by all accounts, I was more than happy laying on the beach looking up at the abundance of stars. There were not that many times in my life that I had seen that many stars, it was only Africa and Chiang Mai in Thailand that I could recall. Yes, I had my chill-out music on, and all was well with the world. That was all about to change as of the next day…

After an early breakfast, we set off on our hike up through the jungle and one of the mountains. The purpose of this hike was to see various flora and fauna unique to this area, and we were not let down. We got to see the 'Howler', a capuchin monkey, rare butterflies, spiders, and toucans. What we had not set out to see, in my mind, was the coral snake. As it turned out, I was the only one to see it, as, at that precise moment, one of the French girls was having a fainting fit, and the others were trying to revive her. I, meanwhile, was fascinated by what had just moved past me in the nearby thickets. I squealed, and Edwin came running over to see what was the matter. I informed him I had just seen something salmon pink moving very fast into the bushes. He got very excited, telling me it was one of the most poisonous snakes globally and was unique to this area! I stood transfixed to the spot while he went hunting for it through the undergrowth, but to no avail. Edwin was quite upset that I had got to see this rare snake, and he had not, and I think for one moment he thought I had made it up. But there was no way I could have known (not being a snake expert) that there would be a pinky salmon colour snake, so he just had to accept his loss! I trod very carefully after that and seemed to bring out all my other senses, with eyes, ears and nose scouting everywhere for the slightest movement of any creature.

We hiked to the base of the stunning Para Waterfalls and had lunch at the viewpoint. I noticed that my left foot was starting to hurt. I put it down to a previous slight stumble I had had on the way down and joined the others for a swim in the river. We were then taken over to a tiny beach near the falls before hiking (or limping, in my case) back to the El Playon base camp. Luckily it was again a relaxed evening with no activity set out. By this time, my left foot had severely swollen, and on the top of it was a big lump that you could roll around!! Anton bandaged up my foot for me while I lay there moaning and feeding myself painkillers, just questioning why did it have to be me? I hobbled out to the beach but was in a much more negative mood. Nobody was talking to me, not even our guide Edwin. The latter really should have been a bit more professional. I decided there and then that. I had had enough of it all. The past few weeks had caught up with me; I was giving up - this trip had won and worn me down! Yes, I decided that I would leave the very next morning - but as it transpired, that was not going to happen.

At breakfast the following day, I informed Edwin of what I thought of him in terms of being unprofessional and not attending to me as a passenger the night before. I told him in no uncertain terms that I was going home there and then. His response was to ask me how I thought I was going to do that? In my mind, it was simple, the boat driver was going to take me. However, Edwin calmly pointed out that should the boat driver take me along the river back home, the rest of the group would have no way of returning to the city. Now I quite liked that idea. There was a vision in my head of them stranded there for a few days until the boat came back for them. Well, that would serve them right! So I informed Edwin that I did not give a s*** (apologies for the language). I had only paid for a 3-day trip and was expected back by the tour director, so a 3-day trip I would have. Poor Edwin took some time trying to calm me down and encouraging me to stay. I decided to call his bluff by stating that I would if the French group voted that I remain. I was convinced they would want me to go! But it turned into a double bluff because they voted for me to remain with them - although they did not adhere to the condition of speaking to me (in English or French). My only regret was that I did not have my penny whistle with me; there would be no need to chat at all then; I could subject them to hours of my relentless penny whistling!

So it was with some reluctance I stayed with the group and my gut feeling that I should have left returned when we came to the next 'supposed' vote. We were given the options of either: going to an indigenous Indian village or going to a remote jungle island that had never been visited or inhabited before. Now the fact that the six French voted unanimously to go to the jungle island meant that that was where we were going to go. My vote, either way, was not going to count. I had the feeling of impending doom, and to be fair, I was not mistaken.

~ ~ ~

Back along the Rio Caura, we drifted, stopping off briefly at an indigenous village of Yekawanas Indians. We meandered around, asking them questions while they proudly showed us their homes and their way of life. Their primary income was fishing and hunting by the men and banana plantation farming (usually worked by the women). Little did I know it at the time, but this could have been the last I might have seen of civilisation for a while, and these could have been the last people to see us alive.

After this refreshing stopover, we sailed along until the engine stopped- it took some mastery for our driver to get it going again. Eventually, we reached the branch off of the river flowing towards the remote jungle island. The uneasiness had not left me, and we were heading into unchartered territory on a non-tourist river in the dense jungle.

We approached our destination late afternoon, a tiny islet with lots of trees. We needed to climb a small hill to reach our accommodation for the night -a makeshift wooden shelter to hang our hammocks.

Our evening meal can only be described as erring on the volatile side that night. Firstly, because I decided to drink copious amounts of the homemade local rum until Edwin very firmly advised me not to do so. Not because he was worried about me making a fool of myself, but because if I was sick, the wild animals would be able to trace us easier! I stopped drinking rum. Secondly, because most of the French group decided that they wanted to go piranha fishing. They were insistent because it had been listed on the itinerary and so far had not happened as a group event. An argument broke out, with the guide initially insisting it was too dangerous to go as it was dark and then relenting. I flatly refused to go. It was firmly pointed out that I must go, I could not be left on my own due to the wild animals! Dinky Doo, although a bear, was small and stuffed and so didn't count as protection. I still flatly refused to go, so one French girl, Adele, opted to stay with me. I wasn't sure how she would protect me, but I worked it out that I could throw her as bait if something came at me. So that was it; the rest of the group disappeared into the darkness down the hill, leaving Adele and me by the fire. We were instructed not to move away from it, as wild animals would not come to us there. For once, I strictly obeyed an order.

It was not long, probably no more than 45 minutes, before we heard the screaming and shouting. I guess deep down, I knew it was coming, so I was not surprised. I was a little intrigued, though, and so I slowly followed Adele away from the fire as she had leapt up at the fate of her friends. There was some shouting backwards and forwards until the group found us - for some bizarre reason, they did not have torches and were following our voices. As I had been told not to leave the fire, there was no way I was leaving it to go down and help them back up.

Amidst their tears and distressed faces, we discovered they had been merrily fishing for piranhas until they thought they felt something alien in the water. In their panic, they had somehow managed to lose our canoe! It had drifted back along the river. My response came as somewhat of a surprise when I advised them to leave the immediate vicinity around me in case I hurt one of them further. They decided it was best to take my advice, and drifted away, one limping due to the cut foot she had incurred during the scramble back through the water and over the rocks.

Edwin took me up on my offer late in the evening when I stated that although he may not want to talk currently, I would be around (where was I to go?) if he wanted to talk later. Taking advantage of that offer, Edwin spoke throughout the night about his guilt and shame, knowing he should not have relented into letting the group do something dangerous. Edwin was hoping to swim along the river in the morning to find the canoe, and since the French had failed to empty the river of piranha, that was a slight predicament! Edwin talked and talked until I eventually fell to sleep in my hammock, but one of his remarks stood out in my mind. This situation could now go either way: if the boat had drifted along the river and lodged against a sandbank, then he would be able to retrieve it and return it to us, and we could continue our journey home. However, if the canoe had strayed along the river back to the Rio Caura, then basically we were stuffed. We would be shipwrecked and isolated on this remote jungle island, myself, the crew and six French people. Nobody would know we were there!

They would not be aware because the remote jungle island was not ready for tourists yet, and was not on any itinerary. In addition, even if we did have a mobile phone between us, there was no way we were going to be getting a signal out there! So this predicament left me with two thoughts: one, that I may be forced to stop being vegetarian and become a pescatarian so that I could eat fish from the river. Secondly, I would make sure I hid a substantial amount of the remaining drinking water from the others (where I thought I would put it, I do not know!).

I awoke in the morning to find that Edwin was not in his hammock. He had gone in search of the missing canoe. We waited with some trepidation, albeit the group decided to keep some distance between them and me! To be fair, though, they had apologised, so I decided not to be too harsh on them. It was not too long later when we spied our hero Edwin in our beloved canoe - I don't believe I have ever been so happy to see such a thing in my life! We loaded up, and we were out of there, probably the fastest that canoe has ever been rowed homeward bound.

That evening, the realisation dawned on me that I had nowhere to stay and was a day late returning. There was the likelihood Cedric had been searching for me. After all, I was supposed to have been meeting him at his office the day before. I decided to take up the offer of the French group to stay in the same hotel as them, it sounded cheap and cheerful, and I would have just enough money to cover my room cost for the night. There was no money for food; however, I was given some leftovers from the trip, and so I settled myself in my room for the rest of the night while the others went out for a drink and a meal. I spent that evening reflecting on the perils of the river trip and tried to focus on the positives. I found few, but that was enough for me to realise that my thinking was progressing. I had travelled through a relatively unknown but beautiful landscape, gazed at a densely star-filled sky and had been privileged to swim with rare wild dolphins.

The following day there was a tapping on the door; it was Cedric! How had he found me? It didn't matter, for here was that lovely familiar, caring face that had looked after me so well so far! But wait, Cedric was not very happy; he had been slightly troubled the day before looking for me when I had not shown up. In his eyes, I had had an extra day on the trip I had not paid for. Without wanting to fall out with Cedric, but being at the end of my tether, I pointed out that I had not wanted to stay. Why had he not thought about the arrangements for how I would return without the rest of the group and only one boat? To top it all off, I had been forced into being stranded on a remote jungle island with a painful swollen foot (which, of course, I had to show him to shock him). Cedric realised he had gone just a little too far. He very kindly took me and my belongings to his office, where he treated me to a substantial breakfast.

I am not too sure who was happiest that I got on the bus that day to go to the airport and fly from Ciudad Bolivar to Caracas. Cedric because he was finally able to be rid of this one-woman disaster zone, although it did mean having to pay my bus fare; or me. Because taking it all in, I had narrowly escaped death twice, I had money and items stolen, had been involved in the suspension of a local guide, I was in pain with a swollen foot with a lump on it and had been stranded on a remote jungle island with six French people!

The relief took over me as I was driven away on the bus, and tears fell steadily. I had not realised my forties would already be so painful and dangerous. I don't know what the other passengers thought of me that day, but I clutched hold of Dinky Doo and did not care. It was one of the last times that I would look forward to going on a flight.

I was not so happy to leave the flight once reaching Heathrow, as my journey involved three trains with my backpack and still swollen foot. I hobbled back to my house from the train station, which was luckily only ten minutes away, and then it was straight to the Doctor. She was not very happy having to treat someone with a foreign object on their foot. The doctor considered sending me to a tropical disease hospital, but a dose of antibiotics did the trick for me. To this day, I don't know what caused it, but the fact that I returned alive was an added bonus. Life really does begin at 40!

They say life is short, and boy had I realised that on this trip. I had been on a challenging hike, had two near-death experiences, and been stranded on a remote jungle island. This only encouraged me to want to travel more and to think about my life. It did not seem like the right time to make significant changes; I was building my career and was soon to become a Team Manager. In hindsight, it is easy to question how suited I was to a 'career', but maybe it was all part of the path set out for me. What I didn't know at the time, was that my manager and colleagues had organised a surprise 40th birthday party for me. Not being aware, I flatly refused to go to the alleged 'works do' due to my painful foot. That was the final Venezuelan legacy, and for once it didn't involve a waterfall!

~ ~ ~

Overall Trip Cost: £1400
(Flight £415, Tour £600, £385 All Other Costs)
Top Tip: In some countries, it is much safer to book an airport shuttle to your accommodation in advance; I cannot stress this enough! It may cost a few more dollars, but it is worth it to ensure you stay alive to enjoy your trip.... you can save money elsewhere later in your trip if you need to. Look on comparison sites back home and book in advance where possible. You will be issued some kind of ticket or voucher. There should be a driver waiting for you inside or outside arrivals at the airport who will hold up a piece of paper with your name on it.

Action shot on Mount Roraima

The 'Lost World', Mount Roraima

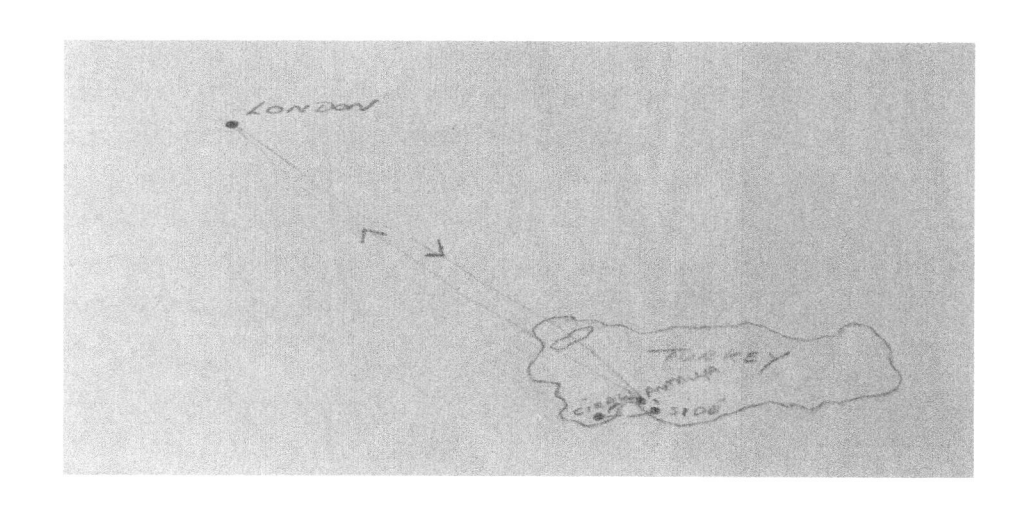

TURKEY ROUTE - 8 DAYS

TURKEY 2006

Nocturnal Treehouse Mandie

Eclipse Path: Africa - Turkey - Russia
I viewed at: Side, Antalya, Turkey
Date/Time of Maximum Totality: 29.03.2006 at 13:55 Local Time
Length of Totality: 03m 45secs

Turkey is formed of seven geographical regions. Ankara is the capital city, contrary to the usual belief that Istanbul is the capital (which is the most populace). Popular places to visit include:- Konya, one of the most ancient cities, renowned for its Whirling Dervishes and Seljuk Architecture; Istanbul with impressive historical sites, modern skyscrapers, thriving nightlife and the Bosphorus River; Ephesus, an ancient site in Aegean Turkey which was at one time one of the largest cities in the Roman Empire; the Turkish Riviera cities of Marmaris and Antalya; Side, with its heady mix of classic ancient ruins and sandy beaches; Cappadoccia, home to the fairytale landscape of unique rock formations; and finally, the Pamukkale Thermal Pools where clear, bright blue mineral-rich waters flow down white travertine terraces. Sounds beautifully relaxing, but why not try a spot of energetic belly dance which has some Roma heritage here, and has been a traditional part of wedding folk music/dance. Or you could try the national sport of Oil Wrestling! The fighters dowse themselves in oil and subsequently face their opponent. Sounds like a bathe in the Pamukkale Pools would be ideal afterwards.

I was now on my third eclipse visit, and I was very much looking forward to this one as it had been five years since my last. Unfortunately, I missed out on two total eclipses, one in 2002, which I stupidly did not go to because it was in similar areas to my Africa trip in 2001. The next total eclipse that I missed was in 2003, which involved cruises to Antarctica that were way out of my budget.

Thankfully, as this trip was shorter, my backpack was lighter. I still packed Dinky Doo and my useful items, head torch, and washing powder; with the addition of superglue which helps fix many things, an overall staple to carry. I felt wisely packed but underprepared as I landed at Antalya airport just one night before the day of the total eclipse. Looking back, I cannot fathom out why I left it so late to get there; anything could have happened, and I might have missed the eclipse. I had not thought this trip through as it was around eleven o'clock at night and not seeing any taxis. I was stumped as to how I would get to my hotel. Christine, whom I met on my Africa trip in 2001, was waiting for me there. Luckily, a tour company representative took pity on me, seeing as I was on my own, and by then, it was almost midnight. He put me on a coach to take me to my destination; however, he clearly did not have that much sympathy for me when he charged me £20 for this privilege. Christine was waiting up for me, and we had a couple of red wines while catching up with each other.

We had also arranged to meet my friend Anna and her mother Barbro; I had met them on my trip to Thailand in 2003. I remember it well, as it was Anna's birthday, and even though she was not on my tour group, my whole group came out for a meal on her 30th birthday. We had arranged for a birthday cake for her and managed to get a table overlooking the sea.

After we left the restaurant, half a dozen of us went to find a bar nearer to our hotel to get drinks. We had heard of a bar area in the marketplace, but all the stalls were closed up as it was very late by then. We were about to retreat when we were approached by two Thai ladies who seemed to appear from nowhere, inviting us to dance outside their bar. I enjoyed dancing with them, but then the others spotted another bar with a pool table just a few metres away. So they all went to the new bar, and I stayed with the ladies. We had a routine, I would continue dancing with them, but if any men came along, I would hide behind one of the large potted plants so they could entertain the men. Our system was working well until one of my group came to fetch me away.

~ ~ ~

ECLIPSE DAY - 29th March 2006

It was lucky that mobile phones had become available since our previous trip together as I was able to contact Anna to coordinate how, when and where we would all meet to view the eclipse in Side. To keep things relatively simple, we agreed to meet at the Amphitheatre in Side, where we would watch the eclipse. That would have been fine had there not been thousands of other people all planning to do the same thing.

With the power of the mobile phone, we were able to track down Anna and Barbro. The four of us settled ourselves into a spot inside the Amphitheatre. We had some laughs with some local schoolchildren fascinated by Dinky Doo and by us, and chatted with anyone in our nearby vicinity. We also explored just outside the Amphitheatre walls; it was a lot quieter out there, considering the thousands of people here to view the eclipse. NASA crew were busy setting up their equipment, and the San Francisco Exploratorium featured a live webcast from the site. A lot was occurring that day.

Not only were we famous for a day, with all the television crews around us, but we were in a venue of profound historical and cultural importance in Turkey. The Side Amphitheatre had served as the centre of culture and art in ancient times when Romans dominated the region. It was pretty eerie sitting there knowing that up to 20,000 people in Roman times watched gladiator and animal fights at any one time! It was also used for more sedate activities such as plays. By the Byzantium era, it had been converted into an open-air church. Today, with its exceptionally designed acoustic walls, it is the perfect venue for concerts and other cultural events, and of course, for viewing solar eclipses.

Total solar eclipses are not just watching what is happening between the moon and the sun in that few minutes of totality. There can be other delights in the sky in the lead-up and afterwards. There is a sense of anticipation and concern if clouds start forming where you are viewing, and you are waiting with bated breath to see if they will pass.

During the partial phase of the eclipse, we decided we did not like being in the Amphitheatre with thousands of people; it was too noisy. So we wandered just outside the walls and found a relatively quiet spot on a small hill with some local Turkish people. We enjoyed their company, and even though they could not speak English, we managed to communicate with a lot of gesturing and mimicking. The elderly lady of their group could see I did not like heights and kept pretending to push me off the edge of the hill; this caused great amusement! Perhaps they did not enjoy our company as much as we enjoyed theirs.

The moon had proceeded to cross between the sun and the earth around 12.38 local time and was creating the effect of a crescent sun. More and more, the solar disc above us was blackening, the sun gradually disappearing bit by bit. The sea was still sparkling blue, and it was quite warm still at that point. Over to our right, we could see large groups of eclipse chasers with their huge telescopes and photographic equipment. Gazing further around our 360-degree view, we could see clusters of excited people with their newly purchased solar eclipse glasses. The crowds became quieter. There was only 10% of the sun remaining, and the sea was no longer glistening; it was a deeper blue. There was a halo effect of clouds near the sun. With only five minutes left before totality, the second planet from the sun, Venus, appeared in the sky. We were elated.

Being a novice eclipse chaser back then, I did not see Baily's Beads (the small red glimmering dots around the sun). Still, I did see the moon's shadow over the nearby temple and felt the shadow whooshing over the land by us. The last chunk of the sun was eaten by the moon, and totality had begun. The 'oohs and ahs' were dissipating, along with the light. At 12:54 local time, we were all in a different world. The sky was of late twilight hues, not completely dark, and on the horizon, there was a light sunset effect. But there, in all its glory above us, was the total eclipse- a completely blackened solar disc with a bright shining white corona around its periphery! We were stunned into silence by its absolute glory. There was not a murmur from anyone, and the silence was deafening, broken only by the sound of a flock of seagulls squawking in sheer confusion, flying home to roost for the night.

We were mesmerised for the entire 3 minutes and 45 seconds, of which we were privileged to witness this most spectacular eclipse. It felt so natural to view the eclipse through totality, with our naked eyes, with no man-made glasses between us and this natural phenomenon. It had been quite cool in temperature, but nobody cared. I stood still, and I reflected, I felt joyous, and I felt humble. I was overwhelmed again at this moment. That is the magic of the total eclipse!

I was woken from my reverie by thunderous cheering and clapping, which seemed to resonate from miles around. There above us, dazzling like a 48 carat diamond on steroids, was my beloved diamond ring holding in its arms the sun and the moon -but the sun was starting to escape! My heart began beating faster, but before I knew it, the diamond ring had begun to slip away. The eclipse returned to its crescent sun formation. From there on in, the sun would gradually become larger whilst emerging away from the moon for approximately 45 minutes until it returned to its full circular beaming glory.

A town bell was ringing. We looked at the beaming faces of those around us and those with tears falling down their cheeks. All our souls overwhelmed in our own way! Everyone was delighted, as this would be an event each one would remember for the rest of our lives. Whether you had or had not seen an eclipse before, this one was a unique and moving experience for all. On this occasion, many thousands of eclipse chasers were very fortunate to observe a magnificent eclipse: Venus had appeared in the sky; our path of totality had perfect weather. the eclipse had not been not marred by clouds, resulting in many effects evident; and we had witnessed the bright corona and the illustrious diamond ring. What more could I say, except, 'Where will I see the next one?"

After having some nibbles with our Turkish friends, we said a fond farewell and returned to the Amphitheatre. We had witnessed something together not often seen in a lifetime. Even the old lady seemed to have warmed to me and gestured fondly one more push over the edge. Our schoolchildren had missed us and were pleased we were back, and they asked to see Dinky Doo again. They were very excited about the eclipse. It was great to know that they had been able to experience this spectacular event away from the classroom. They clambered around us, each telling us in their pigeon English how they had felt about it: joy, amazement, and wonder.

I went to talk to NASA down in the middle of the arena. Among other things, in our reasonably long but compelling conversation, they told me that the eclipse's partial phase had been visible from an International Space Station. They also gave me insight into where the next total eclipse in 2009 could be viewed best: Wuhan, China. I learned all this and more while talking to them with the flies of my shorts open! I was horrified when I returned to my friends, and they pointed this out.

As it was hot and sunny, we headed to the beach for a few hours on the beach. After basking on the beach in our bikinis for awhile, we said our goodbyes to Anna and Barbro for the day. Christine and I went back to the hotel, both full of the joys of spring. The hotel staff excitedly asked us about the total eclipse and our experience of it. We joyfully related everything to them as they listened intently. I was on cloud nine and was in good spirits all day. I must have also drunk quite a few spirits as that evening after dinner, I started belly dancing on stage to a packed audience. I was the star of the show (well, actually, that claim could have been made by the actual belly dancer who had been performing before me). The audience seemed to like me, though, and some of them even joined in.

This stint of belly dancing was not my worst encounter of embarrassing myself in the belly dance stakes. A few years earlier, I had been in Turkey, at a beach resort. It was summer, and the beaches and the restaurants were crowded. I was walking along the promenade with my friend. We saw belly dancing in a restaurant and stopped to observe, as had many other passers-by. I was picked out to come and join in, I was reticent at first, and my friend did not help my case by telling the host that I could belly dance. I was taken to a backroom to don a costume. I had an image in my mind of me dressed in a lovely exotic costume and admired by all. What actually happened was the staff dressed me as a man with a wig and plain baggy clothing, whilst the waiter was transformed into a female! It was too late to back out now; I was committed, my name was being announced on the microphone! Dinky Doo just covered his eyes with his paws in embarrassment.

So myself and the waiter danced our way out, as he gave me instructions of what to do. We danced together, and then amongst the diners. At one point, we were dancing on chairs and then on tables; I was beginning to enjoy this. I could see a sea of faces, a promenade audience, and my friend laughing whilst trying to take video simultaneously. I have now forgiven her! I must have done, for I was here on the stage in Antalya some years later feeling like the star of the show; I put that down to the magic of the eclipse!

~ ~ ~

After my night of high jinks, the following day, we carried out a military operation. Christine and I departed the hotel, taking the bus to

Antalya, where I said goodbye to her at the bus station. The next task was finding my stop for the minibus to go to Cirali. At said minibus stop, I was to meet Anna and Barbro. Amazingly all went to plan.

We had a great time on the minibus on the way to Cirali. For the next one and half hours, we were cooped up at the back and made the most of it by chatting with everyone who was sat near us. We had barely left the bus station when our minibus stopped to pick up a guy flagging down our vehicle. This was Jules from California, having missed the minibus at the station, he didn't give up, and once onboard, joined our party at the back. We had a great laugh and were in high spirits. That was until we got dumped at the side of the road by the minibus in Cirali. We subsequently had to squash into a smaller minivan for those going to our camp. It was not far, though, just down a hill on a track too small for the minibus. We were suitably impressed when we got to our camp, even more so when we spotted our treehouses right next to the beach. We dropped our luggage on the ground and walked onto the beach to drink in the beautiful views of blue seas and distant mountains.

The lady who owned the camp came to greet us and showed us to our rooms. Well, actually, she just stood at the bottom of the trees and pointed up. Thankfully, there were steps up to the treehouse; otherwise, I am unsure how I would have gotten up there, especially with my luggage! Of course, Dinky Doo got up there with ease, not because, being a bear, he could easily climb up, but because he was in my backpack getting a free ride. Anna and Barbro were my neighbours, with Jules a little further along. Being quite excited about our new temporary homes, we chirped out to each other, just like birds singing to each other from their trees.

After a short rest, the four of us set off for the ancient Greek city of Olympos, which was to the right of our camp, just a few miles along the beach. Due to the landscape, we could not get there directly along the coast. So we walked through the ruins and hills until we found a place in Olympos village to eat and drink, ultimately making our way to the Olympos beach.

There was a Romanian guy on the beach acting stupidly by holding a baby turtle. A few people went up to him and told him to put the poor baby turtle down, including Jules and me. He clutched it a bit longer, and then we saw him throw the poor thing into the sea. A crowd of us shouted out at him. I was furious; my nostrils were flaring. I strode over to the Turkish guard at the gate and told him what had occurred. Consequently, he went and had harsh words with the Romanian guy. For me, that was still not enough. I imagined that adequate punishment for that guy would have been solitary confinement, where he would at the least be subjected to one of my extended penny whistle practices!

Climbing up Mount Olympos (otherwise known as Tahtali Dagi) went some way to curing my anger. At the summit, some 7,762 feet high and 2 hours later, Anna and I were rewarded by stunning 360-degree views. We were surrounded by the greenery of trees, distant mountains, ancient ruins, stunning beaches and blue skies. If only there had been a cable car to take us up there, but no, that was installed a year later.

Having expended our energy by walking to Olympos and up the mountain, we decided to relax on the beach the next day. By that time, we had nicknames for each: 'Orange Tree Anna', 'Spiderwoman Barbro', 'Missed the Bus Jules' and ' Nocturnal Treehouse Mandie'. I guess that relates to my not being a lover of early mornings! Suitably refreshed that evening, the four of us ventured out, and we walked to Chimaera. This time we had a new companion, Sargo, the dog who walked with us the whole 7 kilometres; you could say he showed us the way. Chimaera is known in Turkish as 'Burning Rock', the lady who owned our camp had told us to visit there and had given us information about it. The Chimaera is a cluster of small flames that naturally blaze, and at night it looks like how you would imagine hell. It is better to visit in the dark for full effect, which is why we visited after dinner. Taking our torches to explore the rocky slopes, Sargo the dog kept us on track.

Upon our return, we asked the lady from our camp how does Chimaera work. She explained the flames occur where gas (thought to be methane) seeps out and ignites the fire when making contact with the air. Interestingly, although there are not many flames at night, perhaps 20 or 30 of them are still visible from the sea. I guess it was a good idea that we took torches and not gas lanterns; who knows what kind of accidents could happen that way.

My last two days involved primarily basking in the glorious sunshine on the beach. I had said goodbye to Anna and Barbro, but they gave me some sage advice just before they departed. For the sake of Jules and anyone crossing my path, please have a shower! I had been at one with nature living in a treehouse and had decided I would not cleanse; I would go "au naturel". Of course, being stubborn, I refused to wash until I was ready to leave Cirali.

On one of my last meanders along the beach, I sat on a rock thinking back to the total eclipse. This had been a relatively short trip, but I was so pleased I had made this journey. I had been privileged to witness such a spectacular celestial event in the sky in the company of three special friends, Anna, Barbro and Christine. Seeing the total eclipse had stirred up feelings in me, I was beginning to feel a spiritual element from it and wanted to develop more of this aspect in the future. I was daydreaming away to my heart's content when I spotted a baby turtle walking along the sand. Fascinated, I watched him flipping and flapping along until he eventually made it into the sea. I wondered if he was the same one who had suffered at the hands of the Romanian guy, and perhaps he was coming back to let me know he was okay. I put that down to the magic of the eclipse!

~ ~ ~

Overall Trip Cost: £300
(Flight £70, Accommodation £90, All Other Spending £140)
Top Tip: When visiting a particular event, e.g. an eclipse or concert, arrive at more than one day in advance to allow for any contingencies, such as travel disruption. It also gives that sense of anticipation in the lead up to the event.

Wild Elephant Chasing Me!

Walking with Lion Cub

Wild Rhinos Following Me

Venezuela- Lost World

Turkey, Diamond Ring on Eclipse

Argentina, Meeting Penguins

Monkey at Pantanal Camp, Brazil

Ushuaia, Argentina

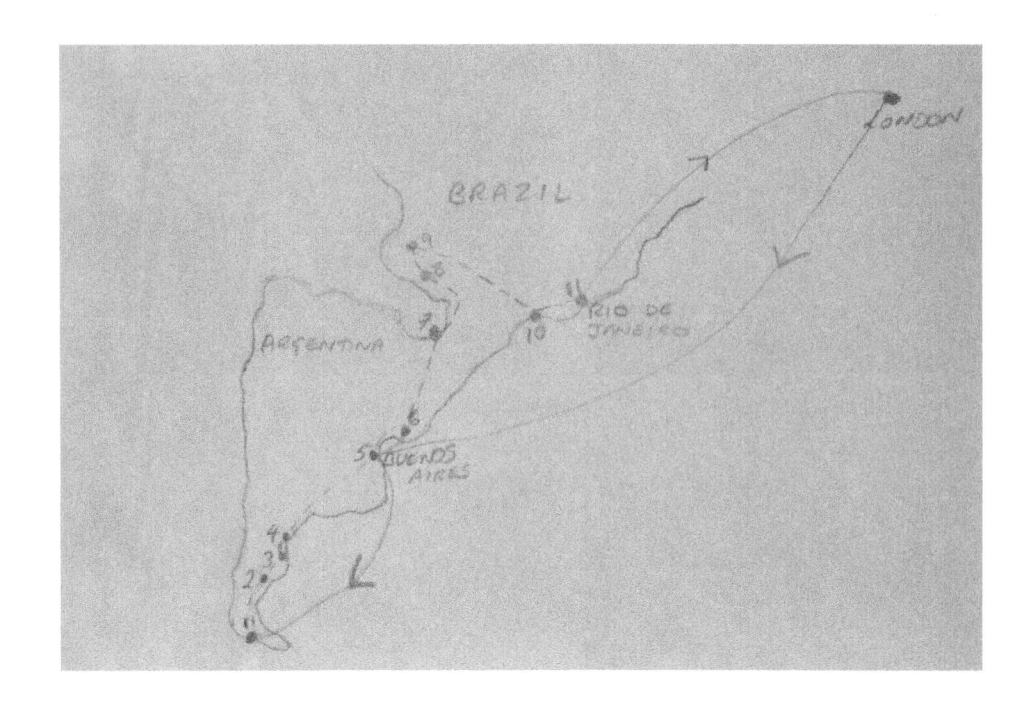

ARGENTINA & BRAZIL ROUTE - 36 DAYS

1. *ARGENTINA - USHUAIA*
2. *ARGENTINA - PETRIFIED FOREST*
3. *ARGENTINA - GAIMAN*
4. *ARGENTINA - VALDES PENINSULA*
5. *ARGENTINA - BUENOS AIRES*
6. *URUGUAY - COLONIA DE SACRAMENTO*
7. *BRAZIL - IGUASSU FALLS*
8. *BRAZIL - BONITO*
9. *BRAZIL - PANTANAL*
10. *BRAZIL - PARATY*
11. *BRAZIL - RIO DE ANEIRO*

ARGENTINA & BRAZIL 2007

Flying Through the Air Like a Ninja!

Argentina has some engrossing firsts, one of them being fingerprinting for identification which they introduced in 1892. Some would say, more importantly, they were the first with Latin music. It started in the capital city of Buenos Aires, to which they would Tango in the slaughterhouse area in the 19th century. Housed in these slaughterhouses would be the world-renowned Argentinian Steak, the beef derived from cattle from over 205,000 Argentine farms. Some of these would have originated near the northeastern Quebrada de Humahuaca, an arid mountain valley with colourful sandstone escarpments. In this same region is Salta with its "Tren de las Nubes" or "Train to the Clouds", the most dangerous railway globally and highest altitude ride reaching 13,800ft. For a more sedate experience, you may prefer Mendoza, renowned for its wine/vineyard tours but also the serene views of Aconcagua, the highest of the America's mountains. Or perhaps Cordoba, the 2nd largest city boasting a mix of colonial and modern buildings and Jesuit mission churches, or the quaint city of Ushuaia, the southernmost city in the world that once served as an exile prison Argentinian naval base. Spectacular scenery and hiking can be found in Los Glaciares, home to the stunning Perito Moreno Glacier, El Chalten or Bariloche, a lakeside town desired for its skiing, trekking, and water sports. If, like me, you love or appreciate nature, visit Puerto Madryn, the gateway to the Valdes Peninsula and famous for whale watching. No trip would be complete without the spectacular Iguazu Falls, one of the world's seven natural wonders, so vast they border with, and via, the Iguazu river, merge through into Brazil.

The Iguazu Falls are just one of the natural wonders of Brazil, which boasts the most significant amount of Amazon Rainforest (60% of it). The Amazon River, which is not just one river but a network of waterways totalling a length of 6,840 kms, flows through Brazil. Here too, you will find the world's most extensive tropical wetlands, the Pantanal. These varying landscapes are components of the 5th largest country globally and the largest country in South America, which incidentally, covers three time zones. The ultra-modern city of Brasilia (shaped like an aeroplane) is now the capital. It replaced Rio de Janeiro to assert its independence from colonialism and revitalise the interior part of the country. Brazil is the only country in South America to speak Portuguese due to the Portuguese colonial influence, which continued over 322 years until Brazil reclaimed it in 1822. When not drinking their national cocktail, the Caipirinha, you might want to try Brazilian coffee. You may well have consumed it back home as Brazil is the largest producer and exporter of coffee, accounting for some 30% of the world's coffee production. Have a drink, sit back and watch a football game with the locals who are football crazy, and why not? They have won the FIFA world cup a record 5 times!

Due to the limited time allowed for annual leave at work again, I opted for an adventure tour to cover the amount of ground I wanted to visit. The one I chose included all the main sights, some unusual ones and would take me to the finishing point in Rio de Janeiro just in time for Carnivale. Dinky Doo had a sparkling outfit in preparation, and my useful items were packed: a head torch, washing powder, superglue and a training golf ball. I had read that this colourful, light, small ball was valuable on long flights. By placing it under toes, heels or balls of the feet and circling your foot around, your circulation would be increased. However, I would need more than a small ball to relax and enjoy my flight on this trip, mainly due to the weather. There were gale force winds a-blowing, and my main concern was as to whether or not the plane would take off in such winds, and what turbulent kind of a ride would it be if that was the case- hold onto your hat Dinky Doo!

That all turned out to be the least of my concerns as when I arrived at the train station heaped up with all 19 kgs of luggage, it transpired that the trains were delayed by the weather. I reached the ticket counter, and the attendant advised that a train was now approaching the platform. There may not be another one for a long time, and I should run for the said train (couldn't he see I was loaded up like a packhorse). Off I sprinted, or lumbered, along to the platform - just to see the train pull away. Had the guy behind the ticket counter known I would not make that train and just wanted to laugh at the packhorse laden female? Anyway, the joke was on him, as a train arrived some fifteen minutes later, on schedule.

It is no wonder that I tank up on red wine on the day of a flight, before I leave home, before and after check-in, and on the flight. It helps alleviate the stress of being on the flight and the usual mishaps. It was no surprise to me that there would be a kerfuffle at check-in. Before that, though, I had to adjust my mindset to the new type of queueing system. It involved queuing in one long line for all flights leaving at different times. I was already on edge when I got to the counter, I can do without that kind of system change..

Having finally reached the check-in desk, the assistant decided she liked my rucksack and proceeded to chat with me about it. This would have been fine, except that she seemed to be oblivious that I was busy sorting my luggage. I realised I wanted to put my sleeping bag into my holdall, so I had to crawl under the desk and onto the baggage belt to put said sleeping bag into the holdall. There was subsequently space in my rucksack, and so I proceeded to manoeuvre my items around, all with a distant chatter in the background. However, the assistant then found a broken zip on my holdall. Everything was taken back out and then returned into my rucksack with an added sleeping bag stuffed in.

After that excitement, I could not relax until I had been through security and made my usual post-check-in toilet visit. I settled myself by a flight information screen with a glass of red wine in hand. I got chatting with two guys next to me, and one of them, lucky for him, was going to be sitting next to me on our flight. He was a chef called Chopsy; I erred on the side of caution by not talking too much, in case his nickname came from using his chef's knife unpredictably!

I am pretty much a creature of habit, so my usual procedure on a flight is to buckle up and check out the person next to me to see how much conversation could be forthcoming. Next is to read the safety instructions, read the film guide to plan my movie schedule for the rest of the flight, and peruse the food menu. Being vegetarian can be very useful on flights where food is served (included in your fare). You tend to get your 'special meal' first, much to the envy of your fellow passengers.

Something about being up in the air draws me to desiring a vodka and tomato juice, which accompanies my main course, with a red wine to follow with dessert. I then have to counteract that with copious amounts of water, resulting in numerous trips to the toilet! It has taken many years to realise that I should be securing the aisle seat to not disturb my seating companions. So it was no different on this flight, buckled up, sat with Chopsy (not much conversation for this flight as we were talked out), films planned, menu sorted. Dinner was served with my obligatory vodka and tomato juice, followed by dessert and red wine, and finally diluted by the water. I settled down to watch my films and doze off, but it was pretty tricky as I needed the toilet and was in the window seat. Both Chopsy, and the woman in my aisle seat were asleep.

In between all of this, I had made friends with Fernando, the flight attendant. I often find that an icebreaker with the airline crew is advising of being vegetarian, followed by ensuring your meal is actually on the flight (this has not always been the case). Fernando had been accommodating, and we had had a pleasant chat.

The following morning, we stopped at Sao Paulo airport for the re-fuelling of the plane, but we were all to remain on board the aircraft. An Italian guy had gone into the toilet and smoked a cigarette, thus setting off the alarm bell. Fernando told this man off, and I mean really told him off by shouting at him and calling upon the Head Steward to do the same. Suitably chastised, the man returned to his seat. Fernando, though, was not content, and he came to me ranting about the situation. With nothing else more entertaining to do at the time, I went along with this, sympathising about the irresponsibility of it all. I mentioned that now, as a passenger, I felt my safety was at risk and that this man should be searched! Fernando liked that idea, thanked me and went off to find his Head Steward to pursue this task. The joke might have been on me as we were three hours late landing at Buenos Aires. This resulted in Chopsy and I running around the airport to find our next flight going to Ushuaia. It turned out that we were at the wrong one, and we needed to get a bus to the correct airport where the domestic flights departed from. I was grateful to finally arrive at Ushuaia, not least because I needed a shower, but surely I would be able to shake off Chopsy now. It seemed very unusual that there would be somebody flying the same route as me all the way to Ushuaia, the remote, Southernmost city in the world. It transpired that the chef was legitimate and went on his merry way to his Antarctica bound cruise ship awaiting him at the harbour.

~ ~ ~

I immediately took a liking to Ushuaia; the pilot had given us a scenic flight whilst coming into land, over snow-capped mountains, some colourful buildings, and the sea. I found the town to be quaint, and I had a good feel for it. The hotel receptionist was accommodating, even more so when I discovered I had misplaced all my booking confirmations for the trip and my mobile phone. Either I had dropped them in the mayhem at the wrong airport, or perhaps on the bus. The receptionist kindly took it upon himself to support me in the mission to retrieve my missing items; however, they did not reappear that evening.

Ushuaia was to be the starting point for my adventure tour travelling to Rio de Janeiro in Brazil, via the coastal line of Argentina, Iguazu Falls bordering Argentina and Brazil, inland to the Pantanal (the world's largest tropical wetland area) in Brazil and back to the coast towards the city of Rio de Janeiro. Before the tour started, I had one full day of exploration on my own and made the most of it by visiting the Naval Base and Glacier Martial. The glacier is named after Luis Fernando Martial. He was a chief of a French expedition that reached the Glacier Martial area in 1883 for scientific purposes. The glacier area is an essential water source for the local community in Ushuaia; however, it is also a popular hiking trail of 6kms (return) for tourists.

Upon returning to the hotel, it was time for a nap before the tour's pre-departure meeting. Fortunately, I met a tour guide called Kiera from a different truck at the hotel who agreed to take me to the campsite later that evening to meet my fellow adventurers. I was to be sharing my twin room with Sarah on tour, who had arrived by the time I got back to the hotel. Along with Kiera, the tour guide, the three of us went off in a taxi to the pre-departure meeting. That is where we were supposed to be heading. However, Kiera stopped the cab at her truck which was off to the left from our hotel. After a while, there seemingly must have been a problem, she sent us off (the meter had been ticking, and she offered no money!). The driver promptly drove in the opposite, but the correct, direction to where our meeting was to occur.

Filled with hope and in jovial spirit, Sarah and I met with our new fellow adventurers, most of whom were from the UK. We got friendly immediately with Helle from Denmark, and the three of us became allies. We were introduced to two of the passengers, Cassandra and Rodney from Berkshire, framed as helpful to us newbies as they had been passengers on several tours before with this company. They were clearly already friendly with our drivers Trudy and Lewis. Aside from previous trips, they had already been on this truck for two weeks heading south to Ushuaia through Chile. I found this very interesting that you could join these adventure tours at any major city on any given route; it was worth noting for the future.

Our home (a big substantial truck) for the next two weeks would be the 'Muppet Mobile'. Sarah and I would be sharing the 'Kermit' tent (those who knew me back then would recall that frogs and the muppets were my favourite things). Time to hoppit!

~ ~ ~

Yes, we were heading out in our truck, and it will be of little surprise to you to learn that it was an early start. I was getting a distinct case of deja vu to the Africa trip by truck. To add insult to injury, not only did we have to get up early at 06:00 am, but we also had to buy our own breakfast. I went for the coffee and chocolate cake option; it seemed as good as anything else at that time of day.

Aside from our short trip on the ferry after crossing the border from Argentina into Chile, we spent the rest of the day on the truck We were on there around 12 hours in total, heading back into Argentina. Our day wasn't finished when we arrived at our bush camp, as we had to set up our tents. Sarah was very patient in teaching me, and I think I perfected it somewhere near the end of the trip. We all got to eat around 21:00, so there were a few rumbling stomachs. Still, once satiated and having socialised, we went to our beds for the night- because, of course, we had another early start.

What a treat, an 05:00 start, leaving camp at 06:00. I cannot function at that time of day, so Sarah packed our tents away that morning. On the positive side, we had plenty of time to sleep on the truck. In terms of scenery, we agreed that we would not be missing anything different. We had noticed yesterday that the landscape was a vast barren desert. It was not what I had imagined, and it went on for miles and miles, with very little in the way of towns and villages in between. The Petrified Forest visit broke up the monotony; it was interesting and humbling to learn the power of nature and how the forest came to be. To think that 150 million years ago, these petrified forests emerged due to multiple volcanic eruptions, covering trees with lava and ash, fossilising them into rocks over time. To demonstrate the power of nature, the heavens opened, and it poured with rain; it was one mad dash to the truck to escape the deluge.

That was enough to convince us as a group it was worth upgrading that night into a hotel; our 'Kermit' tent would have to do without us for a night. I must admit, it was a treat to sleep in a bed that night, after attempting to sleep in the truck and in the tent the night before. Furthermore, we guessed it would be an early start again, and the following day lo and behold, we were up at 05.30 am and on the road by 06.30. Bleary-eyed, we packed our luggage and ourselves onto the truck and promptly all fell asleep.

Now, I hope you have paid attention to my detailing of the landscape because this is when the scene comes into importance. Imagine that as far as you can see, way out into the distance, for many hours of the day and hundreds of miles - nothing changes, you are still in an empty, vast barren landscape. So we were merrily snoozing away, when suddenly out of the blue, there was a loud bang. We were all woken up, not least because some of us had been knocked out of our seats. We were all confused, still bleary-eyed, but nobody was hurt. We looked out of the windows, and we were still in the desert landscape. The door was flung open by our drivers with concerned looks on their faces, checking to see if we were all okay.

So what had happened? Lewis had been driving along at just an average speed. He would have been perfectly visible from all angles- there was certainly nothing to block the view. Yet, one car, and I stress it would have been the only car around at that time of morning, had come careering along the road, crashed into our truck, and ended up in a ditch! Thankfully the alcohol imbibed driver was not hurt, but this was not established until a police car, ambulance, and a fire engine arrived. The fact that all three services had attended was not the strange thing about it; what was a source of wonderment was where had they all come from? Seeing nothing around except these three vehicles amidst the desert landscape with just our truck and a car in the ditch was surreal.

Fortunately, a couple of hours later, a double-decker bus came along and took us to the next town. Amazingly our truck did not even have a dent in it, but the crew had to check it over properly and stay with the police to provide detailed statements. Our drivers gave us strict instructions on where to go and wait for them in this town - do not get lost! What was I going to do? That was part of my repertoire getting lost in new places. I decided it was best to hang onto the tail of whoever would accommodate me and not leave their side.

That evening, once reunited with Trudy and Lewis, we ate our dinner around the campfire. We were rewarded that evening with a beautiful sunset out in the wilderness and seeing a comet. We were all in wonderment and awe; yes, life was good on the road, early mornings were forgotten. The beers came out, and I had my first taste of a 'S'more', which some of you will know is marshmallows melted with chocolate in between two biscuits. What a fulfilling way to end the day.

The contentment would start to go downhill the next day, as personalities were beginning to clash on the truck. We were, however, at this stage attempting to keep the atmosphere light and be civil. The source of discontent was with the particular couple who had been on several of these trips before with this company, which somehow seemed to give them the right to take charge. In particular, they liked to monitor the rota and make sure we were all doing our bit. I'm sure I heard a low growl emerge from Dinky Doo, aimed at Cassandra and Rodney; things were awful if a stuffed bear had taken a dislike to them too.

Aside from them, we had a pleasant day out at a penguin colony. I am happiest when in nature. I am even more joyful when near the wild animals, but not too close they become contaminated by us humans, or want to chase me! After having lunch on a beach, prepared by yours truly, we made our way to a village-like Welsh settlement called Gaiman. This charming little town with only approximately 4,000 inhabitants was founded in 1874 by David D Roberts as part of the broader Welsh settlement in Argentina. Inhabitants still speak Welsh today, and each year there is a Welsh themed festival. Interestingly, the name Gaiman is not Welsh; it means 'Sharp Stone' and comes from the indigenous Tehuelches.

Both Sarah and I liked it here; I found it charming, and Sarah, originally being from Wales, had more of an affinity with it. We went into a small teahouse for welsh tea and cakes, and the owner told us some of the village's history. She explained that the first settlers arrived in 1865, looking for territory to establish a 'New Wales' whilst continuing their old customs and culture. Elements of the settlement still abound with traditional houses, small chapels, and the traditional teahouse. Our bellies full of tea and cake; we were quite content as we made our way back to the truck and then to our campsite for the night.

At dinner that evening, we were subjected to the bossiness of our resident know-it-all couple Cassandra and Rodney and their decision-making on issues that affected us all. There were lectures on truck security and the proposal to go bush camping the next night (instead of a similar camp with access to nice hot showers). This was not so much a proposal as a statement to which we all had to agree. Apparently, we had a democratic vote, but I must have missed that. Maybe I did because I was preoccupied with two ulcers in my mouth and my sore thumb, which I had cut making dinner that night. I subsequently didn't have much to do as I was not allowed to get the blood anywhere - so I enjoyed the ratatouille and rice even more.

Our next day was a full day peninsular tour of the Valdes Peninsular. Although set in the barren land, it is an impressively large and vital nature reserve inhabited by various species of wildlife and sealife. Here we could spot sea lions, elephant seals and fur seals to our heart's content, but no whales - I guess it was just the wrong time of year. I was merrily interacting with penguins, so nothing was going to dampen my spirit. I loved walking near to them and bending down to talk to them. Dinky Doo retreated into my backpack; he had no intention of being pecked at. It was time to leave all too soon, but on our journey to camp, the truck decided it would play up. The differential was leaking oil, and so we had to keep stopping for Lewis to top up the oil (I did not know what a differential was, but it sounded important).

~ ~ ~

Not being overly impressed with the tour company so far, meals not included that should have been, allowing a bossy couple to dominate the tour, and making Sarah and I pay extra for our hotel back in Ushuaia, I was not happy that night when we received more disturbing news from the Tour Manager (who popped up at various stops). We would be treated to a meal that evening because apparently, we had lost a night in a hotel in Buenos Aires. How does that work out? You cannot equate the two, a night in a hotel with a bed and more time in Buenos Aires or a night in a tent with a takeaway!

Anyway, it was onwards to Buenos Aires via the Rio Negro (Black

Water) province, which was the most beautiful scenery we had traversed so far. We could see glacial lakes, forest-covered tablelands, and even snow-capped Andes mountains in the distance. Having reached Buenos Aires with bellies rumbling, we went out for a group meal. This city is a paradise for carnivores where you can easily find a steakhouse on any street as Argentinian beef is famed as a gastronomic delight. The Argentinian cattle raised in the Pampas have a more robust immune system. They are not unnaturally rushed to fatten up, giving Argentina a reputation for having the world's finest steak cuts. I was content with my salad.

After a nice lay in the following morning, I had a day of doing the touristy things. So I headed out into the sprawling city metropolis, magically manoeuvring my way across twelve lanes of traffic on Avenue Julio. It was touch and go at times, but my ability to weave in and out would serve me well on this trip and many others future! It was also time to top up on clothing; I needed new sandals and a pair of my favourite, three quarter length trousers. Dinky Doo came in handy several times when taking photos of famous spots. By strategically placing his head or a paw in a particular position, I could block out the crowds of people. It must have looked like there were no visitors to Buenos Aires except me and my teddy.

That evening four new members joined our group, one of whom was a Scottish guy called James, or 'Jimmy'. As Jimmy was quite loud and upbeat, I was interested to see how this would pan out with our bosses Cassandra and Rodney. The group agreed to go to an all-inclusive meal and Tango Show that evening at extra cost. It was not included in the tour price; no surprise there then. However, it was truly spectacular, the tango dancers were breathtaking, and it was a fascinating experience. Unfortunately, the meal was not that great, and the kick in the teeth came at the end of the evening. We were charged extra than we had previously been advised and were all made to pay a substantial additional amount. We were all livid, but felt there was nothing we could do; even Cassandra and Rodney were subdued into silence. My way of dealing with it was to have fun in the toilets belly dancing while the attendant joined in by doing the Salsa.

Sarah and I set out the next day to Recoleta Cemetery to visit the grave of Eva Peron. Now, who doesn't know of Eva? But did you know she was born Maria Eva Duarte, in 1919? Eva was born into poverty, but by her teenage years had pursued an acting career. It was in 1944 that Eva met Colonel Juan Peron. Two years later, they were married, by which time he was the Argentine President, and Eva had become the First lady. She remained so until her death in 1956. It was my first experience visiting a cemetery with vaults instead of flat graves, so I found this all quite fascinating. There was no greenery or lawns at the Recoleta Cemetery; it was tomb after tomb full of elaborately carved scrollwork and stately pillars. Yes, it turned the idea of a cemetery on its head with the graves being built above ground in the open, in contrast to a dark hidden underground world.

I should have gone with Sarah on the train to the city, but no, I wanted to explore the botanical gardens. Instead, I got lost walking around and ended up some miles away. I then had to get the metro back out to the gardens; I could not face another long walk, not in that heat. I was rewarded with the beauty of the botanical gardens when I finally reached them, and needless to say, I sat straight down and relaxed. Thankfully, I had no children plonked down next to me as in Caracas.

~ ~ ~

Before heading into Brazil, knowing we would have a few long days on the truck, Sarah and I took a day out to Colonia del Sacramento, Uruguay. To get there, we took a 3-hour ferry ride from Buenos Aires (although there is a faster/cheaper one hour ride- we wanted the scenic route!). We were provided with a guide upon arrival, Euglena, who explained the history of the city and the places we visited. She told us that Uruguay had gained independence in 1828 after being ruled by Portugal, Spain and (briefly) Argentina.

Our focus was in the historic quarter, which is a UNESCO heritage site. We walked over the gateway to the historic quarter over a wooden drawbridge and through the Old Town Gateway, the 'Puerta de la Ciudadela'. The quaintness of this Old Town was not lost on us, whilst we wandered through the cobbled streets, the Plaza de Armas, and the 'Street of Sighs' ('Calle de Los Suspiros). We were told that this street dated back to the 17th century when the sailors from afar would arrive after long voyages at sea, and the local women would be waiting for them!

The three of us meandered past the relatively new lighthouse built onto the ruins of the 17th Century Convent of San Francisco. From the lighthouse to the Basilica del Santisimo Sacramento ('Basilica of the Holy Sacrament'), we were walked through the lovely Calle de Portugal, where flowers and foliage spill out of vintage cars. We liked this under-explored street; it really was pretty. It was a hot day, though, and we needed some sustenance. Sarah and I found a café near the harbourfront and ate our lunch. With free time to ourselves for the rest of the afternoon, we wandered around the harbour front and back through the cobbled streets. Our ferry duly arrived, and we headed back to Buenos Aires. It was certainly nice to leave the metropolis for a day and exciting to get another country's stamp on our passports.

On the subject of stamping passports, it transpired that we had all been illegal immigrants at one point! We had been backwards and forwards to the famous Iguazu Falls, which lie between the borders of Brazil and Argentina. On one journey to view them, our passports had not been stamped to say we were all back in Brazil. So that evening, they were gathered up and taken back to the border, stamped, and we were now safe and legal!

We viewed the Iguazu falls from various angles, taking boats out in front of them, hiking trails, and from the air in a helicopter. It was Sarah's first flight in a helicopter, yet I was the nervous passenger (I was up high and away from terra firma). Sarah was absolutely loving the flight, whereas I wasn't. I was torn between attempting to take photos or sitting on Sarah's lap to get away from the window! Lovely as it all was, by the end of the day, we had all had enough of waterfalls. Me in particular, as they reminded me too much of my trip to Venezuela! And so it was we continued our merry way through Brazil.

After a day at a bird park spotting various birdlife and being held hostage by a Macaw that would not let Sarah and me out of the enclosure, torrential rain started to pour down. A storm was brewing, letting loose during the night, and continuing the deluge most of the next day. That would have been fine whilst we were enclosed in our truck all day, but we knew that we would be pitching our tents at some point that evening. The vote was made not to head out into the bush, and we continued driving until the rain eased off and found a scenic campsite. I noticed all was not well in the ranks! Some group members were not happy with having to engage in cooking and cleaning duties (after all, we were on a paid holiday). Others worsened this situation by taking on a supervisory role (need I say more).

I found it quite amusing with the meal process: boxes were emptied from the truck containing crockery, utensils, pans and food etc.; tables were set up, cooking undertaken, eating proceeded, and then the washing up and the flapping commenced! Yes, instead of drying up the used items from the meal with tea towels, they were waved and flapped about in the air and then put back into their respective boxes into the truck. I found this quite ingenious and good exercise for the arms.

And so it was, after a long day on the truck, having eaten our en-route lunch, we reached our Bonito campsite with some of us in a better mood than others. I was more than happy as I went off on a horse ride with Helle and a few others. To say I was a bit nervous on the back of a horse was an understatement after my last brush with a tree in Africa, but soon I was relaxing and trotting along like a professional. After merrily trotting around, we returned to a rather heated discussion around the pool between some of the group members. It seemed to have evolved out of Doris expressing her discontent at her working holiday. Others disagreed with her principles whilst others tried to calm the storm.

~ ~ ~

Now I have never got on particularly well with snorkelling, and the experience the next day seemed to be no different. I don't fully understand what I am doing wrong, which does not help my proficiency, and I end up looking like a rabid contorted fish. Our excursion to the nearby river should have been a much easier experience. We were fitted with wetsuits, the water was not deep, and there were no waterfalls.

Through the rainforest on the way to the river, our new guide Jermaine and I had been flirting together. So my hopes were high! It was upon reaching the river, spotting a caiman on the riverbank, and discovering that I did not like snorkelling in very shallow water, that I refused to go any further. So the group left me at the side of the river. I waited until another tour group came along and started off snorkelling with them but started panicking with my breathing and the shallow water. So it was back to the riverbank again. I was somewhat unsure as to what I should do standing on the river bank alone in my dry wetsuit, as it was a one-way route, and my group would not be returning. But I was not to worry for too long, as a driver appeared and took me back through the rainforest to a car that would take me to my truck. I was almost wishing it wouldn't as all my street cred was well out of the window, and I would certainly not be flirting with the guide.

That night a bbq was set out for us. I was not best pleased as there was barely anything left for me to eat by the time I got to the table! Being vegetarian, there was little variety of food anyway, so I was not on a winner in the first place. I decided that I would be better off having a few beers, that would keep my hunger at bay. It also had the unfortunate effect of a severe hangover the following morning, discovering there was chewing gum in my hair, and I had a headache. This was going to be a relaxing day; that is all I knew.

After my relaxing day, I had an early evening. We were to be leaving early the following day to the Pantanal - home to the largest concentration of crocodiles globally, as it is the world's largest wetlands area. I had been organised and had bought a white shirt and strong mosquito repellent. We had been warned these would be necessary whilst in the wetlands (for crocodiles or mosquitos?) What I was not warned about was not to go to the toilet in the bushes. Now, as that was part of our daily routine when we had nowhere civilised to stop off, this was to bite me on the bum, literally.

At our pit stop at the side of the track, Helle and I sprinted off into the few bushes we could see, only to squat down and find a swarm of mosquitos attacking us on our backsides! The pain was unbearable for us, but we could not stop once we started. We did not know whether to laugh or cry whilst pulling our shorts up and running back to our vehicle. I can only highlight that it was an uncomfortable afternoon on the truck for us both. Yet it seemed amusing for the others, who questioned why we had not put our mosquito repellent on our bottoms. Well, I wouldn't have thought it was the most obvious place to put it. There was no respite for our posteriors as we then had a 2-hour boat ride for the final part of our journey to the resort in the Pantanal. Suitably slathered in mosquito repellent and white shirts adorned, we enjoyed wildlife and bird spotting. I thought I spotted the world's largest parrot, the blue and yellow Hyacinth Macaw, but it was so high up in the sky it could have been a stray Ryanair flight.

That evening I had my first experience of the Brazilian national drink, the Caipirinha, made with local cachaca, sugar and lime. I found it very tasty; it had a bit of zing to it. However, I made sure to take it easy with them as it was a 05:00 start the next morning. I was excited as we were going to have a horseriding excursion through the Pantanal.

The following day, I was not so excited about being on the tallest horse or going as fast as we were. I was quite content to be wading through the wetland areas but not best pleased in the fields when the bossy couple came cantering past. At that point, my horse decided it wanted to join in and started galloping after them. I wouldn't have minded so much if it had happened just once, but this pair clearly found it quite funny and set off my horse on at least two other occasions. I am not sure if they could hear me shouting and then swearing at them as the wind rushed past us, but if they did, they chose to ignore my pleas and carried on! It was a pretty bedraggled Mandie that returned to the resort that afternoon, but also an exhilarated one. I was now a champion horse racing jockey and would look into dressage upon my return to England.

I managed to find some food leftovers but was not too worried, as I had taken a shining to the Caipirinhas.

It was time to leave the next day and take a relaxing boat ride back whilst enjoying watching the birdlife. The highlight was the guide pointing out the Hyacinth Macaw, I got to see it after all, and it was all the more poignant as this bird was at risk of extinction. However, I certainly did not make another toilet stop in the bushes en route!

~ ~ ~

If I thought we would not have to get up earlier for a morning start, I was wrong. The following day it was 04.30, quick breakfast and back on the road. We really must be covering some miles. But truck life was good; Jimmy kept us amused with card games/quizzes and general banter. Discontent amongst the troops was kept below the radar, and we made an effort to get on with each other. We also had Lewis's birthday to look forward to that evening. We had made him a card, and I wrote an amusing ditty for him (it involved changing the differential, reminiscing to our truck breakdown), and we all joined in the singing.

We reached the beach resort of Paraty on the Brazilian Costa Verde. Having completed our truck chores, we needed to get our washing cleaned at the launderette, and shop for our personal treats and necessities. We mooched around our campsite eyeing the other tour company trucks that were arriving. The drivers from all of them were used to meeting up with each other here as they used it as a base camp.

As the day progressed, spirits were high, the beer was flowing, and we were all getting to know each other from the different tour groups. I was on dinner duty with Sarah and Jimmy, and having fed and watered our group, we were suitably pleased with our efforts. We went onto the next task of washing up and drying used items. We had a system, but it seems that was not good enough for Cassandra and Rodney in their supervisory capacity. Well, I had had enough; I lost my temper with them and told them quite clearly and directly (with a few expletives) to leave us to our flapping! I was not pleased with myself for losing my temper with them. I had spent many hours between my travels practising meditation and the art of tolerance- where was it when I needed it? I blamed it on the beers (not my bear) taking effect.

Later that evening, after a few more drinks were imbibed by us all, we were singing and chatting in our semi-circle of camping chairs. During this time a driver from another company was bothering our driver Trudy. This came to a crescendo when he started to play fight with her, and she called to me for help. Now why she picked me, I will never know. However, with my imaginary superwoman cape on, I dived in to assist, and we were all rolling on the floor with me prising them apart. Mission accomplished, I returned to our semi-circle to rejoin the gaiety. Dinky Doo was waiting for me, his paws covering his eyes. The other driver was displeased by my interference and so cajoled me out of my circle of safety whilst taunting me. I did try to take it in good fun, but then remembered I had learned plenty of body combat moves in my dance class back at the gym in England. What a fantastic opportunity this presented to practice them.

So it was with a running lunge and flying through the air like a ninja, I landed on the driver! He tried to beat me off, but my moves were flowing through my mind and out through my legs and arms that were punching and kicking (yes, I had attended boxing classes too!) After the shock and, to be quite honest, the most amusing spectacle they must have all seen for a long time, a few of the group pulled us apart. I was pretty pleased, as, at that point, the driver had me in a headlock! The incredible thing about the whole incident was that I came out of it unscathed! I was indulged and commended by some of the group who were empathetic to the cause (this all started in Trudy's defence). However, I was groaned at and told off by others for my unladylike behaviour. It made no difference; I was basking in the glory of the attention and my heroic efforts.

It was all to take a turn for the worse that night, though. It was late, and it was dark; I was sharing a tent with Sarah, but I had behaved myself, I had not talked into the night, and we were settled down to sleep. I had not bothered to change clothes and had flopped out on top of my sleeping bag in my t-shirt and jeans. I then decided I needed the toilet. I donned my head torch but did not switch it on immediately as I did not want to disturb Sarah. It was all quiet outside, and I could spot the toilet block not too far away. It was, however, far enough for me to fall over a tent's guylines, flying through the air and landing flat on my hands, knees and face! My head torch was smashed, and I limped to the toilet block. I heard somebody call out to see if I was okay; I assured them I was, carried out my ablutions and limped back to my tent.

Hearing the commotion, Sarah was awake upon my return. After I explained to her what had happened, we were in fits of giggles as to the irony of it. I had been embroiled in a fight with a driver with not a mark on me to show for it. But then, by just taking a trip to the toilet, I had returned with ripped jeans where my scratched and bloody knees protruded, a smashed headlight and cut hands. Why had I not learned from my Africa trip when I didn't turn my torch on and fell over the box just outside the tent?

Thankfully, we had another lazy day ahead. I returned to the enchanting colonial town to meander, collect my laundry, and stop for a beer with some guys. Upon my return to camp, I was approached by my sparring partner, the driver, apologising for his behaviour the previous night. He explained he should have been more professional and was worried he would get into trouble. I assured him that I, for one, would not be reporting him; after all, he did have sore ribs and seemed to have suffered already. If I am honest, I was pretty displeased with my behaviour in terms of it not reflecting positively on the more tolerant 'me' I was working towards. I had to forgive myself more than having to forgive him. Some years later, whilst at a travel show in London, I was surprised when a representative from one of the stands ran up to me and tapped me on the shoulder. He had been a driver on another truck and had witnessed the whole event. That is how he had recognised me at the travel show. My notoriety precedes me!

~ ~ ~

It was our last evening in Paraty, and we had been told about a bar nearby where the locals would be practising the Samba ready for Carnival. Some of us wanted to visit that establishment, and I was so excited I headed off in advance with Helle and Sarah. We clearly had not got our directions right; as we went along the lane and turned left, perhaps it should have been right. We heard singing and dancing, and so we headed towards what we believed to be the bar. It turned out to be somebody's back garden, we knew that as we were being chased out of it by a pack of barking dogs! We ran for our lives until we were out of the garden and out of breath! Thankfully we reached our correct destination. It was on our right.

The rest of the group arrived, and we spent the evening dancing, attempting to follow in the footsteps of our local samba dancers. They were very patient with us and were all in good humour. We assumed that as none spoke English, and we did not speak Portuguese (the primary language in Brazil). Still, there was a lot of smiling while jigging around to music.

The next day was leading to the climax of the trip, we were almost at Rio de Janeiro. I was thrilled and excited to be going there for Carnival week, not just for the main parade event itself but also for the various Balls that were to take place. I had packed a few glittery clothing items in my backpack, especially for these occasions, and had ordered my Ball tickets in advance. The first night was the 'Red and Black Ball', where needless to say the theme was to wear red and black and is named after Rio's favourite football team, the Regata do Flamengo. Suitably attired in a red and black outfit (I managed to use some offcuts to make an outfit for Dinky Doo, too), I strutted off with a few others who had chosen this Ball. We arrived and felt like film stars as we walked the red carpet outside with crowds cheering. Once inside and having got our bearings and a drink, I began to scour the scene to see how these events likened to nightclubs back home. The dancing for a start was more exciting in style, and it wasn't long before I joined in.

We enjoyed our evening, and as was the custom at these events, we did not leave until the early hours of the morning. Our taxi driver kept us in high spirits by playing his music loud in the car; perhaps this was a distraction technique. I innocently asked him why he was not stopping at any of the red traffic lights; surely he could get in trouble for that? He replied that he was carrying on through and continuously moving, because if he stopped, as tourists, we could be shot at by people in other cars. I wished I had not asked!

After a day of rest, we headed out to the 'Favela Rocinha'. Our guide explained that a favela is a type of informal settlement or shantytown where residents do not pay taxes. Hence, there is no officially set up electricity, drainage/sewer system or hospitals. Going on this type of visit is always a dilemma. You don't want to stare at locals as if in a goldfish bowl, but this needs balancing with providing an income for the local community. Our particular tour was one where a percentage was contributed towards a new child daycare centre. Everything was explained as we were taken up and down through narrow alleys and into homes and a shop where local art was available to buy.

Unfortunately, the favela can be a dangerous place, not only to visit but importantly for the families who live there. Our guide explained how millions of dollars are gained per month by the drug cartels. These prominent groups truly run the favelas. It was sobering and humbling to learn all this. As we walked along the sewer strewn streets, we were warned when we were not to take photos, and who not to look at or make eye contact with. As we took our last steps out of the favela, we were given that same warning. As we walked straight ahead, I saw to my left an image that will never leave my mind and summed up the whole ethos of what we had been told. There was a young guy in his late teens sitting on a white plastic chair. Nothing unusual about that, you might think. He was calling out to 'hello' to us in a friendly yet underlying menacing manner, with a machine gun in his hands!

~ ~ ~

The next evening we reached the culmination of the whole trip - the Rio Carnival at the Sambadomo, where the top Samba Schools compete in a parade the like of which I have not seen before, or since! I dressed up in a black and silver outfit that had become hidden deep down in the depths of my backpack, and some of the group got out their best outfits. It was a fair distance to the Sambadromo, but we enjoyed the sights en route. Everything was so overboard, the costumes, the food, the music…. everything was an abundance to the eye. We had a great view from our grandstand in the Sambadromo, and we spent the evening amazed and dazzled by the spectacular floats and glittering flamboyant costumes. There was just so much to absorb. It was hard imagining how much work had been contributed by the local communities for each samba school. We drank it all in and stayed until the very last float had passed by. By now, I was used to seeing the ungodly hour of 05.30 but not staying up all night for it, and yet it was so worth observing such a spectacular event.

Finally ready to leave, our group made one last visit to the toilet. As we departed the Sambadromo, the realisation hit us that there would be tens of thousands of spectators competing for the same public transport - and yes, there they were! On every metro, every street, and on the roads. To be fair, nobody seemed to be in a hurry, and there was a lot of singing and dancing taking place. We decided to walk back to our hotel; I followed, not wanting to take the lead and creating extra mileage by getting misdirected.

Having reached our hotel around 06.30, we ate our breakfast and slept away the hours until mid-afternoon. In our last few days in Rio, we switched between lazing around the pool and visiting the various beaches such as Copacabana and Ipanema. One such day by the pool, I chatted with a girl living in Rio but was about to fly home to England. As she told her story, you could see the sheer anxiety oozing out. This young lady had been funded to work as a volunteer in a local favela, in a nursery. One day whilst leaving the nursery, she had been held up against a doorway by gunpoint and was robbed. As if this was not horrendous enough, she had innocently gone to the police. They informed her that she must leave the country immediately as her visit to the police had now put her life in danger! We took turns keeping her company until it was time for her to leave for the airport. I hoped her journey home was safe and that she was back home with her family.

Our last night out was at the 'La Scala Gay Ball', usually held on the final night of Rio Carnival and is the most famous of the week of Carnival Balls. I had eked out all my glittery outfits, jewellery and accessories, for this special moment… but to my dismay, I could not fit in any of them! I had noticed I had gained some weight during the trip, and my costumes had not stretched out with me. So it was plan B, and I managed to tear up some clothes and make something unusual out of them for Dinky Doo and me. The guys in the group took delight in now having something to wear, and so it was that my glitzy tops and bottoms were adorned by them. It was interesting to see how my gold sequined mini skirt managed to fit as a top for one of the guys. One cut up my pyjamas to make a pirate effect outfit, and another sported a silver and black split skirt over his boxer shorts. We paled into insignificance, though, when we reached La Scala. We goggled in wonderment at the bedazzling outfits, often minuscule, worn by men and women parading along the red carpet into the venue. We danced away the night; it seems my practice night back in the local bar in Paraty had been of some use. We were all flagging by 04:00 though, as it was so hot and stuffy, and feathers from costumes were flying everywhere. My body just about made it into the taxi and back out of it upon reaching the hotel. I felt like I had danced my feet off.

There was no time to lay in though, I had to check-out. No more of living it up in style for me in a hotel, which had been provided as part of the tour; it was off to a hostel to share a female dorm for me! As it happened, before I departed, the manager from the tour company who had kept popping up en route had come over to see how the tour had been for us all. I took the opportunity to put forward my complaints. I begrudged paying extra for the hotel back in Ushuaia and paying for meals and optional tours we believed would (or should) be included. In addition, we had been subjected to the bossiness of a specific couple for the entire trip! In my defence, I was not the only one to put forward these issues. I am aware that optional tours are purely that, but we seemed to have more of those and less food (especially for me at buffets!). I guess he kind of wished he had not asked but promised to email me and arrange a partial refund. With that to my satisfaction, I flounced from reception whilst announcing my goodbyes to the group.

~ ~ ~

It was not a goodbye for very long though, as the next day Helle came to visit me at my hostel, and we went out with the expectation of going out on a boat trip. Somehow, despite our research, we could not find our boat and had missed the last one of the day when we finally found the correct port. With the best intentions, I led Helle to where I believed the shopping centre to be, but it turned out to be the wrong one. Still, I bought a CD which I thought had my favourite song from the Sambadromo parade, and this also turned out to be the wrong one! We gave up and went out for a drink with some of the others from the group instead.

The next day was special for it was my birthday, yes, I had miraculously reached another one! Furthermore, it was on my bucket list to visit the 'Seven Wonders of the World' and there was one in the immediate vicinity, the 'Christ the Redeemer' statue. I treated myself and joined a city tour of Rio de Janeiro rather than traipsing around on my own, probably getting lost. Our tour group was whisked away on a 15-minute visit to the Cathedral (the most modern I had ever visited), with a 5 minute stop outside the Maracana Football stadium (the largest in the world at the time). This mammoth football stadium was opened in 1950 to hold the FIFA World Cup (unfortunately for them, Brazil lost to Uruguay, 2-1). Although hosting mainly football matches, it has been known to host concerts and other sporting events.

Eventually, we reached the Christ the Redeemer statue perched on Mount Corcovado. This distinguished statue of Jesus was, according to our guide, the largest in the world at 30 metres high and 28 metres wide at the fingertips of the outstretched hands. We were suitably dazzled and impressed with our stop of 45 minutes there, not having to rush around. The views over Sugar Loaf Mountain and over Rio were tremendous, and we were told that real estate in any area nearby had massively increased in value. We then moved on to Sugarloaf Mountain to view from the opposite direction, back over to the Christ the Redeemer statue and a different perspective over Rio. We ascended the stately Sugarloaf Mountain by going up its 396 metres in a cable car. The 360-degree views from both the glass cable car and the mountain summit were indeed stunning. There was Copacabana beach where we had just had lunch. It was a lovely day out, and one I would need to hold in my memory as I lost most of my photos of the whole trip through Brazil.

I joined Helle and the rest of my ex-tour group for a meal and a drink later that evening. They surprised me with a birthday cake, the singing of 'Happy Birthday' and some unexpected gifts which included a painted canvas material with a picture of, and from, the favela we had visited. So I was not the enemy in the ranks after all. I must have softened some hearts along the way. And it was such a relief not to be 40 any more, making it through to another birthday!

Back at the hostel that evening, my birthday ended with a bang, literally! My fellow hostellers had now become firm friends, and we were celebrating my birthday, drinking, dancing and singing the night away. Some guys had just played a Samba tune for me on bongos, and we were laughing and joking in the kitchen just before midnight. Suddenly, a bang came from the boiler in the corner, and flames came out! We all ran out with our beers in our hands, but after the initial shock of it, some of the guys went back in to sort it out - perhaps they threw their beers over it to put out the flames. Crikey, I spoke to soon, I could have missed on reaching the next birthday!

~ ~ ~

It would be out of character to not have a day where I got lost. And so it was, on my penultimate final day, that I set out to find the elusive ferry I could not find before, Niteroi bound. I set out from my hostel and managed to take the metro to Cinelandia. From here, it went downhill, although I was trying to go uphill to the hilltop district of Santa Theresa,

I just could not find it! It was of no use taking directions, as I was being sent round in circles. Eventually, I found a station attendant who took me to the correct tram departure stop. There was no tram to depart, though, for another 45 minutes. By which time, of all people, Cassandra and Rodney spotted me and joined me at the front of the queue. We went on the tram up the hill, but conscious of time, I took just a quick wander around the narrow winding streets of the Santa Theresa area. It had an arty vibe and seemed a pleasant chilled out spot, but I had to leave in the hope of finding the ferry on time in my quest to reach the island of Niteroi.

With a lot of walking, the help of a taxi driver, a tourist and a policeman, I succeeded in my quest and boarded the ferry. I felt a sense of achievement, it had been a mission, but finally, I was on my way to Niteroi. Having reached the island, I took a short walk around to get views and take photos from a different perspective to Rio de Janeiro. Mission accomplished, I hopped back on a ferry to Rio, trotted back to the hostel, and packed up, ready to leave the following day to make my way back to the UK.

Here was the end of an adventure; on my long journey home to England, I had plenty to reflect on. I had made a few good friends (who I have remained in contact with), had some laughs, experienced some amazing sights/nature, our truck had been hit by a car in the middle of nowhere in Argentina, I had been to a Ball and had been wowed at the Rio Carnival. Contrastingly, I had been in a physical fight and been unscathed, then had fallen over and got hurt the same night. The fight was a battle, not so much physically but psychologically. I thought my character had developed more positively, yet I had also been slowly brewing due to certain people's toxic attitudes and behaviours in the tour group. Although I realised that being within a group of people for the duration of a tour does mean making compromises and trying to be positive, I made the comparison to my previous tour group in Africa in 2001. The explanation I came up with was that I found myself more comfortable with a group of differing nationalities, as was the case in Africa, rather than with predominantly British. Of course, that opened up further questions for me about myself; for example, was I living in the correct country? Despite the highs and lows of it all, the experiences were to prepare Dinky Doo and me for the next trip. I was going to climb to Mount Everest Base Camp!

~ ~ ~

Overall Trip Cost: £2000 (Flights £400, Tour £900, Spending & Other Costs £700)

Top Tip: When travelling to a country with a different language, try to learn as many useful phrases as possible, at the very least 'Please' and 'Thank You'. It goes a long way with the locals to know you have tried to learn the basics. Communication in the country you are travelling to is not always as simple as you would think. There are apps available now on your phone, some of which are free, to assist you with translation.

Brazil, Iguazu Falls from Above in Helicopter   Brazil, Rio Carnival at Sambodomo

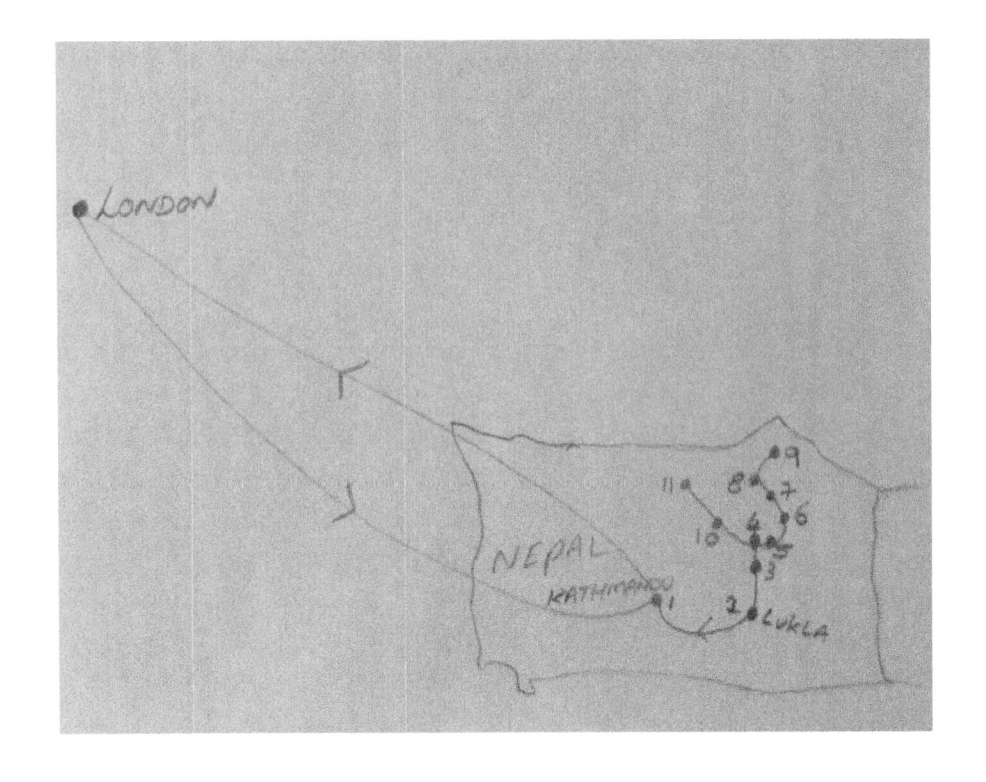

EVEREST ROUTE NEPAL - 24 DAYS

1. KATHMANDU
2. LUKLA
3. PHAKDING
4. NAMCHE BAZAAR
5. TENGBOCHE
6. DINGBOCHE
7. LOBUCHE
8. GORAK SHEP & KALA PATTHAR
9. EVEREST BASE CAMP
10. DOLE
11. GOKYO RI

EVEREST, NEPAL 2008

Up, and Up, then Down, and Back Up

Nepal is a country of contrast with its sprawling city of Kathmandu, its stunningly mountainous areas, and the second deepest canyon in the world, the Kali Gandaki Canyon. The 8 out of 10 world's highest peaks contrast against these dominating the outlying landscape. Mount Everest majestically rises above them, the highest mountain in the world above sea level.

At a mere 60 million years old, Mount Everest stands proudly as a challenge to those wishing to push themselves to its summit and is formed due to the shift of India's continental plate. India's plate crashing under Asia resulted in raising a mass of land upwards, thereby creating the Himalayan range. Due to the continuing shift of the tectonic plates, Mount Everest continues to grow at an average of 44 millimetres each year. Don't leave it too long to climb it then if that is your intention!

My daily existence was a mixed bag in 2008. I had moved into a bigger house and had rented out my previous home to a friend. Having bought a larger house, I needed a lodger to help fund the monthly costs. My work as a manager was becoming more stressful after settling into the role. There were more pressures on those, like me, working in the justice system. I felt trapped. I need some time away to think about my future and perhaps challenge myself. But what on earth possessed me to think it was a good idea to climb the highest mountain in the world, I will never know? It was enough for me to climb out of bed each morning and hike to work and up the four floors to my office! So it was off to the gym and into the hands of a personal trainer who had donated 3 hours of his time. I had decided that my motivation to make sure I actually went through with this climb was to do it in the name of charity.

Not that it helped my mindset when I first stepped onto the treadmill and was put through my paces. It was at that point I started to realise what I had let myself in for!

I had heard about a Children's Home in Kathmandu and got in touch with Indira who dedicates her life to the children living there. The Children's Home became a beneficial distraction from the pain of the training for Everest, as I was able to busy myself with collecting items to take to the children.

The airline (Qatar) had kindly allowed me to take one extra luggage item when I contacted them and stated my mission. A week before I was due to leave, a problem occurred to me. How would I get all this luggage - my big backpack, large holdall with donations in, and my day pack, to the airport? Bearing in mind that my usual route to Heathrow involved three trains in three hours. I was pondering on this dilemma at a works party, and a colleague asked what the matter was. When I explained, her husband promptly piped up that he would donate the taxi fare to the airport. So far, I had seen the goodness in people and the generosity each time I made a request. That was aside from all those who had sponsored me in my hike up Everest. So I set off with a spring in my step, even though it was only February, to Kathmandu....

Aside from a minor scare with the taxi booking to the airport, things had gone very smoothly; this was a refreshing change. I was well packed with my useful items; head torch, washing powder, superglue, training golf ball, and now duct tape. It could fix just about anything if required. I took it off its big bulky roll and wound it round a peg so that there was enough for emergencies and so it was compact and light to carry. Yes, I was prepared, and the outset was smooth so far; even Dinky Doo was surprised at having such an easy ride.

My first flight from Heathrow was headed to Doha, Qatar, where I believed I had a romantic encounter. Things might be looking up. I was coming through security and linked eyes with a gorgeous guy. I then went to the transfer desk, where I was told to go to gate 10. The guy was behind me and said to follow him, which I did until he got into a lift. I do not like lifts, and I lost him going up the escalator, but then he reappeared on the next floor. He called me over and asked me why I did not get in the lift. I explained, and then we had a quick chat in which he asked me to be his girlfriend. Allegedly his name was Vassel, he was going to Dubai, and his family lived in Doha. Something tells me it wasn't a romantic encounter at all. He seemed to know all the staff at the airport transfer desks, so maybe he was undercover trying to find info on me as I looked like a suspect!

~ ~ ~

With only one encounter under my belt, I reached the airport in Kathmandu, where the Kumuka trek representative was waiting for me. The representative and a driver took me to the Hotel Florid, this was much better service than with my last tour company! My hotel was not the most salubrious, but I received a warm welcome from the owner and his wife. I managed to get a nice hot shower before my first experience of a city power cut.

It was arranged for that evening that I would meet with Indira at the Children's Home. As per the arrangements, I was met by Indira's daughter. She led me through the darkness of the back streets to the Children's Home. I could still make out full garbage cans overspilling lining the sides of the streets, crumbling houses and makeshift roofs held down by bricks. This Thamel area seemed to have fallen into despair and disrepair since its popular 'Hippy' days. Upon our arrival, the children said 'Namaste' (a greeting of respect) to me. I sat and drank lemon tea with Indira, and Desmond who was volunteering there for one month. We agreed that Indira would meet me the next day to go shopping for material to make clothes for the children. The women at the local prison would subsequently make pyjamas out of the material, and Indira arrange a visit for me to collect the finished garments.

Desmond showed me the way back towards my hotel; let's face it, the odds are I would not have found it in daylight, let alone in the dark! We went via the Rum Doodle Bar, which is where all the Everest climbers traditionally go. I spotted the wall where all the foot-shaped beer mats are with people's names on who had ascended Everest - my name would be there too upon my return from Base Camp!

With my jet lag catching up on me, I woke up relatively late the next morning. Thinking of power cuts, I rushed to get in the shower. The zipper from my fleece went up into my nose, which promptly started bleeding. Good start to the day! My rush was all in vain, as it transpired there was no hot water until mid-afternoon, so a cold shower it was. I had to be ready, as Desmond was fetching me at midday to take the large holdall of goodies I had bought with me to the Children's Home. The children looked at me with shy awe, whilst we distributed their gifts. The children loved playing with the balloons, and some put their new clothes on. I noticed how little the children had by way of toys; outside they played with old tyres, fistfuls of straw, cardboard boxes, and footballs. Despite what little they had to play with, the children were smiling, shrieking, and laughing. The experience was very humbling overall, and I felt my contribution was very small in the scheme of things. Still, I was made to feel welcome and appreciated by Indira and the children.

My next day was my big move, well actually, I was just moving five minutes along the road to a different hotel. This new hotel was included in my Everest Base Camp tour. Upon arrival there, I lugged my backpack up to my room and settled in. It seemed strange that such a nice hotel did not provide towels, but never mind, I would call reception. They duly bought up some towels whilst giving me a strange look and leaving with my key. Before I could immerse myself in a nice hot shower, the manager appeared; he explained I was in the wrong room, which was why it was not set up, even with towels. And so it was I had to repack all the clothes sprawled around the room and make my way to the correct room.

That evening, at our pre-departure meeting for the trek, I met my co-adventurers, and what made this even better was that food was included! The lineup included: Joey, Bruce and Wayne, all friends from Australia (three fit guys), Gerry from New Zealand (another hunk, what would be the odds!), Emma and Mike from Canada (a sporty athletic couple), Rada and Don from Australia (an amiable and genuine couple), Gregg from Florida, and Annette from New Zealand (my long-suffering room-mate!). I introduced them all to Dinky Doo, although at this point, it was touch and go as to whether he would make it to Everest. I was loathed to carry any extra weight in my pack, luckily for him, I decided that he was light enough to not make much of a difference.

After receiving our itinerary and instructions, we headed out to the Rum Doodle Bar - well, where else would we go? This was the coolest place in town for excited adventurers. We spent our time there wisely, scaremongering each other with the reality of the horrors ahead. Potentially ahead of us lay: rope bridges, glacier crossings, Maoist guerillas (they preyed on unsuspecting tourists, threatening/robbing them), and scariest of all - the flight from Kathmandu to Lukla, one of the world's most dangerous. Upon descent to Lukla airport, the pilot faces a mix of irregular winds, low air pressure, and mountainous terrain, with just a short runway leading to the edge of a mountain.

We were given a city tour the day before departure, a kind of false sense of security really, the calm before the storm. We got to know each other and were taken around Swayambath Stupa, a monkey temple. Of course, the obligatory monkeys were running around pretending to be cute but grabbed any food they spotted. It was onto Pattan and Durbar Square and the Golden Temple. Eventually, we went to the Boudanath Stupa. Here, I took the opportunity to be blessed by a Lama (a monk), as this would keep us all safe on our tour, I hoped! The group watched in awe as I kneeled before the Lama, who chanted at me for what seemed a long time. Finally, he took my Kata (Silk Scarf), gave me oil to put on my forehead and hair, and then threw rice at me. Yes, we would be safe.

I felt I had been quite brave approaching a Lama for a blessing. Previously, my last one took place in Thailand and probably saved my life. So I was, therefore, keen to repeat the practice. I had been with a tour group, and we had gone up to one of the temples. We were shown how to shake sticks in a tub. When it felt right, we would each shake our sticks out onto the ground. You would then go and pick out your corresponding piece of paper with the number from your stick. This was fine for the rest of the group because their numbers had pieces of paper with their fortune written in English and Thai; mine was written solely in Thai. I took said piece of paper to the guide, whose face turned to one of horror, and she instructed me to throw both the piece of paper and the stick back into the temple! No matter who or how we asked her what was written, she would give nothing away. Instead, I had to do everything at the temple that would give me a blessing. I had to ring a row of bells, pour oil from a spoon around a bowl, and be blessed by a monk who tied a piece of string around my wrist to protect me. The whole group were a bit nervous, me even more so.

Our tour guide had gleefully left our group and handed us all over to another. This guide was to take us up into the mountains, but before doing so, the two of them must have had a quiet word about me. This became apparent when we reached our first mountain village. I was chosen to visit a local Shamen, the head witch doctor. The group were fascinated by this and followed at a safe distance, standing in the doorway, eyes agog. I meanwhile was sat down on a small stool. There was an anticipation for the Shamen's arrival. I sat there, deciding whether to make a run for it or not, but the Shamen arrived, and my left arm was lifted into the air. I looked away in case I was to be alleviated of a body part, maybe a finger or even hand whilst chanting started up, and more string was wound around my wrist, and signs made in the air. After my ordeal was over, I was assisted from the stool. At that point, I took flight out to the open arms of my fellow travellers, who were very much in admiration of my bravery.

~ ~ ~

Yes, for my Mount Everest trip, I was now well prepared, as were my group. Our two Sherpa guides and five Sherpa porters were grateful when we told them of my Lama blessing the previous day. We were off, on one of the most dangerous flight paths in the world. We were ready to be led to Everest Base Camp by our Sherpas, climbing 'Sagarmatha' - fondly known as 'The Head in the Great Blue Sky'. The Sherpa are an ethnic Tibetan group native to Nepal, and many are highly regarded as elite mountaineers. They have valuable knowledge of the Himalayan region, which provides them with the expertise to guide climbers up through the peaks, passes and high altitudes of Mount Everest. It has been speculated that a genetic adaptation to living in high altitudes contributes to their hardiness and climbing ability.

Unlike myself, our Sherpas were much more adaptable to very early mornings. I found it pretty pointless being ready for an 05.30 bus to the airport, as our flight could not depart until the fog lifted. However, apparently, this was a usual thing our guides were accustomed to. The time was spent wisely, some felt, by joking and scaremongering about our upcoming flight and the aircraft. The fog lifted, we had eaten our packed breakfasts, and it was time to load our luggage and board the small plane.

We were not sure there would be enough room for us, Dinky Doo, and the luggage, but somehow we all managed to squeeze onboard. It was not the first time I had been on an aircraft with propellers, but it was the first time I had been on one where you could see the pilots and the cockpit from the passenger compartment. Everything that had laughingly been said about the landing was true; there definitely was not a significant amount of distance for landing before reaching the edge of the mountain. But we had an expert pilot to who we were eternally grateful for our smooth and safe arrival in Lukla.

After sorting through our luggage to make sure we had everything we needed for the day, it was time to start our heroic journey to Everest Base Camp. At that point, we were under a false sense of security. It was a relaxed meandering wander for the first two hours, a gentle hike similar to a walk in the rolling hills and dales of England. Even better, we then stopped for lunch, which contained plenty of carbs, noodles and potatoes. It then went downhill for me, not literally as we were going upwards, but after such a pleasant morning meander, I was faced with my first swinging bridge!

Now I have never been a fan of bridges where you can see through the gaps in the floor, let alone those that can move from side to side. I watched the rest of the group pass across the bridge, with the guide doing all he could to coax me across. There were now three options - he would carry me across over his shoulder, I could remain where I was and freeze to death, or turn back (that was looking the most promising at that point). I am not sure which was shaking the most, me or the bridge, as I bravely stepped across, looking only forward, at the guide. Annette kindly walked behind me so that I would feel secure. I spent the next ten minutes wallowing in my glory and bravery, only to be faced with another dreaded swing bridge.

We had traversed alongside the Dudh Kosi River, which looked very blue down in the distance from our height. Our path had been gravel and rock, with steps in some places, but it was undoubtedly manageable at this point. We reached our first lodging of the trek in Phakding at 8563 feet high (2610 metres), and already it was way cooler than in Kathmandu. The only warm room was the dining room, as there was a roaring fire ablaze; our rooms were another matter. Fortunately, Annette and I had purchased matching red fleece thermal pyjama bottoms. I have to admit that I wore mine pretty much day and night for the rest of the trek- they could have walked back to Kathmandu themselves by the end of the trip!

Although I had gone to bed early at 20:00, I could not sleep until at least 23:00, and then that was only for a few hours. My mind was consumed with swing bridges - steel ones, wooden ones, all with holes in the bottom! I kept panicking about not being able to breathe, which, to be fair, was not an unfounded concern as I, by now, had a swollen throat. When climbing mountains at altitude, one thing to prepare for in advance as much as possible is the inevitable lack of oxygen as you climb higher, so where necessary, take along the appropriate medication. I had such medicines, which I did not need to resort to, but others eventually did. I also took along anything else that was recommended. My stock included: Kendal Mint Cake which is helpful as a source of energy, fresh garlic for assisting with acclimatisation, and nappy rash cream. The latter reputedly has other uses. For example, being used as sunscreen, lip balm or moisturiser, rather than purely salving the bottom!

Having been the last person into the lodge yesterday after our walk, I was determined not to be last again. I set off early to conquer the following five suspension bridges (yes, I took to counting them); however, the large herds of yaks beat me to them. It was fascinating to see how the thin, wavering bridges held their weight and how the tiny hooves (in proportion to their bodies) did not get stuck between the metal squares.

In the back of my mind, though, more dangerous than suspension bridges or being last was the threat of the Maoist Guerillas rumoured to be lurking on the trails of Everest. Statements were made in the Nepalese press that tourists were not harmed or targeted by Maoists. However, there were international warnings by Government agencies to be careful on the Everest trail due to the threat of being robbed by Maoist rebels. The system was alleged to be that you would be asked for a donation, and you would be given a receipt for the said donation. There was an informal tariff depending on your nationality: if you were American, you would be asked for the most money; then if German, a slightly lesser amount; and if you were British, you would pay the least. I cannot fathom out the reasoning, but it says a lot about perceptions of the British economy, and for once, I was pleased to be British. If you refused to pay the donation, you would be in trouble. There was a story about a Swedish guy who refused to donate. He carried on walking and thought he was safe; however, a few miles along the trail, he was severely beaten.

I was in the lead for the first three hours. However, after a couple of toilet stops in the bushes to mark my territory (which involved removing a fair amount of clothing items), I had now lapsed behind. I was beginning to feel slightly sick; I didn't know whether it was the thought of more bridges or the height we were now climbing at. I guess I was just lucky that I did not pick a bush with a Maoist guerilla hiding behind it.

However, there was no time to worry about all of that; we were now approaching our first significantly steep climb. We crossed the Dudh

Kosi river five times, winding up through forests on gravel/rock trails which became steeper and steeper and steeper; it was relentless. Our reward, though, was our first glimpse through the trees of Mount Everest standing majestically in the distance.

Considering we had been going up a lot, I noticed we were going down at some stages too. Now, what was the point of that? Upon reaching Namche Bazaar, a town that is a regular staging post for Everest treks, we learned that we were only at 3,440 metres (11,286 feet) in height. I can assure you that my legs felt we had walked a lot higher than that! It was, therefore, not an arduous task to climb into bed at 20:00 and sleep soundly. That was after I managed to get my headlamp to work correctly, although it wasn't really needed as there were no guy ropes to fall over.

The next day was an acclimatisation day, where I learned the importance of acclimatisation when climbing mountains. At the same time, I began my period of reflection on life. As much as I was bored of going upwards (yes already), I duly joined in the acclimatisation hike up a steep hill. This would help when we carried on with our actual trek the next day and from thereon. Climbing the hill that day gave me time to reflect on the very fact that friends back home had told me I would have time to reflect on life whilst climbing the mountain. I could use time wisely to delve deep into what I wanted out of life for my future. However, at this point, all I could think about was putting one foot in front of the other!

The views from the top were spectacular. We could see across to Ama Dablam (a Nepalese mountain at the highest peak of 22,349 feet or 6,812 metres) and Lhotse (the fourth highest mountain in the world at the height of 27,940 feet or 8,516 metres). Standing proud among/above them was our graceful Mount Everest, which, as you may know, is the highest mountain in the world at 29,031 feet (8,848 metres). I trusted our guides would not lead us astray onto the wrong mountain as they all looked quite similar to the untrained eye, just some were more prominent than others. On the subject of climbing the wrong mountain, if you have never read the book 'The Ascent of Rum Doodle'. I highly recommend it if you like a book with a sense of humour (just like this one- but on steroids). The book is a parody of a climb up Mount Everest, yet the author had never left England. I am loathed to admit it, but that book is a cult piece of comic literature, to which mine simply cannot compare in the hilarity stakes.

I was very pleased with myself on the way back down the hill; I was in the lead, I was way ahead. I got chatting with a guy from another tour group, and faithful Annette was not far behind. We were merrily conversing when I heard Annette calling me and one of our guides running towards us. We were going the wrong way! The group had carried on the right path, and we had veered off across the fields. The guide took us both back across the fields to our hotel, where we both promptly laid down for a rest for 20 minutes. Gutted, I was the last back in again.

It was sad to say goodbye to Rada and Don the next day, but when you get to that height on a mountain, you must listen to your body, and if all is not well, you need to get back down to a safe altitude. It had not helped that their room was near some young lads who kept them awake most of the night; anything like insufficient sleep is dangerous to carry on. We made sure that we had a group photo with them before they left us. I was very impressed with our tour company in many respects. In this instance, they were prepared with enough porters to ensure they could take people back down as and when necessary. On a more selfish note, who would I chat with now whilst meandering behind the others?

The scenery was spectacular again, blue sky, mountains, trees, a photo opportunity around every corner. It was surprisingly warm for the height we were at and the fact it was February. It was even more surprising that the trail was relatively level, easing gently up and then down and then back up again. It was the perfect time to do the rounds and get to know everybody, to learn their life stories; quite often, this was interrupted by the passing of yaks. The yak is a bovine cousin of the cow, except this species, has three times the lung capacity of the usual cow, hence its ability to climb the heights of the Nepalese mountains. Yes, I learnt a lot whilst strolling the long Everest trail, and right then I would have liked to have been a yak, not only for the increased lung capacity, but to have those tiny feet, compared to my size 8 canoes!

The meandering was not to last, and we hit the steep uphill shortly after brunch. It was, therefore, a surprise to us all that I was the third person at our goal, Tengboche, located at 12,660 feet (3,860 metres). The village is home to the revered Tengboche Monastery, the most important place of learning in the Khumbu region and considered the gateway to Mount Everest. I believe what propelled me on to Tengboche was plugging my earphones in and playing my music at full blast. There is nothing like a bit of dance music to keep those paws moving forward! We made the obligatory visit to the Tengboche Monastery late that afternoon. A dense fog had set in, and it was getting freezing cold. We watched a ceremony in the monastery, with most of the group staying only half an hour, but Gregg and I seeing it through to the very end. After much chanting, blowing bugles and tea, Gregg and I had to be chipped away from our seats; it was that cold (not really, but it gives you an idea of how freezing I felt)!

~ ~ ~

I was assured the following day that we had walked the worst part of the steepness; I found that hard to believe, we were climbing Mount Everest, for goodness sake. At that time of the morning, 06:00, with thick fog and bitterly cold air, the steepness was the last thing to worry me; I was freezing. It was around minus four degrees. I was half asleep as I stumbled out of bed. I made my last visit to a toilet at the end of the corridor in something meant to resemble a latrine. I wanted to make the most of it as I knew later I would be marking my territory out in the bushes en route to our destination. Still bleary-eyed, in a sleepwalking state, I returned to my room. Well, I thought it was my room, but it wasn't. It was, surprisingly to me, inhabited by a Japanese guy who was just emerging from his bed wearing a look of shock and indignation on his face. He was clearly not impressed that I had appeared in his doorway, and he resorted to shouting at me in Japanese! I wondered if he thought I understood as I retreated with a sheepish look on my face. At least, his tirade had woken me up.

Annette and I set off half an hour earlier than the others, but they soon caught us up. We decided to rest. If only I were a yak. It was hard going that day, and the trail was icy, yet the sun was shining through. I could not work that one out. We were getting enough breaks, but I was not eating much food. In hindsight, I should have made myself eat more of the delicious soups and noodle or rice concoctions (to which I had been adding my fresh garlic). This would have kept my strength going much better than it was. But I did keep going, up and up and up. By mid-afternoon, I was not in the best of moods. My MP3 player was not working for some reason, and we had reached a small bridge(I will use that term 'bridge' loosely) over a river that I just did not want to cross. I was fed up with going up, and I was fed up with bridges. I just stood there looking at what was supposed to resemble a bridge, but which was simply a few planks nailed together by someone who evidently did not have a full carpenter's licence.

Eventually, fed up with my loitering and with no more sympathy coming my way, I was pushed from behind by the guide, and Bruce pulled me from the front. I found a nice spot on the other side where I simply sat down. I decided this is where I could happily stay for the rest of my life, or at least until the group returned from their arduous climb to Base Camp. This was not allowed, and so we all arrived in Dingboche that afternoon, now at 14,470 feet (4410 metres) high.

I was not the only one at a low point. The conversation that evening revolved around not caring anymore if we trod in yak dung; it was just about ensuring we kept one foot moving in front of another. On the positive side, we now had two nights in one place. On the other hand, it was an acclimatisation day the next day which involved traipsing up another steep hill. For the moment, though, we were all content in the safety of our lodge. We chatted, played cards, updated our journals, and I concocted a warmer outfit for Dinky Doo. Our evening was topped off with a nice meal, but I still found it hard to eat much, and my throat was still swollen.

Leaving Dingboche, it was a gentler hike. I was spurred on from having been the second person back down from the steep hill on yesterday's acclimatisation hike. I was beginning to enjoy this stretch of the journey. There was the time and ability to view the spectacular scenery of the snow, mountains and trees. We came to the Scott Fischer memorial stupa. He was a renowned expedition climber who did not rely on supplied oxygen when attempting his ascents to the summit of Everest. Fischer's last expedition to the Everest summit was in 1996, where he died in a snow blizzard during his descent. Although built with his name on, the Stupa stands there to pay respect and remember all who died climbing Mount Everest.

~ ~ ~

It was a shock to us all that I was the first to reach our next destination, and I even had to wait twenty minutes for most of the group to catch up. We were now at our lodge in Lobuche, the highest hotel in the world, at the height of 16,210 feet (4,940 metres). My joy was short-lived as we were off after lunch on another steep acclimatisation hike! To be fair, it was not too harsh, and I made it two-thirds of the way up. All was fine until I sat on a rock to get my breath back, but I lost my balance and fell; I was rolling downhill. This was no good; I had just put a lot of effort into walking up that hill. Bruce caught me to stop me from going any further. Not only had I previously not enjoyed reaching the age of 40, but I was beginning to wonder if I would make it to 50! I sat with Annette for a short while, and we agreed it was a good idea to go back down. It would have been a good idea if we had gone the correct way, but yet again we went in the wrong direction! It was dangerously rocky and slippery and was taking us a long time. Thankfully we were spotted from afar by a Sherpa who hopped like a mountain goat over to us and took us back to where we should have been.

We had not even reached Everest Base Camp, and some of the guys were route planning and talking about the quickest way back. Personally, I could not see what the rush was; the last thing you need to be doing at the heights we were at is speeding about at high altitudes. It seemed to be a lot of macho talk, using excuses to camouflage their sufferings so as to return to lower ground. The next day these discussions continued without Annette having a say. She would be the most affected as I was due to go further on from Base Camp with four of the guys to the Gokyo lakes. We lost two of our group that day, the Canadian couple Emma and Mike, who were suffering from Altitude Sickness; they had to go back down. It was too dangerous for them to go any higher. Our trek that day was, however, quite easygoing, with a few steep ups and downs and rocks to clamber over. Overall it was very manageable (or had my legs just become desensitised).

That day, having time to think about what I wanted in life, I came to two conclusions: I was not going to drink any form of coca-cola anymore, not even diet coke. In my mind, it was not healthy for the body in any way, but red wine and coffee were going to stay! I decided I wanted a healthier nutritious lifestyle for life. Secondly, I would not watch Eastenders (there is nothing wrong with the programme I hasten to add, I loved it) or any other soap anymore. It was purely symbolic of the fact that I wanted to spend my time in different ways with varying activities; for example, learning photography, nutrition, horse-riding and belly dancing. I wanted to look back in old age, not just at my travels but also at having a fulfilling life, not sitting on a sofa. In the meantime, I had a mountain to conquer, and I may have been one of the slowest, but I felt I really was achieving something just by plodding on and continuing towards my goal.

We were not that far from Base Camp and were pleased when we reached our inn at Gorak Shep (at 16,942 feet, or 5,164 metres). We were not so delighted to learn we would be climbing Kala Patthar that afternoon. Kala Patthar, also referred to as Black Rock, is a notable landmark. It has the most accessible close-up view of Mount Everest, and it is steep. Most of the group made it halfway up, and Annette reached two-thirds of the height, as did our guide. For some bizarre reason, he thought I would be safe to go to the top on my own. I was not very happy with him, what if I got lost? I climbed on and was very pleased with myself upon reaching the summit. I was a yak. In that moment, I had all the mountains to myself; and I was intrepid. Nothing could beat me. Well, actually, the wind did. It was so gusty I decided I should make my way back down before I was blown from there over to the tip of Mount Everest!

~ ~ ~

The next day was the big day... our trek to Everest (South) Base Camp. We were all excited; we ignored the fact that it was minus 15 degrees outside. The sun was shining; we were intrepid adventurers. I forgot all the words I had used in my journal to describe this climb so far 'torture', 'ordeal' and 'never again' and 'excruciating' (contributed by Annette). Yes, we all set off with a renewed vigour and a spring in our step. This proved to be a little bit difficult to maintain as we traipsed upwards, clambering over rocks at some points. However, we were distracted from this by the stunning scenery and the summit of Mount Everest looming above us. We even got to inspect a crevasse; although we were pretty wary of it, we did not want to fall down there and end up in a no man's land. Although Bruce might have ended up back home in Australia!

Upon reaching Everest Base Camp, we were elated and celebrated by cheering, singing, dancing and taking numerous photos. I made sure to get pictures of Dinky Doo as an intrepid explorer and me in my pink t-shirt and pink cap for the charity I was representing. Gerry took off his three layers of upper half clothing and presented his chest. He wanted me to write with my bright pink lipstick on his chest, and I heartily undertook this assignment. Whilst there, we were not rushed at Base Camp, and the environment and the scenery were explained to us by the guides. We were by the Khumbu Glacier, the highest glacier globally and very dangerous due to its icefall. This is where expedition climbers would ascend for the attempt at the summit. Although it was pretty spectacular to look at, I made up my mind there and then that I had no ambition to ever go any higher up on Everest. Yes, I was happy at Base Camp.

And here I was standing in all the serenity of a white snowy landscape, gazing up at the way the expedition participants had taken and would take in the future.

Tenzing Norgay and Sir Edmund Hillary had taken the path during their first and successful ascent to Mount Everest's summit in 1953. However, it remains a mystery whether they really were the first to reach the summit or whether this accolade should go to George Mallory and Andrew Irvine during their attempt in 1924. It would be 75 years before a special expedition searched for and found the body of Mallory. They had searched for artefacts to give clues as to whether Irvine and Mallory had indeed reached the summit. There was no definitive evidence. However, one item was missing from Mallory's possessions- a picture of his wife, which he had sworn to place on the summit in the event of success. Where was the photo? At the summit? Nobody knows.

We now know that Mallory and Irvine were just two of over 300 people who have died on Mount Everest; most of these were expeditionists attempting the summit. However, hiking to Base Camp is not to be underestimated and should quite rightly be considered an accomplishment. Several hikers die each year on the way to or at Base Camp. My novice mountaineering body had done me proud.

Our guide explained the impact of the many expeditionists and hikers on this mountain. Approximately 25,000 people each year leave a footfall on Everest. Another impact from this footfall is the increasing litter, and the only way of keeping this down is by volunteering groups cleaning the slopes and making them pristine again. Unfortunately, the waste is increasing; and it includes dead climbers who are either not found or are left where they took their last step. Sobering thoughts for us and made us all genuinely grateful we had made it thus far. We took our final looks, and one by one, we turned and headed away back on the journey towards our lodge. As I took my last long gaze around at this serene and spiritual place, it occurred to me that only one thing was missing. A total solar eclipse; how cool it would have been to experience it there.

As much as the outward journey to Base Camp was strenuous but bearable that day, the same could not be said for the return journey. Most of the group had gone on ahead and had taken all of the Sherpas with them. That left Annette in front of me, walking with Gregg, and me just behind walking with Gerry. I noticed that Gerry slowed down, and he slipped, falling to the edge of the trail. I started to worry, so I stayed with him as we lagged well behind the others.

As fate would have it, we bumped into a group walking towards us, I was slightly in front and started chatting with a few of the English, and as Gerry approached, he slipped and fell in front of them. They helped him up, he looked a bit glazed, so I decided we would have to somehow catch up with the others. That was easier said than done. I could not leave Gerry, but the others were way ahead now. Only Annette and Gregg were in the distant view, and no amount of shouting or hollering could draw their attention. We were only moving forward as much as we were, because Gerry was following in my footsteps. However, we would be back late at night at that rate, and that is if we got back to the lodge without losing our way!

I decided I would have to make a dash for it, bearing in mind we were at an altitude that it is low on oxygen and it is hard enough to breathe just walking, but I ran as if my life depended on it (well, somebody's did). I got to near Annette and Gregg and quickly explained, and we all dashed back together to where I had left Gerry; he had not been able to walk much further on his own. I gave Gerry my water while Gregg kept hold of him and walked by his side. We kept talking to him to ensure he stayed fully conscious. We decided the four of us should stay together rather than split into twos and try and get help because it was getting very late, and hence one pair could get into problems.

It was a long slow, and worrying trek back for us, and then as an added bonus, it started to snow! There was a light at the end of the tunnel, though, when we spotted three figures in the distance coming towards us. It was Bruce and Joey with a Sherpa who were worried and so had ventured out to find us. We explained what was happening, and they took over. Bruce stood behind Gerry, and Joey stood in front, and they marched him back towards the lodge. Our guide took Annette, Gregg and me back to the accommodation to get us soup and have some ready for the others behind us. The Sherpas informed us they were giving a maximum of another half an hour as it was getting dark. If we had not appeared, then a full search party would have been organised. Shame they didn't think of that earlier!

~ ~ ~

If I thought it couldn't get any worse, it did! I guess it had been too cosy in the lodge sitting by the fire the night before, but it was time to face the onward journey. Gerry was feeling better, but now Joey was sick. As we hiked up and down, I felt for him having to clamber over rocks. These were not just ordinary rocks; they were large icy rocks. We were also crossing icy rivers, and at one point, our only way over was the tiniest rickety bridge you can imagine. Let's put it this way, I have big feet, UK size 8 and I could barely fit them on the 'bridge' side by side. I had never trained as a trapeze artist, which clearly would have helped at this point. Oh, and did I forget to mention, it was snowing again!

On the one hand, I was thrilled to reach Pangboche that afternoon, as the torture for that day was least over. However, on the other hand, this is where the group would split. Annette, Gerry, Wayne, and Gregg were returning to Kathmandu while Bruce, Joey and I would be heading to the Gokyo mountain and lakes. I sometimes wonder where I get these bright ideas from? What on earth possessed me to think I would want to climb another mountain straight after climbing Mount Everest Base Camp? It would have been in my best interest to have headed back down with Annette. But no, I had already paid for the extended mountain walk. I felt like I was a Yak, and I believed I was intrepid.

The hike towards the Gokyo lakes itself was pretty pleasant. Although it involved going up again, the scenery was indeed stunning. Chatting with Joey and Bruce, I was slightly perplexed by Bruce. During our conversation, he seemed somewhat churlish with me. It transpired that he did not like the British. Further probing only produced every stereotype you have heard about us. I reminded him there was every chance he was born from British blood somewhere back in his family tree. He sulkily admitted I was right. He was from Scottish stock.

Fortunately, our Sherpa guides were there to relieve the tensions and gave us information about the area we were heading to. The Gokyo Lake region has six principal lakes which comprise the world's highest freshwater lake system. It was simply stunning, with the turquoise lakes surrounded by snow-capped mountains just about visible in the distance. Gokyo Ri, our ultimate goal, stands at 17,576 feet/5357 metres. It has stunning views over the Gokyo lakes and the other focal mountains (including Everest). It would be a less well known, more moderate trek if you were not going via the Everest Base Camp route.

We reached our first hotel that afternoon in good time, and we were all able to relax. Having said that, I took the opportunity to have a workout - where on earth had I summonsed the energy from for extra activity? I was lifting small rocks in each hand as weights and using a large washbag stuffed with laundry as a punchbag! I was even able to have a bucket shower (this involved a small cubicle, a bucket and a hose) with warm water. This was my first opportunity for a wash for over a week since we had left Namche Bazaar. Even Dinky Doo kept his distance from me due to the undesirable aroma permeating from me.

~ ~ ~

The next morning, Joey presented himself and gave the sad news that he was too ill to continue and would head back down to Namche Bazaar with a guide and wait for us there. Fortunately, we would still have two Sherpas with us. I was a lot slower than Bruce, so we could both go at our own pace. The trekking that day was hard going, uphill and icy, and we hiked for many hours; but it was nothing compared to the next day.

Bruce wishing me a 'Happy Birthday' the following day was quite a surprise. Firstly I would not have expected that Bruce would be the person to be wishing me a happy birthday, and secondly, I had forgotten it was my birthday. So straight away, I was depressed because I was rapidly accelerating away from being 40 and being another year older.

In a strange turnaround later that day, I began to hope I would live another year and would happily look forward to another birthday. I really was starting to wonder if I would make it to the age of 50!

We had to traverse via the Cho La pass, and I had mistakenly not looked up how dangerous that route can be. At one point en route, it involved crossing a sheer cliff face with a waterfall dripping down (memories flooded back, pardon the pun, from the Venezuelan Lost World waterfall). Not too horrendous, one would think, except it was making the tiny ledge I was crossing with my size 8 feet very watery and icy. There wasn't really anything to hold onto as the rock face was wet. I somehow managed to sidle across using my walking sticks, digging them into the rock on either side of my feet.

Eventually, having crossed this ledge and reaching the lake area, I noticed my heart rate slowing, and I was starting to struggle to breathe. This became more apparent each time I went for a wee behind a bush. I am not sure that I can explain how taking off your backpack, then shedding your large thick jacket, taking down your trousers, thermals and underwear, conducting your ablutions and then finally having to bring all these layers up again, adorn your jacket and sling your backpack on, can leave you so breathless that you think this could well be your last breath! Literally taking the wind out of you. I tried distracting myself with the two dogs who followed us for some distance, and the remarkable scenery. We were passing by the lakes, and whatever shade of blue each different one was, each stood out against the backdrop of snowy white mountains. Beautiful as it was, my mind kept reverting back to the fact that there was a lack of oxygen.

I decided to tell Bruce and the guides when we reached our final hotel at lunchtime. Bruce stated that we should go back after lunch if I was not better, but I was reticent with this idea purely as he had paid for his trip too, and we had not yet ascended Gokyo Ri. I was impressed, though, that he had shown concern. I ate garlic soup and got a second wind (no pun intended); this got me about a third of the way up Gokyo Ri mountain. I decided I had nothing to prove to anyone, especially not myself, and that I would sit and enjoy the view while Bruce climbed to the summit with his guide. It was a unique way to spend my birthday relaxing against a rock, gazing around at the surrounding snowcapped mountains and iced-over blue waters of the Gokyo lake below. My guide waited silently and patiently until I was ready to descend.

My birthday was finished off quite nicely back at the hotel that evening with a tasty meal and a chocolate log birthday cake made for me. It was fun having our two Sherpas join in (they had always eaten away from us). We played cards, snakes & ladders and pass the teddy (Dinky Doo was not impressed at this) and then headed up for an early night. I would say this must be the earliest I have retired for the day on my birthday, ever. By midnight, I was not sure I was going to make it to the following day. I had woken up laying on my back, my throat was swollen, and I was choking! Although it may not have been the best move, I shot out of bed and sat on the floor gasping for breath and sipping water. I wanted to cry out for help but then was too worried about waking other guests. I did not move from the floor for the next few hours until daylight appeared.

Despite my lack of sleep, I was downstairs by 06:30, gulping back a black coffee, set to go. For once, I was not moaning about being up early. Bruce was ready too, which was just as well as I was waiting no longer for anyone. I can assure you that this is the quickest I had walked throughout the entire trip. Nothing was going to stop me from getting to air; I was on a mission. I felt like a dog sniffing for air, and the relief was immense when we got past the lakes, and a breeze wafted to my nose. I could breathe again, which in turn meant I would be able to go for a wee behind a bush!

My elation soon waned when I spotted the cliff side we had traversed yesterday. It had rained during the night, and the frosty air meant that the water had iced over. So basically, I could see that the ledge I had to cross was an icicle shelf! It looked pretty much like my freezer back home. I thought about not going across and asked if there was a detour, to which my guide gave a negative reply; he seemed to think I was taking the piss. So I tentatively started to sidle my way across, I tried copying my guide, but to be fair, he was having some difficulty too (which really did not instil any more confidence in me). He instructed me sternly not to look down. Well, he was wasting his breath there; why on earth would I want to do that? No, I would not look down; I would just look at the ice in front of my face and continue sideways. But then, I made the colossal mistake of looking across to the other side to where I was headed- it looked like it was a mile away. Why was it so much further than yesterday? In reality, it was only a few metres, but during that moment, both my guide and I knew (he could tell as fear was plastered across my face in sheer terror) that I was going nowhere.

I clung to the iced rock face like a gecko and would not let go! My fingernails seemed to tear through my gloves, making indentations into the ice. My guide tried to coax me over, but I was having none of it. I told him I was staying there until a helicopter came to rescue me! I wanted to cry, but somehow I didn't; I guess that was because I couldn't see how that would help my predicament. That was it; I was going to die here on this rock face. After what seemed to be an absolute lifetime, my guide started to walk back towards me, he held out his walking pole, and I had to hold it and slowly sidle to my left. I could not for the life of me fathom how that thin little stick would help me if I slipped, but faced with a need to go to the toilet, I had to get off that ledge. I very slowly and meekly moved my left foot, then right foot sideways. Inch by inch, I shuffled, whimpering each time I slid, until I eventually reached solid ground, and my guide withdrew his pole.

Back on terra firma at the other side, I couldn't speak to my guide. I just dashed into the nearest bush and then galloped back to our hotel stop for lunch. Bruce inquired as to what took us so long, at which point I almost exploded! Instead, I gulped down my lunch, and we hiked the last few hours back to our hotel at Namche Bazaar for the night where Joey was waiting for us. I was rewarded with a triple room for the night to myself and a "well done" from my Sherpa. Even more of a treat was that there was no hiking to do the next day, and so I took the opportunity to have a lay-in, have a late breakfast, and laze around all day - I deserved it!

Having made a group decision that night, for once it was one I would get a say in. We agreed to head out early the following morning in a bid to reach Lukla. Effectively, in one day, we would be attempting to reach a destination that had taken us three days to achieve on the way up. I was going full steam ahead, with my mp3 player now working and my music blaring. There was nothing to hinder me - except the large herds of yaks. With a quick lunch stop and a bit of manoeuvring around said yaks, we made it just before dark into Lukla and our hotel.

As you will have gathered, I do not like getting up unnecessarily early. Yet, the next morning, we had to rise at 05:30 to go to the airport. We had heard the siren alerting us to the incoming flight arriving at Lukla Airport. Upon arrival, the idea is that you check-in and board the aeroplane immediately due to the volatility of the changing weather conditions in Lukla. This did not happen because although the weather was clear for takeoff at that point in Lukla, the weather had turned in Kathmandu, so we could not depart until 10:00. By then, in my mind, I had been unnecessarily awake for four and half hours.

~ ~ ~

I was very grateful, though, when we arrived in Kathmandu, having safely flown on the small propeller plane and landed without any drama. It was a different case in the van on the way back from the airport. We got stuck in traffic due to a strike resulting in fighting in the streets. We were told by the driver it was all to do with a lack of fuel situation.

I was certainly ready for lunch when I arrived back at the Hotel Florid (the first hotel I stayed at on my own upon arrival in Kathmandu). The owner was delighted to see me and congratulated me on my Everest Base Camp Climb. That was before I bored him and others for several hours, regaling all my Everest and Gokyo adventures. I was treating myself to my first nice cold beer in two weeks, sitting in the garden with Dinky Doo, revelling in the sunshine, when Andre appeared. He had been here during my first stay, he was practising to be a yogi, and today he was leaving. All the staff and I went out the front to wave him off - 20 minutes later, Andre was back! He could not depart as the street

riots linked to the strike were worsening, and cars were being burned.
The following morning I did not feel well at all. Perhaps my body was not used to being at a decent altitude again, and my throat was severely swollen. The hotel owner marched me to a stall near the market, which was allegedly a pharmacy. I was dubious about this but duly opened my mouth while the pharmacist shoved an object down my throat. He proclaimed I had tonsillitis and prescribed various tablets and a bottle of medicine. After that, the hotel owner forbade me to drink more beer!

Around 09:00 one morning, I heard the most beautiful music coming from outside the hotel. I laid there for about five minutes and then could not stand it anymore. I jumped out of bed and went outside in my pyjamas, honing in on the source of the music. It was from a music shop just across the path. This lovely melody was Buddhists chants called 'Incantations', and amazingly, I was able to buy this cd from them. I was particularly pleased as it was perfect for sitting and meditating to.

I had worked out a system for getting things done while there was no power cut, and so was able to shower, visit the Children's Home in daylight, and go souvenir shopping. The rest of the time was spent chatting with various people. On my last day, I was privileged to be given permission to visit the Women's Prison with Indira. There was a process with identity and passport, and then Indira and I were escorted around the prison by the Head Jailor and a high ranking army officer who was saluted by all other soldiers as we walked by. The women were carrying out their daily chores, and I was given an excellent running commentary on how life worked for the women in prison. There was a real sense of community, not just how their dormitories were arranged but also the activities carried out together, such as cooking, spinning, and sewing. We went to the room where the ladies were finishing off sewing the pyjamas for the children back at the Children's Home. I was delighted to see the finished result, and the ladies were so lovely giving me a little handmade purse as a gift. I said a sad farewell to Indira, and then it was time to go to the airport. The prison visit had been a sobering and humbling end to my trip. Still, I believe these experiences help to mould you, give you a greater understanding of the world, and help with the practice of gratitude for what you have. It was sobering to meet friends for whom life was a continuous struggle. It guides me in being more clear about decisions I make and be grateful for having options. My friends back home had been right. This trip would indeed give me time to reflect on what I wanted out of life. In fact, having achieved climbing to Everest Base Camp, I knew that I really was ready for a lifetime of adventures!

~ ~ ~

Overall Trip Cost: £1400 (Flights £355, Tour £645, Spending £400)
TOP TIPS: I would advise not hiking Everest alone. Either hire a Sherpa or book an adventure tour. Book on a tour that allows time to acclimatise. It is crucial to acclimatise - if you have anywhere back home to practise hiking up in higher altitudes, take the opportunity to prepare for your Everest hike. Once on your way to Base Camp, listen to your body. If it needs to go back down, go back down- the chances are if you rest enough, your body could make it back up. Check with your guide/tour company that there are enough Sherpas to allow for this, or hire an independent guide.

Me, Almost at Everest Base Camp

Everest, Yaks on Swing Bridge   En-route to Everest

Gokyo Ri, Lakes & Mountains   Everest Base Camp, I Made It!

China, Clouded Eclipse 2009   Ninyi the Baby Panda, Chengdu

Easter Island, Moai Statue   Kara Riding off on White Horse.

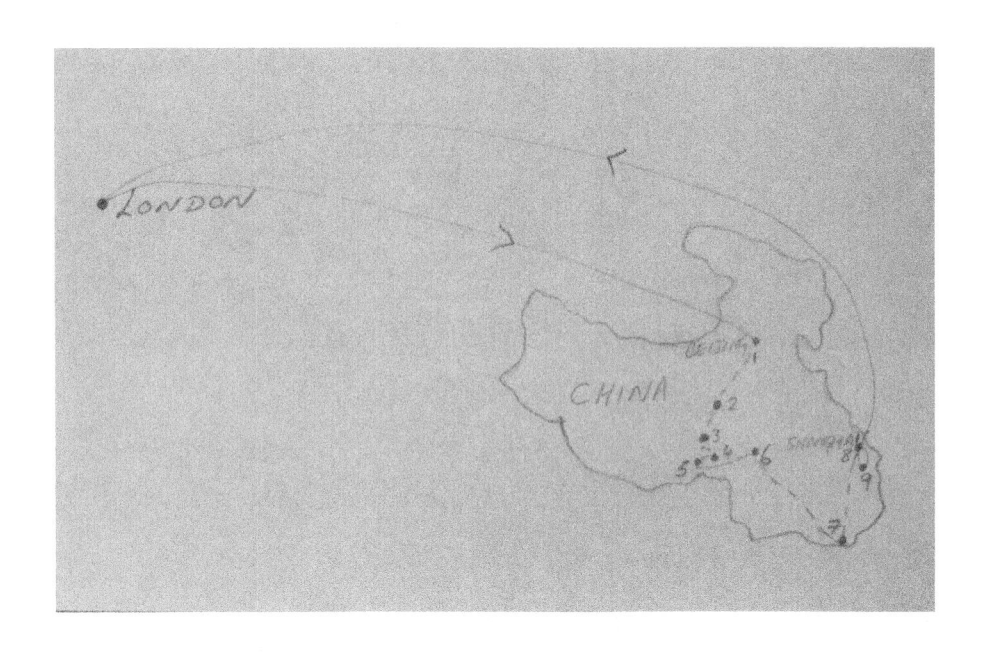

CHINA ROUTE - 18 DAYS

1. BEIJING
2. XIAN
3. CHENGDU
4. LESHAN
5. CHENGDU
6. CHONGQING
7. YICHONG
8. SHANGHAI
9. HANGZHOU & QIANTANG RIVER *TOTAL SOLAR ECLIPSE*

CHINA 2009

Let's Go… to the Panda-monium at the Boring Bore

Eclipse path: India - Nepal - China - Pacific
I viewed at: Qiantang River, China
Date/Time of Maximum Totality: 22.07.2009 at 09:36 Local Time
Length of Totality: 06m 39 secs.

China, with its bulging Beijing, is the 4th largest country in the world and is at the same time the most populated country (over a billion people). Yet, it has only one time zone within its vast expanse. It is believed that ice cream was invented here some 4,000 years ago, allegedly by mixing rice and milk and snow. Another Chinese discovery was tea; this was way back in the 3rd century and was said to have been initially used as a medicine. It has since evolved within its medicinal usages and a wide variety of flavours abound to quench our thirst. After all that tea, you might need the toilet, and you may be surprised to learn that toilet paper was in fact, invented in medieval China during the 6th century. This is ironic as toilet paper is not primarily used, or available in public restrooms nowadays in China! On the subject of toilets, most are still squat style and do not have doors either - this is for both men and women. Ping pong is the national sport in China - you might find the ping okay, but not so much the pong from the toilets!

I had progressed in my thinking for this trip due to past experiences on the various adventure tours. Even though they were pretty reasonably priced, I reasoned I could save money by flying solo, so to speak. I looked at the various tour companies to check their routes and itineraries. I double-checked that I would indeed be making savings. It worked out right, not including flights in either way of doing it, and I would be spending approximately half of what it would cost me on a tour. What's not to like about that.

As it transpired, I would not end up travelling solo (with Dinky Doo) on this trip. I had been telephoning my cousin in Canterbury as was usual and mentioned my forthcoming trip to China. By this time, I was only six weeks from departing and had all accommodation and transport set out for my itinerary- Beijing, Xian, Chengdu, Shanghai, and Hangzhou. My cousin mentioned she had a friend called Linda who was very interested in travelling to China, and she would probably wish to join me. Within a week, Linda was booked to come with me. I had never met Linda before, and we quickly got to know each other whilst making sure she was booked in all the same hotels, same flight and so on. Linda was very personable, and we were definitely on the same wavelength. Linda was also a very spiritual person interested in alternative medicines and was very excited to view such a celestial event as a total solar eclipse. This was to be my fourth one.

The day of departure arrived. I drank a few red wines to pluck up the courage for the journey ahead, triple checked my documents and was packed up with my useful items; head torch, washing powder, superglue, training golf ball, duct tape and an umbrella. I figured the umbrella would be just as useful as a sunshade as well as keeping off any rain. I went through the usual last-minute (dis)organisation, which this time involved a trip to the hairdresser. The day before, I had attempted to cut my own hair in a bid to save time. This was a false economy as I cut my hair too short on one side, and so there I was only a few hours before my flight in the hairdresser's chair having my locks evened up. I then had to rush home to catch the first of three trains that would take me to Heathrow airport. In my mind, it was not an auspicious start at the airport with thunderstorms and lightning cascading through the sky outside. However, I did manage to successfully meet up with Linda. I had previously told her she would recognise me by the little teddy bear sticking out of my pocket.

It was time for a glass of red wine (another pre-flight standard procedure for me) with one of the salad rolls I had bought with me. I always take my own packed lunch (which usually takes up most of my hand baggage allowance). This is for two reasons: airports always over-inflate food and drink prices; secondly, it has been challenging to find food I can eat, so rather than starve, I like to make sure I will be fed for a week in just one journey! It turns out that I did not need to bring my food store with me, as the food on the flight was more than adequate, and by the time we had transferred through Dubai airport, I was well fed and watered and was ready to sleep soundly.

I wanted to nod off, but instead, I chatted with a Chinese lady who was sat next to me. Yuon was a teacher who had three female students and a male teacher in tow. We had great fun with me practising my mandarin with them, and Yuon advising me of the local cultures. She stated this involved two main things: the first was spitting, and the second was throwing rabbits- rabbits, I was horrified until we realised her pronunciation was a little out, and she meant throwing rubbish!

Yuon did not, however, warn me of the landing procedure in Beijing, which involved health officials coming on board to take our temperatures from our foreheads. They carried out this with a handheld machine and wore masks. It was our welcome to China, as was the humid hot air outside the airport.

~ ~ ~

That evening in Beijing, Linda and I ventured out to eat. We had gone to the nearest restaurant to our hostel and were the only westerners in there. The staff did not speak English, but all came out to serve us. My pigeon mandarin was not enough to translate throughout the saga that was about to commence, not just that first night, but for most of the trip. Yes, eating out was a steep learning curve for us both that first night. For me, it was the realisation that sharing food is much more the norm in China and that ordering food would be for all on your table. I do not share my food, and I was not about to start. It took a while, but I managed to assure the waiter that I would be ordering and eating my own salad. I did not dare order anything other than that as I was unsure what creatures could be served up hidden in a sauce - I had heard too many stories. Linda learned that you should check the portion size and ensure that you are ordering for one person. Poor Linda ended up with a meat dish with rice that would feed six people. When looking at the menu price, she had read it as costing £4.80; however, it ended up costing £14.80! This is expensive when you consider my salad was only £2.50 with bread and a pot of tea.

We spent the next three days visiting the usual tourist sights, although how we managed to pack it all in with the searing heat, I do not know. My eyes must have been deceiving me because I thought I even saw some drops of perspiration on Dinky Doo; it really was that hot. Naturally, our first port of call was the Great Wall of China. Thankfully we had taken our umbrellas to shade us from the beating sun as we climbed the steep steps at the Mutianyu section of the Great Wall. We had chosen that area because it is quieter than the very touristy section of the Great Wall at Badaling (where it gets very crowded). It was tranquil when we visited Mutianyu and yet was still well set up for a visit. Except for those dratted steep steps up. Having said that, I should not be so harsh about them. Not after reading about the blood, sweat and tears put into constructing the Great Wall over 2,000 years ago in the 7th Century BC. It is believed that over 800,000 people were involved in creating the wall, of which 400,000 died due to giant falling stones, disease, exhaustion, and even animal attacks. After the exertion of walking up and along the wall, I took the easy route back down - by toboggan! Yes, sacrilege, I know after all the hard work put into building the steps, but it was also fun, and because it was so quiet, I was the only one on the track. It took me all of 5 minutes to get back down to the bottom.

That evening, Linda and I were more cautious with our meal choice. Linda managed to get a meal that did not feed six people, and I got my vegetarian meal just for myself. However, the fun began when the chopsticks came out. Linda was quite nifty with hers (I swear she had practised before leaving England!). In contrast, I looked like a demented stick insect, with fingers flailing around and managing to eat one mouthful out of every four attempts! A spoon was discreetly delivered to me; I was hungry and would need to eat as much as possible ready for the day of touring ahead tomorrow.

It was an early start heading out by metro to the vast expanse of Tiananmen Square. It was a plain-looking square but was nonetheless full of history and culture within its 215.730 square metres (53.31 acres). This square is home to various official buildings, some of which hold arts. A prominent one is the Mausoleum of Mao Zedong, Chairman of the Politburo Communist Party from 1945 until he died in 1976.

Standing proudly high above all in the square was the Monument to the People's Hero, a 10-storey obelisk. However, Tiananmen Square is most globally renowned for the 1989 Tiananmen Square protests. I recall watching a horrific event on television back in 1989, otherwise known as the 'June Fourth Massacre'. There had been a build-up to that day, starting with student protests on 15th April 1989; they were calling for greater freedom of speech and less censorship. There was a military crackdown on 4th June, where hundreds of people died, and thousands were injured. The Obelisk would have been silently standing there witnessing it all.

One image stood out for millions of people (including me) around the world, that of 'Tank Man', who stood with a plastic shopping bag in each hand facing off some tanks heading towards him. He was pulled away to safety by two men. Nobody knew who he was, and I wonder if he ever admitted to family or friends to being 'Tank Man'.

We crossed the road to the City of the Forbidden Palace, so named because initially commoners were prohibited from entering without permission- well, that's me out then! Except my Chinese Yuan were accepted, and I was allowed inside to view this vast heritage site consisting of many (980) buildings. Thankfully, visitors do not have access to all the buildings; I would say that over 8,700 rooms are just a few too many rooms to visit. I doubted we would make it around the 60% of buildings that are open to the public. I was one of the 14 million people that would be visiting the Forbidden Palace that year. All of us viewing the most prestigious collection of Chinese cultural artefacts and the world's most extensive collection of well preserved medieval wooden structures. Whilst appreciating how the splendour of these palaces could attract so many people, I was not overawed. I took to wondering why there were no birds on the roofs of the buildings (apparently, this is due to roofs being specially designed so that birds do not land on them). There were so many people there, I had been struggling to get any decent photos without people in the way, even when using Dinky Doo to try and block them. This contributed to my discontent at this site, so we decided it was time to move on.

Linda and I retreated from the crowds at the Forbidden City. We headed to the Summer Palace, or the Yihe Yuan "Garden of Restful Peace", where we meandered around the lakeside. The Kunming Lake is in the centre of the Summer Palace park and is so large that it takes up approximately 75% of the whole site. It is an essential landscape feature of the Summer Palace along with Longevity Hill. The Summer Palace itself, we found out after we had rested and recuperated, is 270 years old. It is home to the most extensive and best-preserved royal garden in China (if not the world), covering some 1.1 square miles. The royal gardens are renowned as a masterpiece of landscaping combining the nature of the hills and open water lake with the artificial features of the halls, palaces, temples and bridges. We were able to spy down onto the majestic features by wandering up 200 feet through various other magnificent features. These included the "Hall of Dispelling Clouds", the "Tower of Buddhist Incense", "Through the Wonderland", to reach the top of Longevity Hill and the "Hall of the Seat of Wisdom", exhausting isn't it? We were, and so sat down to recuperate with the vain hope of becoming wise people and not walking too much further in the heat. We had covered several miles that day and were faced with one more day of culture, heat and temples before moving on.

And so it was, the next day Linda, Dinky Doo, and I found ourselves at two less-visited temples. The first being the 'Yonghe' Lama Temple, the 'Palace of Peace and Tranquility' - they clearly haven't experienced my penny whistle! I found it quite surprising that this most revered Tibetan Buddhist temple outside of Tibet was less visited. Perhaps that is partially why I took to it. It was easy to navigate the ornate, colourful temple halls built on a North to South axis that ascended in height and importance as we moved around the complex without the crowds. The astonishing finale was an 18 metre high Buddha carved into a single trunk of a Tibetan sandalwood tree.

Leaving the Yonghe Temple, Linda and I must have clearly looked wearier than we actually were in the eyes of the loitering rickshaw drivers. They clearly felt the 550 metres to our next temple was a step too far for us. I put them straight using my mandarin, "boo yow" (I don't want). Maybe that is not really what I was saying, for they found it hilarious enough not to pester us anymore! Or perhaps it was my cockney accent, but I was proud of myself with my pigeon mandarin as we entered the Confucius Temple. Where better to reflect on learning of culture than a temple dedicated to the greatest thinker and educationalist in ancient China, Confucius. The Temple of Confucious was initially built in 1302, with later additions made in both the Ming and Qing dynasties, making it the second-largest temple constructed for him. It was, however, reasonably easy to navigate within the primary four courtyards. We oohed and aahed as we wandered around the main structures before heading back out to the 'Chujian Bai' or 'Touch Evil' Cypress Tree. Being 700 years old, it must have seen a thing or two during its time. Legend says that people thought the tree could distinguish between good and evil people. Of course, I felt the need to touch it. Had I passed the test, was I on the right path? Remember, Confucius, say…"Good people strengthen themselves ceaselessly", I must be almost perfect!

Well, maybe not perfect, but footsore by that evening. So having a massage recommended to us by our hostel actually seemed like a very favourable solution to the spreading aches and pains of three days trotting around. We had confirmed our next hostel and our airport transfer at the other end, and so had just enough time to melt onto a massage bed and be lightly caressed with gentle hands. What actually happened upon laying on the said bed was that I was pummelled and bent into various contorted positions. I thought I was back in Thailand having a Thai massage. And what was he doing to my ears? What a strange sensation it was with him investigating them inside and out. I could stand no more. Using the flight as an excuse, I took an early departure from his gnawing hands, with Linda not far behind me.

As it turned out, we were right to be concerned with our timings, as it was a bit of a rush to get to the airport; however, we made it on time, only to find out the flight was going to be an hour late leaving. Perhaps the pilot was on a promise, or his dinner was ready on the table for him at home because we still landed on time at 22:00. We had landed in Xian, and things were about to go downhill from here for me that night.

~ ~ ~

The downward spiral began with our Xian airport pick up not being there to meet us, despite having confirmed with the shuttle company that same morning. We had walked out into the Arrivals Hall where drivers were waiting with their cards held up with names on. Mine was not there. We had walked past them, and I tried to get back through in front of them, but security tried to stop me! I got through. I then tried to go along past the waiting drivers shouting out 'Han Tong Inn' (our hotel) but just got blank looks. It got more embarrassing when I asked the security guy for help. He called loudly across the other side of arrivals to get a female who could speak English to come over. Her only suggestion was to get an airport shuttle bus, then she made an escape.

I don't know if it was embarrassment, stress or tiredness (or all of these factors) because I then thought I heard a loudspeaker voice say, "Mandie, your transport has arrived". I had called the girl over again (via security, whose eyes were rolling at me by now). She relented into phoning the Han Tang Inn after assuring me there was no speaker call made for me. The girl advised that apparently, our pick up car had broken down, so we had to get the airport shuttle bus. It was very late by now, and we gave in. Linda wanted to get a taxi at the other end, even though our accommodation turned out to be only a few minutes walk from our drop off point. It was raining when we got there, so we jumped in the taxi. The driver had a bit of trouble finding our hotel, and we all ended up getting stressed as it seemed the hotel just did not exist. We finally found the hotel, checked in and fell onto our beds. It was at that point I realised my daypack containing my documents, money, and Dinky Doo (basically all my valuables) was missing!

At 01:00, I was walking with the lady from the hotel reception just ten minutes along the road where we had got in the taxi to see if we could find our driver. Our early morning excursion was to no avail. However, around 04:00 the receptionist was knocking on my door. The driver had arrived with my bag - he wanted a £30 reward. I was too tired to negotiate a fairer compensation, I needed my bag. Dinky Doo, although pleased to be back in my possession, had a stern look of disapproval on his face at my carelessness!

It will be of no surprise to learn we got up late the following day; the arrival in Xian had been too much for both of us. Once adequately recuperated, we took a taxi out to the Wild Goose Pagoda. We bought our entrance tickets to the outer grounds and then another into its tower, where we climbed seven floors to reach the top. We were rewarded with magnificent far-reaching views over the city, and we took our time there as we knew we had seven storeys of walking back down.

Something weird then happened when we left the Pagoda to get a taxi back to the hotel. There were no taxis around, which we found strange for a touristy area, and we could not hail one down. The taxis would slow down, shake their heads and drive on; it was baffling. Eventually, a taxi slowed down enough that I could jump in; he was trying to tell me to get out. I was too busy encouraging Linda to get in. So lumped with us both with me refusing to get out, he soon realised that he was outnumbered and would have to drive us to our destination!

After a siesta, lunch and refreshing ourselves, we walked along the road to the Bell Tower (famous for its bell) and Drum Tower (famous for its drum) for more views over the city. We could see where they were building a new subway (I suspect it's completed by now). We ended the day with a wander around the Muslim quarter, mostly known for its Great Mosque, traditional buildings, and famous snack & commercial streets. Footsore, I retired to the hotel bar whilst Linda went to a nearby clinic for acupuncture for her back (rather her than me!). To be fair, she did come back feeling more relaxed, albeit with several pin pricks in her back.

No trip to Xian would be complete without a visit to the Terracotta Warriors. We ventured out first in a taxi, then train, and finally bus to reach our destination. We were tired already, and so to assist us in the abundance of information we were about to digest, we enlisted the help of a guide, Lily. She took us to a golf cart-style vehicle to transfer us to the main entrance; it promptly broke down. I am sure we could have walked, but Lily would have none of it. A second cart came along, and we were on our way to the entrance, just a few minutes drive away.

Inside, firstly we went to pit one, it was an incredible sight. The Terracotta Army is a unique collection of thousands of terracotta soldier, horse and chariot sculptures portraying armies of Qin Shi Huang (the first Emperor of China). These precious artefacts were discovered in 1974 by a group of locals digging a well who came across fragments of a clay figure. Here in their hands was the first piece of evidence of thousands of clay figures occupying 600 pits connected by tunnels and vaults. Little did they know at the time the sheer importance of their find and the archaeological significance.

Lily told us about a German guy who dressed up like a terracotta warrior and jumped over the barrier to stand with the real ones - he wasn't discovered until after 20 minutes. He was then deported back to Germany. Lily liked to relate these stories. There were several more anecdotes to come our way, making our tour even more enjoyable. The end of the excursion was not so pleasant for me, as I am not a keen shopper, especially when I am there to sightsee and when the items are overpriced. I, therefore, took no pleasure in visiting the jade shop and loitered outside whilst Linda was made subject to the sales spiel.

We said a fond farewell to Lily, who waved us off and pointed us in the direction of the buses returning to the city. Unfortunately, we seemed to board the one bus that would take the longest time (the number 914, beware). We were so late back we only had time to have a quick look at the Great Mosque, no time to go in, as we had a flight to catch. There was a pattern emerging of getting to airports by the skin of our teeth!

~ ~ ~

Our next destination was Chengdu, the home of the panda (it is a little known fact that globally all pandas belong to China, no matter what country they are in). For me, this would be the highlight of the whole trip, other than the total eclipse. There was no doubt that we would be visiting pandas - we were in panda city. And so it was the next day we set off with a keen group of tourists and our guide John. At this point, I could fill the following few pages with panda talk (although Dinky Doo might get jealous). I was in panda heaven seeing: adult pandas, red pandas, pandas feeding, pandas climbing trees, pandas playing, pandas sleeping, pandas drinking milk- anything panda. It was Panda-monium!

And yet, there was more. I had pre-booked to have my photo taken with a baby panda. Although this was an expensive experience (£100 at the time), for me, it was priceless and something that I would not forget. I spent a lot of time choosing the right outfit to wear that day. Should I wear something neutral, or black and white to fit in with the panda? Definitely not red, as that might upset the panda. In the end, it was totally irrelevant as I was provided with a blue plastic gown, gloves and slippers. Not my best look, but it was all for the good of the pandas and made sense. Ninyi the baby panda, I shall use the term 'baby' loosely as he seemed rather large to me, was placed on my lap. It was fantastic, we both sat there while he held my hand and nibbled on a peach whilst the staff took photos and video for me. Ninyi looked at me a few times, and at one point, I quietly clucked at him. He seemed to like that and turned a more towards me; the staff were a bit warier than I was and shuffled forward to make sure he did not make any more sudden moves. My ten minutes with my newfound friend seemed to fly by. It was my legs afterwards where I could tell I had been sitting there so long holding the weight of a 30-kilogram mammal on my knees!

It seemed appropriate that evening to attend the Traditional Chinese Medicine Hospital with Linda. She would investigate the possibility of back treatment, and I would see if there was something to ease the numbing of my legs above the knees. Instead, I was distracted by the proposal of having some of the excess fat around my belly dissolved. I opted for the 'Tui Na' massage by Dr Miaow (I am not sure if they were jesting me with her name); I just hoped she would not dig her claws in me! In fact, in comparison to my last message, Dr Miaow was quite gentle while she pummelled in essential oils for weight loss around my belly and hips. We both knew that it would take more than one Tui Na treatment to get rid of my amount of fat, but Linda had sufficient treatment for her back until our next stop.

Our bus back to the hotel was an exciting experience on an old clapped out vehicle. Of course, it was packed full. However, there was still room for a chicken, who somehow managed to escape its basket and proceeded to terrorise us all, including the driver fluttering around to its heart's content. Our laden bus was moving so slowly, most vehicles were overtaking. Even a vendor cycled past on his trike with a large cannister of steaming sloshing soup. Another had six chickens hanging upside down, perhaps our terrorising chicken would be joining them? I slept soundly that night dreaming of pandas and chickens; all that was missing was a cockerel to wake me up early for our next part of the journey.

~ ~ ~

When booking a tour, it pays to look into the finer details, which we did not do when we booked a trip to Leshan and Mount Emei. And so it was the following day at 06:30 (that is the first thing I did not check, how early we would have to get up), Linda and I boarded our bus. It must have been a rare vintage model by the looks of it. We turned out to be the only westerners, and with a guide that only spoke Mandarin. After revelling in the glory of being the star attraction, we suddenly realised that we would somehow need to know some information. How long would we have at the toilet stop? Was it a toilet stop or a tourist attraction? Where were we? Were we on the right bus? This was further exacerbated after our first stop at a Jade factory (yes, another one). I conversed with a lady via her daughter in hand gestures and my pigeon Mandarin; it subsequently fell to the children on the bus to translate. There seemed to be a trade-off for this; we had to spend more time with the children and have every known photo opportunity with them. Their parents were proudly pushing them forward with one hand and their camera in the other. I am not entirely sure that the children were so happy about this, but they duly played along.

The tour company did manage to fit in one tourist site worth visiting that day, which was the Leshan Giant Buddha carved into a cliffside. The children translated for us the guide's rendition of the Giant Buddha's story. It was along the lines of this being the largest Buddha in the whole world at the height of 71 metres. The Leshan Buddha sits staring over the confluence of the rivers Min and Dadu - you can physically see this by the way they overlap. It is most apt that the Leshan Giant Buddha is protected as a UNESCO World Heritage Site, as legend has it that the Buddha is there to protect all those on the river. Most of our information came from a young Chinese girl named Casey, who was on this tour with her father.

I was not so impressed by the lunch they took us to, which, although it was included in our fare, did not offer much for me as it was not vegetarian friendly. I was subjected to communal seating at a round table with chopsticks and with the food being shared. As we know by now, I do not like to share my food or sit with strangers who have more access to my food. I wasn't sure if I was being impolite, not slurping my noodle soup from the bowl like all those around us. I think the final straw for me was the chopsticks. I agree you should try to fit in with local cultures, but my chopsticks seemed to be contorting themselves into various positions whilst I looked like my fingers were stick insects on heat!

I was still hungry, but then dismayed to find our next stop was an ebony museum - please stop already with the shopping breaks! I was soon suitably cheered up and impressed with our next point, at the Tea Exhibition, the beautiful, graceful ladies in symmetry with each other displaying tea-making skills. The finalé was a showstopper with a young lad flinging around a teapot with a very long spout, just as if it was a pair of nunchucks, and finishing by pouring tea from it. Naturally, afterwards, there was a shop to buy tea.

I am not sure if we had worn our guide down, but the next day we had a different guide to take us to Mount Emei; she certainly was not the most tolerant or friendly of them. By now, we had also found another translator out of the children, little Mick, who was very polite and willing to assist us. I found it strange that Mick was on this two-day tour on his own, with no adult supervision, aged twelve. Perhaps he secretly had a parent there who just wanted to offload him onto us two unsuspecting westerners for the trip duration.

Our guide reluctantly relayed information to us through Casey and Mick, so one can only hope that the following information is correct. Mount Emei is the highest of the Four Sacred Buddhist Mountains of China, at the height of 10,167 ft (3,099mtrs). The mountain is believed to be a place of enlightenment and is the location of the first Buddhist temple built in China in 1AD. There are 76 temples in the Mount Emei area, most of which are on the mountain, and it certainly did seem like we got to see a lot of them. The Temples at Jinding stood out for me, not just because of their eloquence but we were able to get a cable car up to them, which meant less walking. We traipsed around the sites, following our group. They seemed to think our names were "Let's go" because they just kept repeating it! By the end of the day, all of the group seemed to have learnt these two words of English and seem to like practising it on us, especially the guide.

After lunch, as we walked past some monkeys, one of them snatched the bag of food from Casey's father. It happened so quickly. The monkey was eating when suddenly it leapt at Casey, who was just standing nearby and bit her! We did not realise how bad it was until we got to the next temple. I gave her anti-septic wipes until she could get some medical help, nobody seemed as worried about it as Linda and I. Her knee got worse throughout the day, and Casey's father would not take her to seek first aid. I really felt sorry for Casey with her badly swollen, bruised knee and hoped it was not going to get worse post trip.

The ultimate goal was to reach Mount Emei Golden Summit Temple, which we did after two hours of walking up winding slopes around the mountain. It was worth the walk, a golden spectacle with its most notable feature being its unique head. I know a few people I could consider two-faced, but this statue beat them all hands down by having ten faces. They faced ten directions, each depicting the Bodhisattva's "Ten Truths of Universal Worthiness". A sight to behold, I cannot lie.

After the Wannian ("Ten Thousand Year") temple renowned for its outstanding 62 ton and 8 metres tall Buddha Samantabhadra statue, we walked the 2-4km to the monkey area. This was a strenuous but beautiful walk, and the scenery was lush. You could have your photo taken with them at the monkey area, but I did not want one. This was due to believing one had weed on me from up in a tree (it could have just been where he jumped across the tree and the rain shook off it) and Casey's earlier biting monkey experience. Also, I had enough of photo taking. We were still subjected to being planted into family photos by people outside of our group by this point. I wonder how many people are sitting looking at a picture of me right now, with a giant Buddha behind, a temple or a mountain, or a river, and their child!

I was grateful for our long walk back down through the lush scenery as we were to spend the rest of the day on our tour bus, making our way back to Chengdu. We waved our fond farewells to each other. We had all got to know each other through our communal eating and photos. It was mostly our attempts over the two days to communicate with each other, not very successfully, that had been fun for us. "Let's go", we all shouted one last time and laughed!

~ ~ ~

After a day of rest, Linda and I set off on our journey to Chonqing to begin our Cruise along the Yangtze River. Getting the train to Chonqing was easier than I thought it would be; you looked up your waiting hall number at the train station and then went through the security to your waiting hall. Once there, it was signed which gate to go through. Once through the gate, it was easy to find the platform, mainly by following the crowd. It was easy to find the carriage as they had their respective numbers on each side. with the seats inside the carriage all numbered individually. Round one complete. It was straightforward at the other end too, we followed the signs to the taxi area and queued there. Although there was a relatively long line, it did not take long as there was plenty of taxies. This would take us to our pier for our luxury cruise ship. Round two complete.

Initially, I could not see our luxury cruise ship on the whole stretch of the river and so was convinced ours had departed. Now, outside appearances are deceiving because what looked like a giant rusty tin can externally ready for the scrapyard turned out to be an elegant floating hotel on the inside. We checked-in, finding ourselves in a luxury twin room with its spotlessly clean ensuite toilet and shower. There was a tv, bright white clean towels, and even hot water as an added bonus!

At lunchtime, however, my frustration at the communal dining table commenced. I did not expect to go hungry on a ship where the fare was comparatively pricey! I decided this needed to be nipped in the bud. I approached the staff several times throughout meals on day one to explain that as a vegetarian, that did not mean I wanted to go hungry. The problem kept arising as there was not much food being put out on the table in the first place, and to be fair, the meat-eaters would naturally want to eat vegetables and rice too. This, however, left very little on the table. I could not fathom out what their problem was with setting out a buffet. It had been a long hard struggle but by day three, I finally managed to get my own meal, which was promptly set down on the table, and I was left with a bowl of lettuce leaves and tomatoes.

I couldn't fault the ship for its activity programme, though, and the following day I was up in time for Tai Chi on the deck. Linda had gone in search of the spa rooms for acupuncture for her back. After the Tai Chi session finished ten minutes later, I was ready for my breakfast and a relaxing morning. This turned out to be a good plan, as in the afternoon, we were taken out on our first excursion to visit Fengdu the Ghost City. Seeing there were steps involved, it was sweltering hot, and

I did not have much energy due to lack of food, I took the chairlift. I was picked out of the group, I don't know if this was my penance for being lazy or not listening properly to the guide's talks as I was so hot, but yes, I was picked out to lead the way. Did they not know my track record of getting lost? I was wearing red, and apparently, that would protect the rest of the group. Does that mean if anything was to happen and I was first in line, I would take the fall for the rest of the group?

I noticed I was being videoed for the third time that day. The first was in the morning doing Tai chi, the second coming up in the chairlift, and the third was leading the group. I really did deserve to become famous or capitalise on this. In fact, we were just about to cross a bridge that signified prosperity; there was also one for longevity. You could make a wish for one of these; I was greedy and requested both. Later, you could wish for a baby (and choose a girl or boy) in front of the fertility god. That one I was not so bothered about (it was not long after my last tour where I had to tolerate other people's children), the money and long healthy life would do for me thank you very much!

Aside from a lack of food again for me at dinner, it was a lovely evening. After dinner the staff put on a show, they performed different types of acts and danced. After the show, Linda and I went up on the top deck. It was soothing lying there relaxing under the stars on a warm balmy evening.

Where the ship lacked in providing food for me, they certainly made up for in their provision of activities, excursions and commentary on the stunning scenery. After an early morning Tai Chi session again, I showered and then joined all my shipmates up on deck. We excitedly witnessed our passage into the "Three Gorges", famed as the most scenic stretch of the Yangtze River. Journeying 193kms of the river, the cruise ships pass through the 3 adjacent gorges of Qutang, Wu and Xiling, culminating their journeys at the Three Gorges Dam.

We were now entering the first of these, the Qutang Gorge, the shortest but most majestic of the three. Starting from Baidi City and passing through the Kui Gate, the following five miles contained several scenic spots, all pointed out to us. The Kui Gate is formed by two mountains, with Mt Baiyan ("White Salt Mountain") on one side and Mt, Chijia on the other. They set a precedent for the rest of the chalk walled mountain cliffs lining the edge of the fast-flowing river racing through, forming an imposing picture. Of the numerous picturesque spots along the route, one that stood out for me was the "Rhinoceros Looking at the Moon", as the rock formation did indeed resemble a rhinoceros looking up westwards towards the moon. Perhaps it was one from back in Africa that followed me, now immortalised, and here to haunt me?

Whilst the rhinoceros continued in his meditative state, I took plenty of photos and ate breakfast. We subsequently entered the second gorge - the Wu Gorge. This 27-mile gorge is known as the cloudy/misty section due to its narrowness winding through the mountains, hence less sunlight entering. The entrance to the gorge was brightened up by an arched red bridge, used to connect areas of Wushan county, and said to be amongst the highest of bridges in the world. We drifted under the bridge and along the river; I would have liked to have seen the trees in the winter when the leaves turn red. However, for now, I would settle for this scenic stretch of the river home to the "Twelve Peaks of Wushan". Each rock formation on the mountain was intriguing and fun to work out what it was and if it looked like its namesake. My favourite was the 'Goddess Peak", resembling a slim, graceful female standing high up amongst the clouds and the mist. This goddess was high enough to be one of the first to view the forthcoming solar eclipse; what a magical moment it would be for her.

After drifting along for several hours through the Wu Gorge, trying to spot any sign of habitation (but finding none), we had reached the border of the Wu and Xiling gorges. From here, we were carted off on a smaller ferry for our excursion of the day down the Shennong Stream. It was along here for approximately 20 miles (out of the entire 60-mile length) that tourists would be taken on small sampan boats to view the most scenic spots. This stunning narrow gorge is comprised of "Mian Zhu Gorge", "Parrot Gorge", and "Longchuan Gorge". We were treated to deep jade colours of the river, steep cliffs, cascading waterfalls and dense green vegetation.

I must have made it only made it just as far as Parrot Gorge in the small sampan when I began feeling too hot and struggling to breathe. I was trying to distract myself with the intriguing wooden hanging coffins. It was a marvel in how they could have gotten there on the cliff faces; it remains a mystery to all to this day. It was no good. When I heard our guide saying it would be cooler 'inside' the mountain we were visiting, I must have had my first experience of a claustrophobic panic attack. It was very embarrassing as Elise was in mid-flow on the microphone, and I stopped her once, then changed my mind, and then stopped her again and told her I was not well. So we had to turn the boat back - I don't think it could have been any more embarrassing! Perhaps it was down to malnutrition! I was shaking like a leaf as I got off the sampan, but everybody heartedly waved goodbye to me. I dozed back on the ferry until the others got back. Helen and Dean (a couple from London) came and sat behind me and checked I was okay when I woke up. We chatted and laughed the rest of the way; they definitely cheered me up. I was glad to be back onboard our ship, and for once, was not bothered about how little might reach my plate.

On our final cruise day, the main event was our visit to the Three Gorges Dam. It was a fascinating tour; we stopped at platform 185 and then the Observation point tower of Tanziling. With only a few years under its belt of being operative, the purpose of the Three Gorges Dam was to increase the Yangtze River's shipping capacity and to produce electricity. It was to become the world's largest power station, and the sheer scale of it was overwhelming.

When I saw it, not all construction was complete. We were told that by 2015 there would be an elevator to take the small boats through a ship lock which would only take approximately 45 minutes rather than the 3 hours it took currently. However, there was some controversy and mixed feelings over the building of the Three Gorges Dam. On the one hand, there was the potential for floods downstream that could affect millions of people, and the Dam provided flood storage space to reduce this risk. Another positive was the implementation of technically advanced large turbines to limit greenhouse gas emissions. The downside was that over a million people had been displaced due to the Dam's construction. What's more, there had been a significant impact on ecological changes in the vicinity, for example, increased land erosion.

Once back on the boat, it was time to finish packing up as there was only one hour before docking at Yichang. When we docked, the staff let us stay on the boat for one more hour so that Linda and I did not have to rush about. We had to get a taxi as there was no other way to the airport from the dock, so we shared with Helen and Dean, as there was only one taxi left. Why had we loitered around on the ship when we should have been concentrating on ensuring we could get to the airport!

It was a case of deja vu when we arrived in Shanghai, the hostel staff were not at the airport to pick us up to transfer us to the hostel - they had forgotten about us! They were not about to forget me when I reached the hostel. When we got to the City Central hostel, there seemed to be a further problem. Stefan on bookings and reception had not changed my dorm booking into a twin room. So they wanted us to go into a dormitory. I stood my ground, and we got a twin room even though they had said they were full.

We only had one full day in Shanghai (although we would be returning here post-eclipse). So we decided to escape this city and visit Suzhou as it seemed it would be more picturesque, like Venice with all its canals. And so it was we got up ready for our 08:00 departure on what would turn out to be a very different itinerary than we had planned. The only part of the day which was remotely like what we had believed to expect was our lovely sampan canoe along the canals of Suzhou. It was very much like being on a gondola in Venice, except our rower did not sing "just one cornetto, give it to me". We got taken back to the hostel by 16:00 instead of 18:00 as we had previously been told, and, they had tried to squeeze in the obligatory shopping stop at a jade shop! In true Victor Meldrew style, I complained to Stefan about our tour.

I can safely say that Stefan was glad to see the back of us the following day when we set off to Hangzhou. Arriving at Hangzhou, we had to wait a long time for a taxi in a massive queue. However, our time was used wisely as a man behind us contacted our hostel. He then wrote down the address in Chinese for us to give to our taxi driver. Surely we would reach our hostel with easily now? Wrong, our taxi driver could not find the hostel. He got irritable, especially when I pointed to the meter. He turned it off, and unsurprisingly, not long after, he found the hostel.

As we had nothing planned for the rest of this day, Linda trotted off to get an X-Ray (mainly as she wanted to check to see if her backbones were aligned, which would be cheap enough to do here). Meanwhile, I spent my time preparing for the total eclipse, which was to occur the next day. My preparations were predominantly chatting to everyone staying in the hostel to find out if they were also there for the eclipse. I found one group of female friends who were indeed here for it, and they too were making last-minute plans.

It is at this point I must stress the choice of my location for viewing this eclipse. You may remember that back in Turkey in 2006, NASA had told me exactly where the best spot to be was, Wuhan. I had chosen to ignore that advice as I had discovered such a phenomenon as the Qiantang River Tidal Bore. I had researched that a massive tidal wave would roll across the width of the Qiantang River at a tremendous height that could be surfed on, and this would occur at the time of the eclipse. However, our main concern at the time was the weather. It had been satisfactory to date, but predictions were lots of clouds for the next few days; it was not looking promising down by the river. However, I had carried the image of such a rare phenomenon in my mind for several years. Nothing would shake that image out of my head, not even with the prospect of a bit of cloud cover. And so it was that two of the friends were going to catch a train to Wuhan that night (they had listened to my rendition of the NASA story and clearly saw something in it that I did not). The remaining two friends Cilla and Mary, were accompanying Linda and I the next day to the Qiantang River.

~ ~ ~

ECLIPSE DAY - 22nd July 2009

This would be the one day I would not mind an early 04:00 start. Amazingly, all went to plan. Cilla and Mary met us downstairs at the reception at 05:00. The taxi arrived on time and managed to get us to our destination without getting lost. Actually, our driver was very informative too. He told us how in Chinese folklore the eclipse occurs when the sun is swallowed by a huge dragon. They call this 'Ri Shi' (eat the sun). To prevent the dragon from eating the whole sun and scare it away, a lot of noise and commotion had to be made, banging on pots/pans and drums, and using firecrackers. Would the dragon emerge today and swallow the sun, spitting out the glowing sun before being frightened away? We doubted we would see much of it judging by the thick clouds covering the sky.

We arrived at the Six Harmonies Pagoda viewing spot at the Qiantang River. We set out our picnic, camera equipment, and I found a viewing spot for Dinky Doo. The authorities had the event well organised. There were specific exit and entry points, eclipse viewing glasses were handed out, and there was a running commentary on the loudspeaker (not that we could understand it!). Everyone was in good spirit and claiming their piece of land in preparation for nature's show soon to begin.

Nature did indeed give us a show - of thunder and rain not long before the eclipse, and a lot of clouds! We were teased during the partial phase with glimpses of a crescent moon shining through the clouds sporadically for approximately an hour. We kept positive, and at around 09:00, suddenly, the clouds lifted and then we were treated to a flash of the diamond ring around the sun's periphery.

I did my usual during the lead-up and got excited and kept changing between my camera and eclipse glasses. I was trying to remain optimistic for totality. Here was the longest total eclipse of the 21st century at six minutes and 39 seconds long. There would be plenty more time than usual during an eclipse to experience it, yet I kept missing it between the clouds! Oh well, at least there were fireworks in the distance across the river.

The river. Where was the tidal bore? Where were these high rolling waves that had been predicted? Well, they were certainly not on the Qiantang River as far as I could see. They were more likely to be back in Bristol, England (apparently, they have some of the highest tidal bores in the world back home on the Severn Estuary). This boring bore was more of a rolling wave across the water rather than gaining any height, certainly nothing for surfers to surf on. It was a mixed bag of feelings, really, as the image I had built up in my mind did not happen. Still, on the other hand, we had been lucky after all that cloud cover to see some snippets of the eclipse. Why had I not gone to Wuhan?

On our last day in Hangzhou, Linda and I decided to visit the West Lake. We invited along Henry, a guy from the UK who was also staying at our hostel. The West Lake is a large freshwater lake with plenty of park area surrounding it. The lake is divided into five sections by three causeways. Hence, there are several islands, some natural and some artificial. The three of us decided to go on the West Lake boat cruise, which took us to the "Three Pools Mirroring the Moon Island". I found it refreshing to be somewhere in nature, as I am not really a lover of densely built-up areas, no matter where it is in the world.

We got talking to three Chinese lads whilst floating along on the balmy water. We were getting to know each other, the usual small talk (age, where you live, and what you do for work etc.). Henry was telling us about his work in an office back home. Then just casually threw into the conversation an occurrence when he was working as an Elf in Lapland! It just suddenly tickled me, and I couldn't stop laughing. Firstly, because of the way he casually threw it into the conversation. Secondly, due to the picture in my mind of him dressed as an Elf! The Chinese lads looked bemused and, in the end, asked why I was laughing. It was tough to explain to them amongst fits of giggles. I am not convinced they ever fully understood.

We chatted more with the Chinese lads for a while as we walked around an island looking for a sign to the Broken Bridge. Sometime later, it dawned on us we had literally walked around the island and had gone past where we started. We had gone full circle, perhaps more than once. It transpired that there was no sign for Broken Bridge, it was under a different name, and we got pointed to it in the right direction. I was told afterwards that the Broken Bridge is not broken but that it appears like that in the winter when the snow is on it, confused? We were!

After more meandering around by the West Lakes, Linda needed to get back to the hostel to get her luggage and go to the hospital in the hope of having an MRI scan. So I got on a public golf cart, taking the scenic route to the Pagoda. It cost only £2 and went past some fascinating sights which most I did not get a chance to photograph as the driver seemed to speed up each time. I wanted to go over the Su causeway to get a view of both lakes. I stayed on and paid the driver another 10 yuan, enjoying the ride, and so remained in my seat. The driver suddenly realised I was still there, sat in the same place, rooted to the spot! She tried to get me off, so I offered her more money saying 'Pagoda'.

Luckily there was a Chinese girl on the cart by then who spoke good English and translated for me. The driver thought I was mad - wanting to go to the same pagoda. The driver suggested it would be easier for me to get a taxi - but I remained in my seat and offered more money. The pair could not understand my logic, but the driver took another 30 yuan and off we went. In my explanation, I had said I wanted to get a photo of the Golden Bull, which I missed before, and so this time, the driver made a photo stop for me there. I chatted with the girl who spoke good English about the Chinese culture, and she told me that it was still the law in urban areas that families could only have one child. If they had a second child, they had to pay the government as a punishment. If they have twins or triplets, that was okay, and they wouldn't get a penalty. I asked about the holes in babies clothes that show their bottoms. Apparently, this is so they can go to the toilet easily. This then raised another question for me, I could not understand what happens with babies and their clothes with holes if they are in the cot at night and the parents are asleep- the girl replied, 'maybe they shit the bed'!

After a delightful day of visiting the West Lakes riding round in circles on the golf cart, I opted to take a bus back to the hostel. I wasn't sure I was boarding the right bus. After I had delayed it at the bus stop trying to find my hostel leaflet to show him, the driver motioned me to board the bus and sit down. He figured out we were going the right way, and so I paid my 2 yuan. I pointed out my hostel - as we drove past it!

Later, Linda and I said our goodbyes to our newfound friends at the hostel, set off in a taxi to the train station, caught the train to the airport, and took our flight back to Shanghai. It was nice to see a familiar face back at the hostel; yes, Stefan was there to greet us (although I am not entirely convinced he felt the same way). I booked a City Tour of Shanghai with him, and I was particular about what I wanted to visit on said tour, which did not include ANY jade shops. I really do not think I could have been any clearer and had high hopes.

At 08:00, we were ready for our Shanghai city tour; in total, there were eight of us were from our hostel. The guide arrived and proudly welcomed us to our Hangzhou excursion - but we had just come from there and had no intention of returning so soon. After checking out the finer details of where we were heading, the guide, Julia, took us out to the correct minivan. Our first stop was the Oriental Pearl Tower, which I didn't venture into. For two reasons: there was only lifts to reach the top, and I don't like lifts, and secondly, it was high with a glass floor, and I don't like heights. Linda kindly took my camera up there for me and took photos which were enough evidence to pretend that I had been up there! Our next stop was to the riverside of the Bund river to take some pictures. We could not walk alongside the Bund river as it was under construction due to the Expo fair of 2010.

After a quick tea break and a toilet stop, we visited the Jade Buddha temple. They had a pond there with lots of koi fish. I expected us to be taken around the back to a jade shop; however, amazingly, we escaped that. But yes, it was all too good to be true, as our next stop was a pearl factory, and naturally, there was obligatory time for shopping! I was rewarded for my patience with a buffet-style lunch; I didn't have to share my food at last.

I enjoyed our afternoon of sightseeing. We visited the Shanghai Museum with its collection of ancient Chinese art, the French Concession with leafy boulevards consisting of historical buildings and the Old City. I had never pictured Shanghai as having an Old City and was pleasantly surprised when we arrived there. The boundary had been marked by the Old City Wall. It had survived from 1554 until the end of the 20th century, and there were, in fact, still some parts left. The Old City had been the urban core of Shanghai, with its City God Temple and my favourite, the Yuyuan Gardens. Ironically, the gardens are not really gardens but large ponds with zigzagging bridges, pavilions, and pagodas. Either way, these really were worth the visit.

I thought we had got away with not having another jade factory saga and was delighted with Stefan. He must have listened to me after all. I was wrong; no more than twenty minutes into our drive back to our hostel, they managed to squeeze in a stop at the jade factory. I was hopping mad; on two counts. Firstly, Stefan had lied. Secondly we were flying home that evening, and now we would be late back to the hostel, and in turn, we would be in a rush to get to the airport! My disdain was not lost on the driver and Julia. I explained our predicament, but it was all relatively futile, although they cut the visit slightly short.

Of course, we were indeed late back at the hostel; I did not have much time to lay my wrath on Stefan (he had a lucky escape); I would have loved to penny whistled at him for a few hours. But it was just after 18:00hrs, and so we rushed to have a quick shower, eat, do final packing and checks and catch a taxi to the bus station. From there, we would take the airport shuttle. We just about caught it, just as it was pulling away from the bus stand. Exhausted, we arrived at Pudong airport but decided it was best to get check-in and security over and done with so that we could relax on the other side before our flight. I did my usual last-minute gift shopping, chocolates for people at work, little nic-nacs for friends, a chopsticks for my Dad, and a bookmark for my Mum.

I watched films and slept soundly most of the way to Dubai airport, where I would transfer to my London flight. I was half asleep whilst walking through security at Dubai airport, when I was awoken abruptly. I was stopped from going through and was asked what the long metal object was in my bag. I kept looking at the picture; I was baffled. I would struggle with this kind of question when fully alert, so asking me when I am half awake would not elicit much. Then I remembered it was the bookmark I had bought for my mother! I believe that he would have questioned me more had it not been for him getting in a kerfuffle with another passenger. I took the opportunity and made my escape.

I made it to my flight to London; it was time to reflect. I wondered what had been wrong with Linda's back, and had it been cured after all the alternative treatments? And what a long trip this had been with so much packed in. Highlights for me were Beijing with its Great Wall and sledging back down from it. Culturally it was Xian and the Terracotta Warriors; but the most cherished experience was a baby panda sitting on my knees in Chengdu. We had been the sole westerners on the giant Leshan Buddha & Mount Emei tour with children as guides and had escaped Shanghai to boat along canals in scenic Suzhou. Of course, our unique nature highlight was Hangzhou with the total solar eclipse (albeit through cloud) but no river tidal bore. That alone made me realise I had developed in one respect; I had taken responsibility for my decision to go to the incorrect place for the eclipse. Rather than riddle myself with regret for not listening to the NASA advice, I adhered to my decision and made the best of the situation. It wouldn't deter me from venturing out to see future eclipses. If anything, it inspired me to plan/prepare, increase my total eclipse research, and, yes, enjoy them again. Bit by bit, I was learning more whilst being drawn in by the magic of the eclipse.

~ ~ ~

Overall Trip Cost: £1800 (Flight £450, Accomm. & Excursions £900, Spending £450).

Top Tip: Take out a business card from your accommodation in case of getting lost or a driver not speaking your language; you can then just point to the accommodation name and address.

Top Tip 2: you may wish to download a VPN before you travel, as Facebook, Twitter, and many more social media sites are not currently officially available in China.

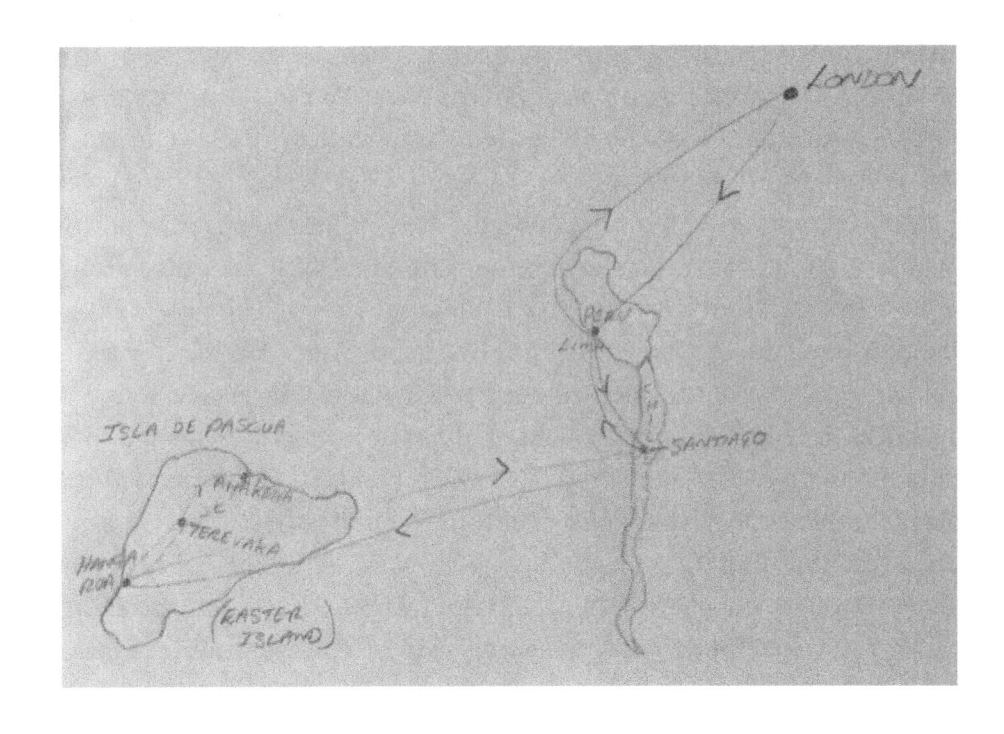

EASTER ISLAND ROUTE - 16 DAYS

1. LONDON - LIMA
2. LIMA - SANTIAGO
3. SANTIAGO - EASTER ISLAND
4. EASTER ISLAND - SANTIAGO
5. SANTIAGO - LIMA
6. LIMA - LONDON

EASTER ISLAND 2010

There's a Worm in My Water

Eclipse path: Pacific - Easter Island - Chile - Argentina
I viewed at: Easter Island
Date/Time of Maximum Totality: 11.07.2010 at 13:34 Local Time
Length of Totality: 05m 20secs.

Easter Island, or Isla de Pascua, is the world's most secluded inhabited island lying in the Pacific Ocean in Oceania, a remote 2,360 miles from the coastline of Chile. The island has several names. The more commonly known Easter Island was so named by the Dutch admiral Jacob Roggeveen, the first European to land there, on Easter Sunday. Rapa Nui is the name given to this isolated island by the indigenous Rapa Nui people. This is the one they still use today. There was a steep decline in the island population by the time the Europeans arrived. Oral traditions state that this derived from civil warfare and cannibalism among the inhabitants.
The Indigenous Rapa Nui people are believed to have settled on Easter Island around 300-1200CE, having most likely migrated there from the Marquesas Islands of Polynesia. The Polynesian Rapa Nui bought with them a wealth of agricultural skills and traditions. Despite previous beliefs that war and/or disease had wiped out the Rapa Nui, they have survived, representing 60% of the current Easter Island population. They have held onto their traditions, beliefs, culture, and traditional music of choral singing, chanting and natural instruments such as conch shells.

Whilst researching for my fifth trip to see a total solar eclipse in 2010, I came across a promotional video from a company organising an eclipse festival on Easter Island. Their video showed a packed festival with people smiling, dressed in cool clothing, and casually dancing in the sun to an upbeat version of a song with the lines "where's the sunshine, where's the sunshine…". This filled me with images of me dancing, wearing a belly dance outfit, with the sun shining down on me, and I was smiling and happy. Little did I know it at the time, but the reality was going to be very different.

Now with a combination of their promotional material and my imagination running wild, I was hooked. Excitedly I ran round to my friend Jason's flat and showed him the video - he too was up for it. Jason wanted to go primarily for the festival with the eclipse, whereas I wanted to go for the eclipse with the festival. It was agreed, we would go to this fantastic festival on Easter Island, home of the Moai statues and the indigenous Rapa Nui people.

Thankfully, although it was a very early start at 04:00, the journey there was not too eventful. The rest of the trip was going to be far too full of drama, although, of course, I did not know that then. My main concern was how on earth I would get my luggage to Heathrow, let alone to my destination. I had packed my useful items; head torch, washing powder, superglue, training golf ball, duct tape, umbrella, and a few pink sacks (large thick plastic bags used for waste recycling). These would lay flat in my pack, taking up little room. They would be great for sitting on if ground wet or dirty, as an emergency cover for daypack or poncho, and putting litter into, if out in a group. As I would be camping in a remote area, I needed to take at least the bare essentials: tent, sleeping bag, lilo, tiny camping stove, and then, of course, clothing/toiletries etc. My pack was weighing in at 24kg, I would say the most I have carried in weight, and then there was my daypack, again at the maximum weight limit, and I somehow still had to fit Dinky Doo in there. I wished Jason was there to help me, but he had taken a flight the day before, so I set off as a lone packhorse.

I was pleased to see my luggage off at check-in at Heathrow and even more delighted to relax into my seat after a few red wines on the plane. The journey there had exhausted me, and it was only 10:00. I slept soundly until the food came round. If there is one thing that can wake

me up when I am sleeping like a baby, it's the smell of food!
I was alert enough to get through the transit at Miami airport. I had heard nightmare stories of how long it could take to get through their security, so I was prepared with a laid back approach to it (although maybe I was just still half asleep). I had also heard negative rumours about border control and to be on guard. So I was on guard, but as it turned out, I had a very friendly Immigration Officer, which I must admit was a pleasant surprise. I was beginning to wonder if it was a trick, or maybe he fancied me? I saw a romance blossoming as we discussed the jobs we both had in common with each other.
We had both worked in probation style jobs, working with offenders, and he seemed more than happy to chat about this. On the one hand, I thought this would help me get through, but on the other hand, it probably took longer than it would have done due to the length of our conversation. I wondered what else romantically we had in common, but there was no time to delay; I had another flight to catch to Lima in Peru. When I arrived in Lima and discovered my brand new security wire netting had been removed from my backpack at Miami airport, I felt betrayed by him. His chatting with me was all a ruse whilst they scoured my pack; I was sure of it.

~ ~ ~

I spent the night in Lima to have a break away from flying and get a good night's sleep before flying on to Santiago. Upon reaching Santiago, I had a two-day break before flying on to Easter Island, and I wanted to make the most of it. What actually happened was that I overslept the next day and ended up having to rush around on my last day. I liked the hostel and the area I was staying in, and it felt very safe. That did not stop me from almost getting into a confrontation in a local cafe. I was standing in a queue at the counter. I heard three people behind me talking about me in English, saying that I looked German (they must have thought I only spoke German and wouldn't understand). Now Germany had beaten Argentina in the World Cup the day before, so perhaps I should have been worried, except I was in Chile. I turned around and calmly explained that I was not German but would take their comments as a compliment. We laughed it off whilst two of the friends apologised for their drunk and leary friend, who probably still thought I was German.

I am sure I would get a lot further and get much more sightseeing accomplished if I did not spend so much time chatting with people. That day was no different, and so it was, I only had time to rush up Cerro San Cristobel on the funicular (the railway taking you up the slopes of San Cristobel hill). I hurriedly photographed the surrounding parkland, peeked at the Virgin Mary statue, and took in some views over the city before having to rush back to the hostel before going to the airport. I returned there, quickly put my mp3 player and phone on charge, collected my luggage and spruced myself up, ready for my airport pick up with no time to spare. The beauty of a shared airport pick up is that you share the cost with other passengers. I was just getting friendly with my co-passengers when I suddenly realised I had left my mobile phone and mp3 charging up back at the hostel. The driver and passengers were very accommodating and agreed we must go back and retrieve them.

Perhaps something was warning me not to go Easter Island, and it all became a bit of a mission at Santiago airport. There was not much time before my flight, and I seemed to be the only one concerned about that! The check-in assistant was having problems finding my ticket; I showed her I already had my boarding card. Ironically this had been in a bid to save time, mission not accomplished. Eventually, I got to the boarding gate, and there I found some of the crowd who were to be my neighbours on the campsite on Easter Island. I started chatting with a Scottish woman called Alison, who came over to me as she heard me talking about the festival. Alison was with her family, her son Jamie and her daughter Julie who was there with her partner Alex and child and a friend. It turned out I was sat just behind Alison on the plane, and I was across the aisle from a newfound friend, Kara from Australia, and so it was the flight passed quite merrily. Kara happened to be seated next to two DJs playing music at the festival (they may well have ended up being the only two). It would turn out to be very fortunate for us to make friends with the DJ's, as when we arrived at Easter Island airport, we realised it was a long way to our campsite and the Scottish family, Kara and I had no way of getting there!

~ ~ ~

The DJ's took pity on us as it was late at night and said they would transport all their equipment to the campsite in their pickup truck and then come back for us. This was great, except they ended up having to take the vehicle three times on the 15km round trip on rough terrain. This had evolved due to their amount of equipment and various people having jumped on the bandwagon, so to speak. By the time they had loaded up three times and deposited people and equipment in the middle of the night, it became apparent that both people and luggage had become confused. It was pitch black, and we had to navigate over unknown land to pitch our tents. The Scottish family came to help as we just kept falling over and then having fits of giggles. Kara was not laughing so much when she realised her tent had not arrived. However, we agreed she would share mine for the night if it was not on the last run; luckily for her, it was.

I am not the best at putting up tents. It really is not my forte, so the Scottish family helped Kara and I to put our tents up in the dark of the night. We decided if anything needed adjusting, we would do it in the morning. In amongst the calamity, Jason must have heard all the chatter and came to look for me. We were excited as we had both made it and had a lot to look forward to! We joined the others around their campfire and had a couple of beers, not noticing that by then, it was well into the early hours of the morning. It was time to hit the lilo, and although my sleeping bag had seemed quite thick, I was still quite cold. I was so tired, though by then, that I still managed to sleep soundly.

I awoke to the pitter-patter of rain on my tent - this should have been a warning of things to come! I peered out of the tent and was faced with a bracing wind and a downpour of rain. The good thing about tents is when they are close enough you can talk to your neighbour. Kara and I agreed it was not a good plan to go out in that weather, but we had a dilemma about what to do about breakfast.

I had food supplies but was to discover that my tiny cooking utensil would be of no use at all over the coming week (it was a small iron rectangular stove where you put the fire lighting blocks on). My Scottish family saved us, they invited us to their campfire for breakfast, so we at least had one meal under our belts.

~ ~ ~

I think the first day really set the scene, and it was not a pretty one. It was quickly established that the campsite was not set up ready for us customers. The shower and toilet cubicles were not adequately built up. There were no food or grocery stands as was promised, only a third of the DJ's had arrived, and there would be no music for two days. So off it was for Jason and me into the main town of Hanga Roa, which was about five miles away. Not too far, you would think, except it was not the easiest of terrain to master, especially not when it had rained. We traversed from the slopes of the Terevaka volcano (the highest point of the island at 511metres), which seemed to melt away under the rainfall. Luckily, we were offered a lift into town in a truck with a fellow camper at the site gates.

We quickly realised it was not going to be cheap to eat during our stay. My shopping consisted of lettuce, tomatoes, bananas, rolls, two tins of peas, dozen eggs, two cucumbers, red peppers, two cartons of wine, totalling a horrendous $40. Where is the local Lidls when you need it! Of course, in reality, this is what happens when there is an eclipse who wouldn't want to cash in, and at least, in this case, the money was going directly to the locals.

Wandering around town, I met my new wine sister Mary, and Mary had literally just met her new life partner Brian. We all hit it off straight away and returned to camp with a few wines under our belts. It was great meeting lots of our fellow campers, and as if to say all was going to be okay, the sun came out. A rainbow appeared, which seemed even more spiritual as we were on a very spiritual island. Simultaneously I happened to be talking to a very spiritual new friend, Nacho.

The camp was in different sections, and I wandered around it. I encountered the Denmark crew and Karl from Germany in the far corner, Marek from South Africa, and many others from the "over the hedge section". I eventually returned to my own area of the camp, which had been named "Camp Dead Horse". It was so-called due to somebody finding the skull of a dead animal and sticking it on a wooden pole in the middle of our camp.

It was coming to the time of day when I would need to finish setting up my tent, setting out all my items so that I could find them, and inflating my lilo. This was all in the hope that I would not get washed away during the night. Yes, the first couple of days were a time of settling in, making new friends, not cooking much so drinking fruit vodka and eating little. The DJ's were setting up their equipment, there was rain, then sun and the camp slowly transformed into something mildly resembling a festival site. I reminisced back to the promotional video of the festival-goers revelling and dancing in the sunshine, lucky them!

By the third day, Scooter and a couple of other guys who had paid to attend the festival had volunteered to finish building the shower and toilet units. I, therefore, braved it into the newly built shower block, hoping for a lovely hot shower- it was not to be, so cold shower it was! I like to think I can put up with most things in life, but cold showers and early mornings are not included. The volunteers had done the best they could; the water was not under their control.

As we were suitably refreshed and woken up, Kara and I took a short walk down the volcano slopes to the "Ahu Akivi", the sacred site of seven moai statues. These were the only ones on the island facing out to sea, and one of the legends is that they represented the first group to reach the island. They stayed there and looked out to sea to guide the rest of the Rapa Nui people. They are aligned with astronomical precision looking towards where the sun sets during the Equinox, resulting in the belief that this site originated as a celestial observatory.

There are another 900 Moai statues on Easter Island. They consist not just of heads (as is a common perception); but also of bodies that cannot be seen as they are sometimes submerged below ground. All were originally lying down, but some have been re-erected. The average height of a Moai statue is 13 feet tall and 14 tons in weight - the heaviest one weighing 86 tonnes! At some point, the figures were moved across the land. Still, nobody knows how, as there was no availability of wheels, cranes or even large animals to transport them.

We had a fun evening later sat around the fire, again hosted by my Scottish family. We ate, chatted, laughed and joked. We were in high spirits. It was Kara's special birthday - her 40th and I presented her with a card I had made, which we had all signed. Alison gave her a watercolour of the view she had painted earlier that day. Our fellow Japanese campers just across from us had a cake for Kara; she was truly spoilt! There was an intriguing end in store that evening for Kara. Just as we were going back into our respective tents, a tall, handsome man appeared on a majestic white horse. The next thing I knew, Kara was swept up onto the back of the white horse riding off into the night. Part of me was thinking how romantic it was, but then I started to worry about her being taken away like that. Kara reappeared the following day as if nothing had happened, taking it all in her stride, or canter.

~ ~ ~

The next day it all began to liven up; I was approached to see if I would like to volunteer somehow. I agreed and was taken to Johanna, who, if she telepathically liked me, then I was in. I really could not have cared either way, as I had plenty of lazing around to do and wandering around chatting to all my new friends. It seemed I had passed the test, though, and so I was stationed on meet & greet. I felt it wise not to warn people about the lack of facilities on the camp. Especially not the recent lack of water in the few toilets and showers, and cheerily motioned the way for them to drive their trucks. Luckily for them, at that point, there was a track to drive on. A couple of hours later, I was instructed to take a break. It seemed more like I had been sacked, so I took the opportunity to have a salad (I was not going to get anything cooked) and chatted with some of my neighbours.

Our calm turned to storm after we found out there was no drinking water. Worse still, the previous tank from which we had been drinking water had small worms in it! Somebody had thoughtfully brought a sample over to us as evidence. This was the start of a revolution, which heightened when a volunteer came over to announce that the organisers were refusing to go into town to bring us water. A large group of us gathered and stomped off up towards the office! However, halfway there, a messenger came to tell us that the organisers had had a change of heart and had gone into town to get fresh water. I would say it was a lucky escape for them. There was a band of disgruntled vegetarians. After all those years of not eating meat, I was not the only one upset at having digested worms!

To be fair, it was probably quite hard work for the two organisers left on camp to sort out all the shortcomings. The main organiser had not been allowed to fly out of Santiago to the island, as he was a known drug dealer and had been arrested! I questioned what I had gotten myself into here, and it was still relatively early days. What more could happen?

~ ~ ~

That evening the festival proper began. By now, the DJ's (the few who had bothered to make it to Easter Island, the rest of them must have had a premonition and made the wise choice not to come) had set up their gear. The music began. I will use the term 'music' loosely as it was not entirely my thing, but I decided to embrace it. I gave up embracing it by around 06:00, by which time I was one of the few to have retired for the night. I had not read the promotion clearly as I had failed to read the bit about 24 hours per day music, loud music! Now the ball was rolling, and there was no stopping it. I can honestly say I was not part of the clan that had complained about there not being enough music. It was light relief for me when there was some respite from it!

After a week on the island, things had begun to settle into a daily routine: wake up to music; dress myself and Dinky Doo; and try to cook breakfast but give up and head to my Scottish family to use their firepit. Kara would disappear into her tent with her handsome Rapanui man and hand out fruit vodka to me; whilst I would be mooching around chatting to fellow campers and drinking red wine with my wine sister Mary. The weather routine consisted of rain early in the day followed by cloud and then sun, with sometimes a rainbow thrown in. Night routine was dressing up in something weird and wonderful, and dancing the night away. There was a break in my routine on the eighth day when I was able to get a hot shower, and I was able to wash my hair for the first time. I am glad I did not wash it before with the worm water shampoo!

By now, there was quite a close group of us who would meet up regularly to put the world to rights. Our motley crew consisted of Karl (from Germany), who liked to fly his kite; Bam Bam from the USA, who had the most outrageous laugh and sense of humour; Marek from South Africa playing his neat guitar; and Scooter (from Australia) who had the best outfits for dressing up in. In the immediate neighbourhood, aside from Kara and my Scottish family, there was Alice from England and Sean from the USA. It was a standing joke about our various neighbourhoods. We had created Camp Dead Horse with its skull of a dead animal, Camp Over Yonder (it was a bit further out divided by a hedge), Camp Rainbow (as a rainbow was seen coming from it) and Camp Worm Water (we know why that is so-called!).

It was time to go exploring, and so it was on the ninth day I ventured out with Scottish Julie's partner Alex to the Ana Kai Tangata Caves. We walked for miles, over rocks and up and down through various terrains via the Ana Te Pahu- "Banana Caves" so named due to the sweet potatoes, taro and bananas that wildly grow there. We eventually found our destination, the sea cave (Ana Kai Tangata cave) that literally does open up into the sea. We stood inside the cave and looked out through the large hole in the cave wall, watching the ocean lashing against rocks and the subsequent spray blowing away. We weren't the only ones admiring the views, and got chatting with four Chilean girls. They kindly offered us a lift back to near our camp, and so we squashed into the back of their car. We still had a few fields to cross after we sprawled out of their vehicle, but our camp was a sight for sore eyes for once; we so easily could have been wandering the fields for hours.

Upon my return, Kara got the fruit vodka out (no dinner for me then!). Karl appeared and offered to take me on his hired motorbike for a trip to Anakena beach. It didn't take long to reach the white coral sand beach, which lies in a small bay. Anakena is edged by coconut palm trees and is home to the "Ahu Ature Huki", a solo moai statue (the first one to be raised up in modern times), and to the "Ahu Nau Nau", a row of 7 moai statues with their backs to the ocean. After a swim in the warm turquoise blue Pacific Ocean, and after a magnificent sunset, we were driving back under the dark night sky, and the stars were shining brightly. We had stopped briefly to look at them when a car pulled up, and a Rapanui guy came over to check both us and the motorbike were okay - I guess we may have looked a bit suspect!

By day ten, I had gone into survival mode. I found that by using my feminine wiles (I cannot claim to be a Ray Mears, being more of a 'Fay Mears'!), not only could I get people to do my shopping as they were going to town and I was not, I was able to get them to cook for me too! What was I to do without a campfire? My lovely Scottish family provided the firepit, and Kara, her new boyfriend, or Karl cooked my meals. To that end, my new nickname became "Princess".

The next day saw the start of an exodus from the festival and campsite. Many people were disillusioned with the festival, which, to be fair, was a pretty lame attempt at a festival. It was more like a rundown bar with a few locals. The landowners provided themselves as security (which involved drinking copious amounts of alcohol and creating a sense of unease). Then there would be a group of about thirty or forty of us festival-goers trying to liven things up with fire skills, juggling, acrobatics, and my belly dancing. We had woken up on exodus day to foggy, rainy weather, which had also dampened the spirits, and it really was quite cold. I was relieved that Jason did actually return with my shopping; I felt it was touch and go as to whether he would also attempt an escape! I finally ventured out to see if Karl was still around; he was but had been found asleep in the bushes. I had lost Bam Bam, my Denmark crew and Marek. They were fortunate to find accommodation in town; there was never going to be an abundance of it due to the tour companies booking up the majority years in advance.

It is times like this when you see the best in people, and the Rapanui families were starting to take people in (often for free) as they felt sorry for us. The track up the side of the volcano to our campsite had become practically impassable, and we were becoming cut off from civilisation. I solved this issue by drinking fruit vodka and hatching a plan to stay in Karl's tent due to him having a lovely thick mattress and a nice well-insulated tent. That night, I watched while Karl was strutting his stuff out on the dance floor, sneaked out of the festival party and hijacked his tent. When his head appeared through the zipper late in the morning, I refused entry, to which end he took up residence in the abandoned large tent of the Danish crew. Meanwhile, Kara had hired out my tent to a Chilean guy. I had a bit of a surprise when I returned to my tent late morning, and there was a pair of long legs sticking out of my tent. He was clearly taller than my tent and must have been really uncomfortable due to my lilo slowly deflating!

~ ~ ~

ECLIPSE DAY - 11th July 2010

This was not a day for despondency and low mood; we all gave our best to send out positive vibes. I was challenged with this initially as I wanted to have a shower and had to wait outside the female block. At the same time, a guy inside took his time preening himself. I was banging on the door, shouting out that there was an eclipse to see. The door was eventually opened, and I was allowed in. That was fine, but the guy decided to continue his vanity mission, indicating that I was free to use the shower. Well, I was not going to do that, being a prude, and herded him out. I never got to know his name but referred to him from there on in as "Naked Shower Man". So my day suitably brightened up, and now wearing my best belly dance outfit, I headed out with the rest of the group down to the beach to claim our spot for viewing the eclipse. I got as far as the camp gate and was offered a lift on the back of a motorbike. It was not too onerous a decision: walk seven kilometres over that dratted terrain with my friends, or escape on a motorbike - I went on the motorbike.

I met with the rest of the group down at the beach, and luckily for me, they were very forgiving and were still talking to me. We had a fantastic view; we were slightly upwards on the beach amongst some rock platforms, and so was able to look over the throngs of crowds on the sand and out to to the ocean. More importantly, we were staring almost face to face with the Moai statues, standing majestically overlooking us. All were placed with their backs to the sea; alas, they would not get to see the eclipse. In contrast, Dinky Doo had a prime position.

The weather was in our favour, and the sun was shining brightly. Perhaps it was those positive vibes we had been emanating that morning. The eclipse would commence at about 12.40, and totality would be at about 14:11. The totality was to last 4 minutes and 41 seconds, a pretty great time span as it is not often that they last that long. There were approximately four thousand eclipse chasers in total that had come to witness this celestial event, and we were not to be disappointed!

The partial phase, when the moon began moving between the sun and the earth (around 12.40 local time), teased us with that first little nibble out of the sunlight at first contact. As the moon slowly covered the solar disc, biting larger chunks out, the surface blackened, and a crescent sun appeared (it would look like a waxing crescent moon). The subsequent shadow bands danced their thin wavy lines across the cloudless sky as we gazed in awe. And here was an added bonus- we were honoured by the presence of the two planets Venus and Mercury, with Sirius (the brightest star in the sky) and Canopus (the second brightest star) in the clear blue skies above us. This was a particular treat for those of us from the Northern Hemisphere living in built-up urban areas not usually privileged to see these.

As the crescent sun disappeared, Baily's Beads appeared, showing tiny specks around the rim of the sun, throwing out the last rays of sunlight. And here came my favourite part of the whole process - the Diamond Ring. Here glowing out before us on the now darkened disc in the sky was a luminous diamond ring, and below a shadow had crossed the still Maoi Statues. Shortly after, with hardly time to get our breaths back, the totally eclipsed sun was the proud owner of a corona which could be seen shining in all directions around the moon! It was time to make the most of the next 4.41 seconds of totality. I was too excited. I wanted to drink it all in but also make photographic memories of it too. Externally I was as quiet as all those around me, all of us emanating an eerie silence, yet internally I was bursting. A tirade of thoughts was thundering through my head!

Was it thundering in my head? Or was it stampeding of the wild horses in the distance who were confused by the change so quickly from day to night? The sky was dark; on the horizon, there was a slim red sunset, and seabirds flitted past us, ready to roost for the night. I was distracted momentarily by Alex going down on one knee proposing marriage to Julie. How romantic. What a thoughtful idea to propose during an eclipse with an actual diamond ring underneath the one above us dazzling in the sky. Julie quickly said "yes"; she wanted to see the rest of the totality.

As totality slipped away, the moon's shadow eased away gradually, and the sunlight began to appear again from the western edge of the sun. The corona disappeared, and if you looked quick enough, you would have got a glimpse of Baily's Beads before a thin crescent of the sun became visible. By now, people were singing and cheering, and there was traditional tribal dance down on the sand. We partied with the Danes, and I had a real good laugh with Marek. He thought my martial arts flying front kick (from my body combat class) was hilarious and said my opponent may not be scared, but he would die laughing! Unfortunately, in my excitement I dropped my good camera, it broke.

That evening we returned to camp reluctantly, as we had all had such a magical day down at the beach. I would go as far as to say that the spectacular celestial event we had witnessed had eclipsed the FIFA

World Cup Final Match 2010. This was happening simultaneously in Johannesburg. I am sure the Dutch supporters would have agreed with us as they lost 0-1 to Spain! We, on the other hand, on that tiny remote island, contentedly danced the night away in the festival tent and saw in the dawn of a new day.

~ ~ ~

It was a day that many more of my neighbours left the campsite in droves, all seeking shelter in the main town of Hanga Roa. I felt I was hardcore and was one of the dozen of us who stayed. Mabye it was the lure of Kara's fruit vodka. I was sorry to be saying goodbye to my Scottish family and Karl, especially as he would be taking his tent.

I lasted one more night, but conditions were getting quite treacherous on the side of the volcano. We were warned by not leaving soon, we could be trapped there. Taxies could not get to the campsite as the track was now completely waterlogged; if you had a 4 x 4 vehicle, you might have been lucky enough to escape. One of the deciding factors for leaving was a distraught female telling Jason and I that several of her valuable items had been stolen, including her wallet. She suspected the landowners. After all of the warnings, Jason and I decided not to take our chances and began to pack up. As luck would have it, I spotted a local just about to drive off on his tractor, and I ran to him begging for a lift into town. And so it was that day that Jason and I ended up on a trailer with all our luggage and a water tank full of tiny worms. Many people laughed at us as we trundled into town on the back of that tractor. We were too busy rattling around due to the rough terrain, praying that we got to town with our luggage intact, and not being drenched by worm water to be concerned at being the source of such amusement.

Upon reaching Hanga Roa, we looked at each other; what were we to do next? Where were we to go? Our tractor driver had the solution, we would stay with his family. Well, as it turned out, it was a wooden house he was building next door to where he, his mother, siblings and nieces lived. The house was being built for his mother to live in, and was at that stage a shell with no window. But we were not complaining, it was a roof over our heads, and we were very grateful. There was no point in Jason and I debating which room to sleep in; they both mirrored each other. Neither had an advantage over the other of en suite, glamorous decor, windows or even a door to argue over.

We decided to get out of the family's hair the next day. So Jason and I hiked up the Rona Tau volcano - you really would have thought that we had had enough of volcanos. But no, we could not resist an hour and a half trek up a steep trail! The journey was worth it; the crater had water with green patches on it and looked a bit like the Okavanga Delta. We walked around the crater rim. The highlight of the day for me was on the return to town when we spotted several wild horses trotting alongside the road.

Back in town, we bumped into many of our camping compadres. To be fair, it was unlikely with just one main road that you were going to miss anyone. The studio of the local tattoo artist was bulging at the seams from eclipse chasing tourists, proudly emerging with their new tattoos. The feeling was that if you were going to get a tattoo anywhere, then this would be the place. I was tempted to succumb to having one too. I would dwell on that dilemma whilst cooking dinner for the honu family that evening, aided by Jason. We were waiting for our tractor driver, and when Hamuera got home, he had had a bad day at work. His wrath was mainly because he had been up to our previous camp. The landowners said that the festival organiser had to pay his wages, not them, which Hamuera disagreed with, and so they had argued. Hamuera would be going up there the next day to get his wages, and would fight with the landowner and pluck his eyes out if his money was not there.

It was undoubtedly all kicking off on Easter Island. I had seen Nacho in town talking about the problems from our former camp that the festival organiser was having with the landowner. He was trying to charge her treble their original agreed amount for the use of his land. There was the chance she could be held to ransom.

~ ~ ~

After dinner, Hamuera, Jason and I sat around the table listening to music, drinking beer and chatting. I did the meerkat dance, which they thought was highly amusing. Hamuera told me not to say "estoy callienta", which means I am hot/horny and do the meerkat dance at a disco - the locals would think it was a mating ritual dance!

My dancing prowess was to be exhibited later that night at the local nightclub. I was surprised and impressed that such a thing existed on this small island. The night began at the house of a guy called who I had recognised because I had seen him on a documentary film about Easter Island. It was a mellow start to the evening with a bbq and jamming session out on the porch. I felt like a fish out of water because I don't take drugs, I don't play any musical instruments, and I certainly do not sing. I was getting cold; it was time to warm up, so we headed to the disco around 03:00. I was enjoying strutting my stuff with my meerkat moves and belly dancing/pop dance combo, but Jason was starting to feel uncomfortable. I must admit there were quite a few eyes on us (but I put that down to my dance moves). Jason drove us home in Hamuera's car, which I thought was pretty impressive as we had no clue where we were. Yet, somehow, he managed to navigate the town and find the alley leading to our temporary home.

The next, and what turned out to be my unplanned final day, started off pretty standard - for one thing, the rain was still pounding down. Then it gradually turned surreal. I was walking along the road. Previous camping companions were pointing at me and saying, 'that's her'. I thought this odd, but maybe I had achieved fame as being a Princess? I was then informed by some friends that a guy from the local Consulate was looking for me. I carried on to the internet cafe, and then it all began to make sense. Reading my emails, I discovered an email from the Santiago Consulate stating that my mother had been taken ill and had been rushed to hospital! My friends helped me make some calls to England as I was stunned, I was to return home as soon as possible, but first I had to find the local Consulate representative. I walked out of the internet cafe, unsure which way to go when I spotted Jason in a taxi. He jumped out, gave me a hug and said he would help me sort things out, and we jumped into his cab. The taxi driver would not take any money for the journey, which was so good of her. She had been circling the town with Jason, had gone to the police station with Jason and so knew the situation.

Back at base, at home with the family, we tried to get in touch with the Consulate worker Ryan. I managed to eventually make contact by phone; he had been out looking for me (and had been over the past 24 hours!). He wanted to come and see me to make arrangements to help me get back to England. I thought he would not find me as I was not at a hotel that could easily be found; I was in a back street out of town. As luck would have it, as soon as I mentioned the family name, he told me to wait there - he knew the family well. Ryan pulled various strings, and everything was sorted to get me on a flight back to Santiago asap. And so it was the following day I bade my sad farewells to my Honu family and Jason, after which Ryan drove me to Hanga Roa airport.

I often think back to that morning at the airport and what the scene must have looked like to a bystander. Ryan assisted me with checking in, and miraculously, I was upgraded to Business Class. He waved goodbye; I went through security to the waiting area, where I promptly burst into tears due to the mental exhaustion and overwhelming of it all. I went to board the plane, and tall, handsome Ryan returned to me, rushing through via security and into the queue to give me a hug and wish me well. It seemed like a scene from Casablanca, with a bittersweet romantic goodbye between the man and the woman, whereas in reality, it was very different!

It was a long journey home, consisting of several flights and several trains back from Heathrow to Southend. Despite having been on one of the most spiritual islands, I was glad to be home. It had been an exhausting and anxious journey back to England, and it had given me time to reflect on what we had all gone through. The campsite conditions had been horrendous, not only due to the lack of facilities, but also having worms in our water. On top of that, we were subjected to a week's worth of torrential rain on the side of a volcano; it was just wretched. I was grateful, though, that we had experienced the most magical eclipse in the company of the Moai statues. I dispelled feelings of disappointment at my trip being cut short and not seeing most of the other Moai statues or the remainder of the island. I had more vital priorities. I threw my luggage into my house and jumped into a taxi to the hospital. There was my mum lying on the hospital bed, laughing and joking with the nurses and doing her party trick to prove she was okay, flinging her legs up in the air! I did not know whether to laugh or cry; she was fine and could not figure out why I had dashed back from halfway across the world.

~ ~ ~

Overall Trip Cost: £1200 (Flights £600, Festival £300, All Other Costs/Spending £300).

Top Tip 2: Create a travel information document that you can leave with trusted family or friends back home and email to yourself. The document will contain important details for your papers, e.g. insurance, passport details, drivers licence number, home address and mobile number; the names, addresses and contact numbers of Consulates in the cities nearest to where you are travelling; and bank account details. See Appendix 1.

Eclipse on Beach   Just another wet day Breakfast!

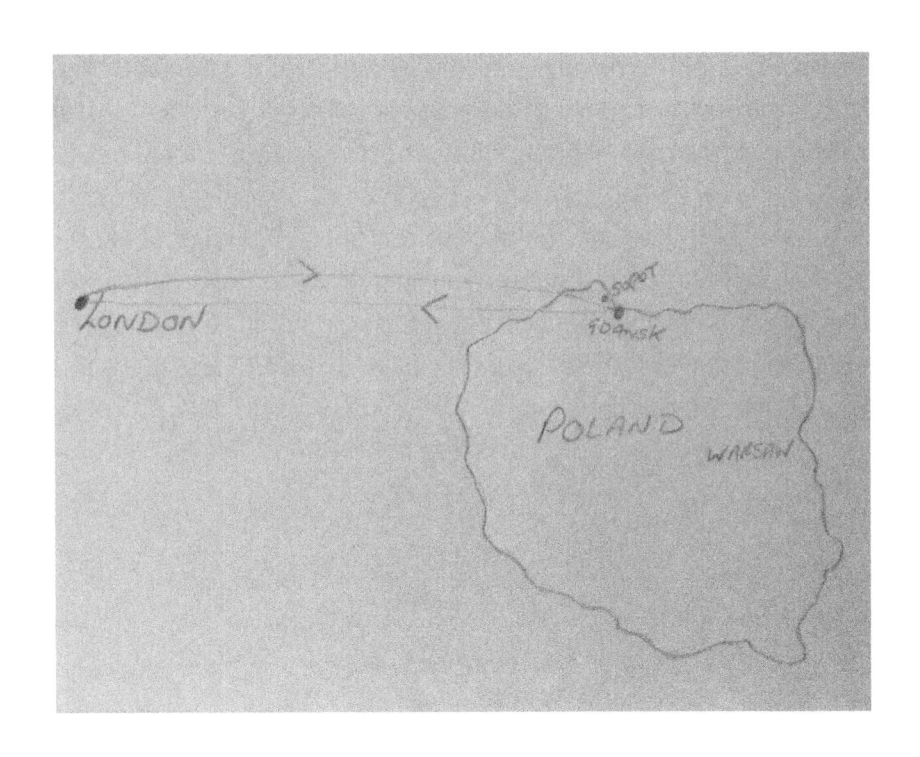

POLAND ROUTE 2011 - 5 DAYS

GDANSK, POLAND 2011

Spreadeagled like a Starfish

Poland has an impressive list of inventions to its name; amongst them are: radiation for curing cancer (invented by Marie Curie), vitamins (Kazimierz Funk), condoms (Julius Fromm), the bulletproof vest (Jan Szczepanik), vehicle windscreen wipers (Josef Hofmann) and the modern make-up (Max Factor). When not making things, the Polish have various traditions, one of which is to say goodbye to winter. This takes the form of making human-sized dolls called Marzanna, and when spring begins, the dolls are drowned!

I had been on a few trips to Poland (although not to the capital city of Warsaw), namely Poznan, Krakow, Zakopane and Rzeszow, and each had been an adventure. For example, I was on a day trip, had been on an early flight, and was eating my breakfast on a bench in Rzeszow. I spotted a crowd around a television crew, I could not resist. I had to see what was occurring. As I approached, the crowd dispersed, cheering, and the various presenters dotted out into the crowd. They thrust their microphones into the faces of onlookers - me being one of them. With a microphone now inches from my mouth, I was asked in Polish and then English, what did I like about Rzeszow? For some reason, unknown to myself, in my poshest voice, I replied, 'ooh, it is very up and coming'. Even Dinky Doo looked up at me in surprise, whilst the presenter smiled, lost for words and make a quick getaway.

This particular trip to Gdansk, Poland was for my birthday and was just a quick jaunt away; here I was hurtling like the speed of light towards 50 - would I make it? My friend Michelle wanted to accompany me, she liked Poland having been before with me to Krakow. And so it was that we set off very early (02:00) on a cold, dreary winter's day to Gdansk. We chose Gdansk as it had a quaint old town and had several spas with very reasonable prices (cheaper than in England) as my birthday treats. We also wanted to visit nearby Sopot as it is a city twinned with Southend on Sea where we lived. Also, it had a pier that attempted to, but could not match the length of our world's longest pier.

It seemed too good to be true that everything went smoothly at the airport and on the flight. Even when we reached arrivals at Gdansk airport, our booked shuttle driver was waiting for us with my surname on a placard. Yes, the journey was going well. However, we had only been in the country for half an hour, when we were in a car crash! Michelle and I were sitting, enjoying the snowy scenery. We did not chat with the driver as he could not speak English. We wanted to let him concentrate on the icy roads. The motorway was very ice-bound, and we were getting concerned as the driver seemed to be going quite fast for the weather conditions. The next thing we knew, the driver skidded on the ice, and we bounced from one hard shoulder to the other, sliding across the ice at least five or six times. There was a long drop down to the highway below each time we hit the barrier on the left! Parts were flying off the vehicle, and I thought I saw sparks coming off the wheels. Michelle and I looked at each other; we thought this was it!

After what seemed like an eternity, the badly bashed vehicle came to a stop; it all happened so quickly and yet was in slow motion. The driver came round and let us out of the one door that would slide open. We all stood out in the freezing cold, with Michelle and I not knowing what to do and the driver not wanting the Police called. A few vehicles pulled up, and one of them, another taxi, offered to take us to our hostel. There was some mention of payment. Before I exploded at the driver, Michelle insisted that our shuttle driver would be paying as he had almost killed us! I thought we were being taken to the hostel, but we stopped at the hospital (hostel - hospital, sounds similar). The left shoulder side and arm of my body were sore, and Michelle had hit her head. We were both so grateful we had put our seatbelts on as our injuries could have been a lot more severe, or I might not be here to tell the tale!

We convinced the driver that we wanted to go to our hostel; we just wanted to get to our room and lay down. Arriving at the reception, the staff were so lovely after we relayed our awful experience. We had managed to get our suitcases out of the van's luggage compartment. However, my brand new case, which I had purchased just a few days before the trip, had been seriously dented and ripped and was unable to close. The Receptionist sent us to our beds; however, she gave us the wrong door key, and we walked into a room already occupied by two people. Back we went downstairs to get the correct key and to finally get some rest. The Receptionist redeemed herself by handling the luggage situation on my behalf with the owner of the shuttle company. To his credit, he appeared later that day with a brand new suitcase for me. As we were asleep, he left a message to say we could have a free return shuttle to the airport upon our departure.

~ ~ ~

After a few hours, we were famished and so walked into the town to eat. My bowl of soup appeared, and I was about to take a mouthful when I noticed something strange floating in it - chunks of meat (I am vegetarian). I called the waitress, who merely replied, 'it is okay, it is only bacon- not meat'. Needless to say, the bowl of soup went back to the kitchen.

After the day we had endured, it seemed a good time to go to the hotel across the road and book some birthday spa treatments for the next few days. Considering we were in Poland, we were surprised how valuable my pigeon German was to come in handy, particularly with the lady at the spa reception. We managed to communicate with a little German and a little English, and I assured Michelle that I knew what we had booked.

Although my left shoulder and arm were still in pain, Michelle and I roamed around in the bitter cold the next day to see the sights. What spurred us on for this was that the museums were free on that particular day, so who were we to miss out. We found the St Nicholas Church; Town Hall, and Artus Museum, formerly known as the Junkerhaus (where merchants met socially). After a quick snack, we visited the Amber Museum (housed in the former prison) and the Prison Tower. It was here the Security Guard thought it was fun to put my hands in the antique shackles so that Michelle could get a photo of me. He felt it even funnier to leave me there and walk off.

Looking forward to our pre-booked jacuzzi session late afternoon, we turned up only to discover it was not working. We were disappointed and returned to our hostel. I sat on my bed, heard a creaking noise and then it collapsed on one side. I just looked at Michelle in disbelief, and all we could do was laugh!

We decided to finish the evening off with a nice meal in a quiet cafe down by the canal. We ordered dinner, but it was apparent it was not going to be so quiet. There were only three tables in the cafe. One we were sitting at, an empty one, and a noisy one comprising five British men having a raucous time together. They were friendly and got chatting with us, and they kept making jokes. The jokes and stories were so believable we thought some of them were true, but then they would laugh again.

The conversation turned, and they asked us if we had heard about the earthquake in Christchurch, New Zealand. They told us that it had been a powerful earthquake and it had destroyed parts of the city, 185 lives had been lost and thousands of people injured. We thought they were joking, as perhaps they might think it funny to make up a story after hearing Michelle's New Zealand accent. They promised us they were not kidding, and we rushed to our hostel to see if the story was on the tv news. They had been telling the truth, Michelle was distraught as her daughter was working in the city centre of and living in Christchurch. The hostel staff were very accommodating and provided a phone for Michelle to contact her daughter, who thankfully was fine. However, there was an air of sadness over us due to the destruction, lost lives, and so many injured.

Neither of us could sleep that night, Michelle with Christchurch on her mind and me with a swollen, bruised arm and shoulder. However, as it was my birthday the next day, Michelle and I soldiered on. We took a short train ride to Sopot, just twelve kilometres away. We wanted to visit Sopot as it is twinned with Southend on Sea, there's a road sign as you enter Southend to confirm this. We wandered around Sopot and came upon the only building of note there, the Crooked House. Before getting notions of this being a quaint olde-worlde building, I should mention it was built in 2004 as a modern shopping centre. It is fairytale-esque style though, and has the Polish version of a Hollywood Walk of Fame.

Sometimes fate just throws a curveball. I unexpectedly came across a Doctor in the Crooked House who advised she could eliminate the fat from my hips for a very reasonable sum of money. Who was I to decline that offer? An appointment was made for me to return in two days, I was assured it would be a simple, painless procedure. We then ventured back out into the snow to see if there was possibly anything else of note. We found the Molo Pier. We were pleased to discover it was shorter than our world-famous longest entertainment pier in the world in

Southend on Sea (which is one and a quarter-mile long). Back on shore, it was the first time I had gazed across a sea totally iced over, and that could be walked on. Of course, we just had to experience this novelty.

After an excellent birthday meal, Michelle's treat for my birthday, we walked back to what I thought was the train station. I believed it was the train station as there were lots of people heading out of there. I am not sure why I did not notice they were all teenagers and that the building I had walked into was a High School. I simply thought the strange looks I was getting were due to the relatively large birthday badge I was wearing. Having found the correct train station and recomposed ourselves back at the hostel, it was time to head over to the Spa Hotel for my birthday massage package. I had opted for the Slimming Treatment, which started with peeling, exfoliation, and then a body wrap. I was left alone in the room with the zen music playing gently and the candles glowing softly. After being slathered with essential oils, I was gently swaddled in a wrap from my neck to my feet. What I had not accounted for was a claustrophobic feeling, and I spent the next twenty minutes trying to wriggle out of my cocoon! I was unsuccessful, mainly because I was up on one of those beauticians beds. If I wiggled too far on either side, I would have gone over the edge and fallen to the floor.

And then came the massage! Having had Thai massages previously, where I have been bent into positions that I didn't think my body was capable of (I really am not bendy) and walked upon, I usually go for the relaxing option. Now either my German had not been that great when booking, or the Receptionist's English had not been great, but here I was laying down being pummelled! The words 'ow' and 'ouch' seemed to have no effect whatsoever, and I was to endure this for the entire allocated 30 minutes. I must have looked like a broken person when I re-entered the hostel; even Dinky Doo was of no consolation to me now. The young guy at reception strongly advised that I go to the hospital. And so it was that I ended up in a Polish hospital on my birthday, in a foreign country, at night, on my own. I had turned down Michelle's offer to accompany me; she was feeling ill after her massage.

It transpired, thankfully, that I did not have any broken bones, but my ligaments were strained from my shoulder to the elbow. They were very friendly at the hospital and gave me a copy of my x-ray as a souvenir birthday present! I finished my hospital jaunt by waiting across the road at a takeaway pharmacy for my painkillers. A considerate taxi driver was watching/waiting to ensure I was safe and escorted me back to the hostel. The painkillers helped me get my first night of sleep since our arrival.

I should have made the most of that night's sleep as it was the last one I would get on this trip. Being the final day, and the day of the treatment on my hips, Michelle and I went back to the Crooked House in Sopot. I was courageous and, seeing only six vials, thought I could handle it well, as it would be only six injections. How wrong was I? Forty two injections later (yes, I counted them all!) out of what ended up being nine vials, I emerged into the waiting area. If you had poured water in me, it would have spurted it out of all the pinprick holes! Taking one look at me, Michelle whisked me off for one of my favourite foods, Pizza. I was fine at first, but then the itching and soreness started creeping up through me. It was followed by swelling and bruising. I had left the crooked house with a crooked body.

It was our last night in Poland, and we cracked open a bottle of red wine to celebrate; I was also hoping it would ease the pain and help me sleep. It was not to be! There was not one position that I could lay in that had any modicum of comfort. Dinky Doo, perched in his usual place on the pillow, observed all my flailing silently. Eventually, I laid flat out on my front spread-eagled like a starfish in one last ditched attempt to get some sleep.

It was time to return home, and I intended to be the first on the plane. I was going to get a large exit seat, and no one would stop me! Not even the airport shuttle driver arguing in German that I must pay for the shuttle or he would call the Police (it was meant to be free!). Michelle was left behind as I set off like a greyhound onto that plane, with the seat belt loosely wrapped around my bruised/swollen waistline. The pain was worth it, the injections worked, I lost weight, and I had another birthday behind me!

Although this was only a short trip, Michelle and I reminisced about it for a long time after the event. We both agreed you just couldn't make this one up; so much had happened in such a short space of time. Yet again, a lesson was being given on how short life can be. We could have easily have been killed in that car crash, and still, there was more pain and suffering. Yes, the injections were self-inflicted pain as I had chosen them. I definitely did not regret them, though, as they made such a massive difference in my body shape and confidence. Overall, I felt stronger in myself, even though at work they were trying to break me down, and the pressure was too stressful. My journeys away were becoming more and more important to me. I had reached a pattern in my travelling where I would have one lengthy trip per year and several short trips away with friends. I noticed I was becoming unsettled; I was brewing up for a longer trip.

~ ~ ~

Overall Trip Cost: £220 (Flights £40, Accommodation £60, All Other Costs/Spending £120).
Top Tip: Check what access you have to medical care in the countries you are visiting. I cannot stress enough the importance of buying travel insurance! I have met backpackers in dire situations and no insurance to fall back on. Check travel insurance comparison sites. If you intend to travel often, opt for an 'Annual' policy which covers you for multiple trips a year - but do check the number of days you can spend travelling (policies can have a limited amount of days). These are better value.

Sopot, Crooked House   Sopot, Walking Out on the Sea

Koala at Sanctuary

Eclipse Day Sunrise, Port Douglas

DUCK Vehicle, Kuranda

Bondi Beach, Christmas Day 2012

Kuranda Kangaroo at Sanctuary

Uluru (Ayers Rock) at Sunset

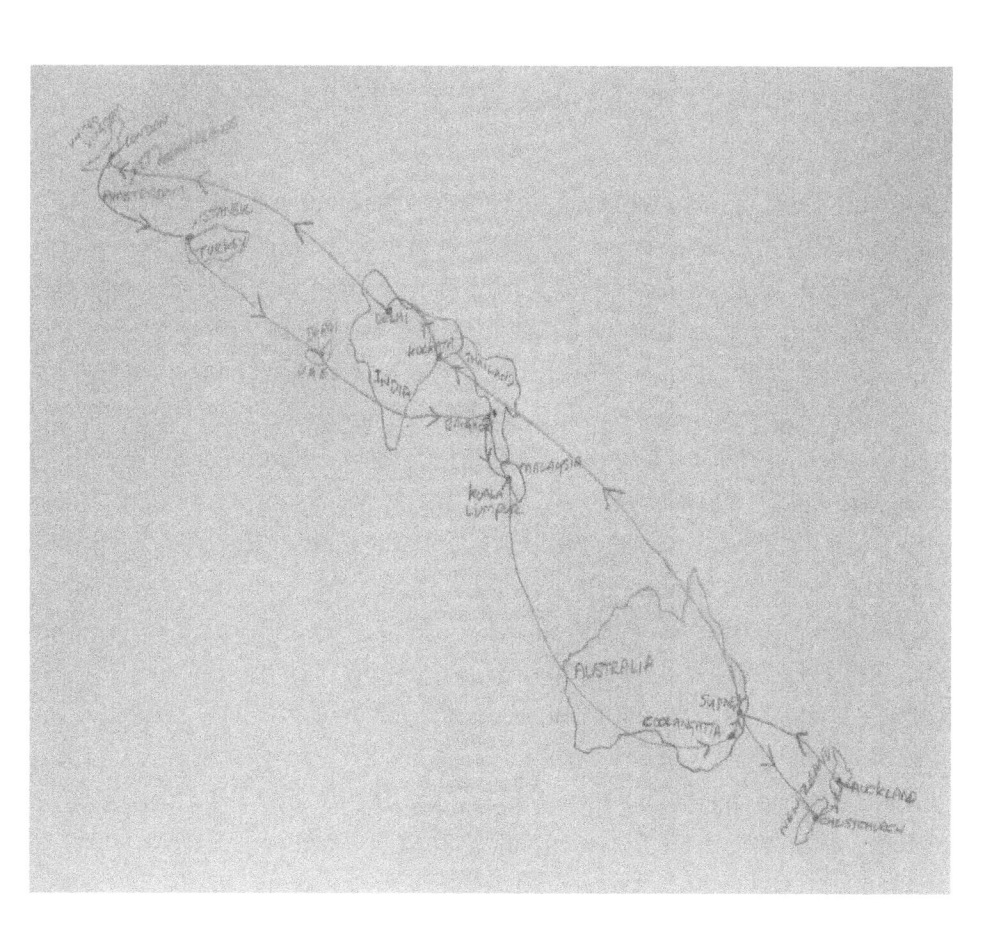

AUSTRALIA ROUTE - 4 MONTHS & 18 DAYS

LONDON - ISTANBUL - DUBAI - BANGKOK - KUALA LUMPUR - COOLANGATTA - SYDNEY - CHRISTCHURCH - AUCKLAND - SYDNEY - KOLKATA - DELHI - AMSTERDAM - LONDON

AUSTRALIA ROUTE 2012 & 2013

This sixth total eclipse trip was to be a life-changer for me. I was setting out on a 4-month adventure resulting in losing my job of 12 years, my partner, and the 'old' me. The Local Authority I worked for and had dedicated my life to for the past 13 years was refusing to give me a career break stating that I would have to resign to go on such a long term break. An ensuing debate went on for several months prior to my departure, in which I was eventually granted my desired career break.

Simultaneously, I split from a guy I was in a committed relationship with. He was devastated that I was intent on making this long trip and begged me to stay. I decided I could not be with someone who would not support me in this or any future journey, especially if there was no intention ever to join me and be a part of them. And so we parted ways just days before I left. I could not dwell on this as I was busy buying one more property while earning a salary (to prove earnings to the mortgage company). My mum was not too happy that I was leaving for so long, but I left her in the capable hands of a few trusted friends. It was hard saying goodbye to friends.

My quest was to find a more spiritual me; this was not a light bulb moment but a yearning for many years to find my 'inner hippy'. I was seeking a life with less stress, culminating in reaching my life plan of living in England for approximately 8-9 months of the year and travelling the world the rest of the time. No more reliance on tours with early morning starts; now was the time for the independent me to venture out on my own! I would be using my savings to do this backpacking and would be staying in hostels mainly. Although I was on a shoestring budget, I had decided that as I was going to be on the other side of the world, I would not stint on seeing or experiencing things during this one time chance, e.g. the Great Barrier Reef.

I had decided that Australia was too far away to take just one flight, and so had broken up my journey into stints of up to 7 hours. Hence, it took two weeks to get to Australia and longer to get back. I would be going via Istanbul, Dubai, Bangkok, and Kuala Lumpur. Returning would be via New Zealand, India, and Amsterdam- Netherlands... phew, I am exhausted just writing it all!

~ ~ ~

Overall Trip Cost: £6,000 (Flights £1,200, Acc. £2,100, Transport/Spending/Tours £2700)

The power and imagination whilst travelling, holding up a rock, facing the next challenge, overcoming fears, believing in yourself, believing anything can happen...

ISTANBUL 2012

Belly Dancing Like a Native, with a Swollen Eye

Strangely, Istanbul is not the capital city of Turkey, but it is the largest, with a population of over 13 million people. It straddles the two continents of Europe and Asia. There are many ancient architectural delights in Istanbul, from the Aga Sophia to Galata Tower, Blue Mosque, Basilica Cistern, Chora Church, Topkapi Palace and Dolmabahce Palace. Istanbul has been the inspiration for several noted authors such as Ernest Hemingway. It was at the Pera Palais hotel that British author Agatha Christie wrote her famous novel "Murder on the Orient Express".

Considering I am not a lover of flying, I have never been so glad to set foot on a plane as I was on the day I set off on my travels. When I awoke, I did not imagine my journey there would be as horrendous as it was. I had made my final checks: food perishables eaten or given away, the car was on SORN (untaxed on the driveway), flights reconfirmed and online check-in complete, etc. I triple checked my daypack for passport, insurance details, travel money and most importantly, Dinky Doo. He was now the proud owner of several new outfits for the varying climates. Naturally, my backpack was packed full and heavy as usual (around 20kgs). I had included my usual useful items: head torch, washing powder, superglue, training golf ball, duct tape, umbrella, pink sacks, and now had a couple of additions. Labels would be invaluable for the hostels to clearly indicate my food box. Although not so useful in dorm rooms, I had a door stopper to keep unwanted strangers out of my hotel rooms. Safely prepared, I was ready to be picked up for my promised lift to Stansted Airport. And what a lift it was! My friend Michelle turned up with her partner driving her car. They were an hour late, by which time my anxiety levels were hitting an all-time high, and half a bottle of red wine had been drunk. I had forgotten how scary her partner Gushi's driving was and spent the whole two and half hours there holding on for dear life. Gushi was oblivious to the effects of his antics. He was smoking, singing, driving with no hands on the wheel- just his knee holding it in place, and taking the scenic route, getting us lost! Thankfully I arrived at Stansted airport in one piece and used my flight to Istanbul to recover.

I had the foresight not to plan too much for my 3-day stay in Istanbul and could sufficiently relax after the pre-departure car ride. There was just one strange occurrence, which was with my left eye. I woke up on the first morning to find my eye was very swollen and puffy, not too weird, you would think, but precisely the same thing had happened on my last visit to Istanbul. I walked along to the same chemist and requested the same medication, with some gesturing and the Pharmacist's brief understanding of English. Now I did not mind ordering medicines in such a manner for my eye; however, there was an additional complication. I needed to request something to aid the cystitis I had developed - and yes, it was just as embarrassing as you can imagine it being. I had been in the Pharmacy long enough gesticulating that all four staff were involved in assisting me. This resulted in a queue of local people, who were not bothered by waiting and seemed more entertained by my medical predicament.

I was staying in a hostel in the Taksim Square area, so all popular locations were relatively nearby: Republic Monument; Galata Tower; Istiklal Street (for shopping and markets); Dolmabache Palace and Clock Tower etc. However, on this short trip, I was being slightly slothful and spent most of my time in the hostel chatting with other travellers and drinking. It didn't take much to encourage me to start belly dancing, much to the backpackers' delight.

I did venture out to the plush Pera Palais Hotel as it was on my 'bucket list' to have an afternoon tea there- it would be the equivalent of going to the Ritz Hotel in London for the same experience. Back in the day, the Pera Palais Hotel had been a stop-off point for the rich people who had travelled on the Orient Express to Istanbul. They would be transported from the train station to the hotel by ornate sedans (best described as a single enclosed small carriage with windows carried by four people). Two backpackers from the hostel accompanied me, and we had all made an effort by dressing in our best gear, which was smart enough to gain entry. The staff were cordial and escorted us to the elaborate and plush tea room. I was particularly impressed with my cake as not only was it chocolate, but it was topped with a gold leaf. You see how we backpackers can live sometimes!

I was pleased I had conserved my energy the next day, as I needed it to visit the Florence Nightingale Museum. If only my Indira Nightingale from the Children's Home in Nepal was here to accompany me. I just know she would have loved to have experienced the museum of her idol and namesake too.

It turned out to be a total military operation in preparation and getting there, which was very appropriate as the museum is indeed placed inside a Turkish Military Base. To visit, you must arrange with your hotel to send a letter to the museum to request a visit; a copy of your passport must accompany this. Having duly followed this process, I set off to search for the museum. This involved transportation by metro, ferry and bus to get there. I walked in circles from the bus stop, being misdirected by a Police Officer, a passer-by, and a bus passenger. It was hot, and I was getting stressed as I had to be at the museum at an allocated time.

I eventually found the museum and reported at the main military gate. All I can say is that my visit to the museum was a lot shorter than my journey there and back. Still, it was an engaging enough experience to make the visit worthwhile. After the army confirmed my identity, I was searched, and my bag was placed in a locker. Process completed, and I was accompanied around the museum by a Turkish Army Major who made the experience in the museum very engaging. All I had known about Florence Nightingale previously was that she was a nurse referred to as "the lady with the lamp". I learned that Florence had laid the foundation of professional nursing and established a London hospital

(St Thomas's). This pioneering woman would have the highest distinction medal in nursing named after her; the Florence Nightingale Medal, and new nurses would be required to take the 'Nightingale Pledge'. I left with a newfound admiration for Florence and could see why my Indira Nightingale was so in awe of her.

I was let loose by the Turkish Military back into the heat and big wide world to find my way home. Amazingly I found my hostel, and I was happy returning to a few cold beers and belly dancing/socialising.

I had thoroughly enjoyed my time in Istanbul. My eye was cured, ulcers and cystitis had cleared entirely, guaranteeing continued hip gyrating belly dancing. I was pretty excited starting out on this trip, and I set off to my next stop, Dubai, with a spring in my step.

~ ~ ~

Top Tip: Find out if the town or city you are in has a travel card that offers cheaper priced travel on buses/trains/metro. Some transport systems are cashless now and rely on prepaid card payment. In Istanbul, I used the Istanbul Kart on public transport.

Istanbul, Tea & Cake at the Posh Pera Palais

DUBAI 2012

A Desert Surprise

Dubai is both an emirate and a city of the United Arab Emirates (UAE). There are seven emirates in the UAE, of which Dubai is one. Within the Dubai emirate, there is Dubai city, which, although it is the largest city, is not the capital (Abu Dhabi is the capital). Dubai is renowned for its gold which you will find in many Souks, Malls or even ATMs. Dubai holds a world record for the longest gold chain, measuring a staggering 5,522 metres. Do not be tempted to steal the gold as you won't outrun the Police in Dubai; they are privileged to drive supercars - think of the Lamborghini or Ferrari. Not in the wildest stretch of my imagination can I see an England Police Officer motoring around in one of those through the streets of Manchester, London or Southend!

Arriving early morning at Sharjah airport, not Dubai (around 25 miles away), I had had the foresight to book transport to take me into Dubai. That was unlike a Swedish flight stewardess, a British couple I had met on the flight and a French guy. They all hitched a ride with me, and the driver was very accommodating; in fact, he did not charge any extra. To be fair, they all offered to chip in, but being my new spiritual self, I declined their offers.

Many people flying onto a further destination would usually only transit through Dubai. This was one of the reasons I felt that aside from the convenience of breaking up my flight, I would enjoy some time there and see what was on offer. It was to bite me on the bum a few years later when I visited America. President Trump had not long been in office and was prohibiting travel to and from certain countries. A list was produced that denied you entry into the US if you had travelled to these countries within a specific period. Dubai was not on that list, and yet I was questioned as to why I had visited. It was touch and go as to whether I would gain entry. I explained it was a funny story about my

Dubai stopover. I put it in the context of my fear of flying and breaking up my journey and taking two weeks to get to Australia. Luckily the immigration officer found it funny. My passport was returned, and I took a hearty step into the USA, still unsure why I had been questioned about visiting Dubai.

~ ~ ~

During my few days there, I mixed it up a little in Dubai with the tourist sites: the Souks (markets), a haven for gold shopping, a Dhow Boat ride and a walk around Dubai Mall. Next to the mall, I just had to see the world's tallest building, the Burj Khalifa, a staggering 830 metres high and with 163 storeys. I had no desire to go inside and up to the observation deck as I don't like lifts and so it would have been a long walk up! I saw the Bur Khalifa just after sunset as it got dark. It was impressive at nightfall lit up with the Dubai Fountain water display occurring right next to it. The Dubai Fountain is set on Burj Lake, the world's largest choreographed water display, and I was captivated by it. The dark sky contrasted with the shimmering sprays of water which danced in patterns to varying genres of music from classical to contemporary. After all my sightseeing, I took some time out to relax on the popular Jumeirah beach. However, I am unsure how relaxed I was after reading the long list of prohibitions. Notwithstanding, I laid practically fully dressed on the white sand beach, occasionally taking a dip in the warm, clear blue sea.

In Dubai, my favourite experience was the Desert Safari. Yet, it was also a pretty hair raising one with our jeep driving up and down through the steep dunes! It is one of those activities that does not look so scary until you are experiencing it. We were navigating narrow ridges of sand and hurtling up and down near-vertical inclines in the sandy dunes. I was also slightly worried about the baby in the back of the jeep. He had only just been fed his milk on the way to the desert but amazingly slept through it all. Our small tour group watched the sunset and were then transported to a camp set out purely for tourists. Although this was rather touristy for me, I decided to make the most of it. I enjoyed a free short camel ride, free henna tattoo on hand, complimentary tea and dates, and then a big buffet meal. We were treated to the spectacular displays of a whirling dervish dancer and finally a bellydancer. She really was quite impressive, and it pains me to say it, but she was way better than me; but then I bet she can't play the penny whistle! What a lovely end to my stay in Dubai; I would highly recommend the desert safari and taking the time to stopover in Dubai as part of your journey if you can. I found local people to be polite and helpful and felt safe at all times. I was already gaining confidence in my travels.

~ ~ ~

Top Tip: Be respectful of the customs and cultures in the country you are travelling to. It is worth reading up before departure so as not to offend locals/ authorities unintentionally. Be aware of when to dress modestly and where showing public affection is acceptable.

Riding the Steep Desert Sand Dunes

BANGKOK 2012

The Land of Noodles, Smiles and a Laughing Driver

Thailand, as you look at the map, resembles the shape of an axe. Generally, you would find it more hilly and countryside like in the north, with the cityscape of Bangkok being central, and with beaches and islands being more southerly. They all have a common theme, temples, as there are over 35,000 of them throughout the land. Dubai may have a lot of gold trade, but Thailand has the world's largest gold Buddha, weighing 5.5 tonnes and standing 15 feet tall. Thailand is a country of extremes. Here you can find the smallest mammal in the world, Kitti's hog-nosed bat (or 'Bumblebee' bat), and also the world's largest fish; the whale shark that can reach a length of 40 feet long. Thailand also holds the world's largest water fight, the Songkran Festival for Thai New Year, on 13-15 April.

Bangkok once had plenty of water, as canals were the primary way of navigating the city, for there were barely any roads back then, until the end of the 19th century. Now you can wander the streets and choose from a plethora of street food stalls. Perhaps eat a scorpion on a stick and wash it down with a Red Bull drink that was invented in Bangkok - the guy who invented this became a Thai Billionaire. There are over 200,000 millionaires (in US dollars, not Thai Baht), in Thailand and 95% of them live in Bangkok. Live like a millionaire and treat yourself to a massage, but be prepared; a Thai massage is not always relaxing. You could be stretched and twisted into various positions and may even be walked upon by the practitioner!

I arrived around 07:30 in Bangkok, and my shuttle driver was dutifully waiting for me. He seemed a pleasant guy, but we did have a slight communication issue - I didn't speak much Thai, and he did not speak much English. He did, however, try to explain to me that he had visited my hostel the day before. Perhaps it was part of his route planning. He seemed to find it quite funny and kept laughing to himself. As we neared my hostel and drove along back streets that grew smaller and turned into alleys, he began to chuckle to himself again. When the vehicle could go no further to his credit, he walked me and my luggage to the small back alley amongst shacks where my hostel was situated. I was slightly concerned about what I would find in this accommodation due to my laughing driver, but it was okay, and I settled into my clean and crisp ensuite room.

I had visited Bangkok once before, back in 2003, and was absolutely petrified of it on my first day. I remember walking out of my hotel, which happened to be on a busy crossroads. I took one look at all the chaos taking a few nervous steps, and then fled back into my hotel! This time, I wasted no time in getting out and about, walking around in an attempt to familiarise myself with the local area. I kept my eyes peeled for any street food stalls that did not offer purely weird and wonderful meaty objects (such as frog kebabs). I favoured something plain like sweetcorn or the typical noodles- most meals come with a noodle option. I was clearly not paying enough attention to the ground I was walking on, though, when I found myself sinking in fresh wet cement, much to the amusement of the locals. Due to the heat, the cement had set by the time I walked back past later. You could see two lots of paw prints on there, mine and those of a dog that had been following me.

I had been given a tip-off for an atypical attraction in Bangkok, and so it was the next day I headed off to the Forensic Medicine Museum. I love to experience the unusual, and it's not every day you get to see a metre-long tapeworm dangling from someone's bottom! I must add, though, that I took to eating rice immediately after my visit - noodles had somehow lost their appeal. You needed a strong stomach for a visit to this museum. Human (both adult and child) body parts chopped up and pickled, skeletons, a room dedicated to various parasites and how they affect the human organs, pictures of gunshot wounds and a mummified body of a famous madman who had eaten children's livers were just some of the stomach-churning visual onslaughts.

I skipped lunch that day but mustered up an appetite to eat at my local café that evening. I had found a lady who cooked the perfect vegetable stir fry with tapewo…, I mean noodles! Thankfully, she also had rice, and she cooked the meal fresh out at a stand - all for the bargain price of $1. One of the locals eating there the night before had set me up with my routine. Order my food, take a plastic cup, fill it with cold water and ice from the Esky (portable cooler box), fetch my cutlery and await my meal. Perhaps I should have been a bit more careful with my choice of drinking non filtered water (it wouldn't have been the first time of having worms in my water). Still, hey, it was free, and I was living and eating like a local; I was in my element.

~ ~ ~

For some unknown reason, perhaps because I was just following the three backpackers from the hostel to Ayutthaya, I found myself in a 3rd class carriage on the train the next day. We were going to visit the temples there, and apparently, we were experiencing a more down to earth way of travelling. It was undoubtedly that going by the smell coming from the nearby toilet. It turned out we were on the wrong train. We gave our goodbyes and thanks to the locals, who had heartedly given us the bad news with smiles on their faces.

Having found the correct train to Ayutthaya, we dashed for it; I slipped and broke one sandal, but we still made it onto the train. I spent the rest of the day wearing one sandal or walking barefoot. It was pretty useful, as we were visiting many temples and hence, no shoes allowed.

Reaching Ayutthaya, we bargained for a tuk-tuk just to get it to what the usual price should be, the price set out for tourists. Having wasted by then fifteen minutes of our lives, we set off on the rounds of the temples. We found out afterwards that we could have walked between some of the sites, but to be honest, we all agreed the few dollars it cost us for the tuk-tuk was worth it due to the heat. We would have enough walking to do in and around the temples, and I only had one functioning sandal.

We visited the giant 37 metres long Reclining Buddha located at the entrance to Wat Lokkayasutharam temple, draped in a marigold sarong and the main attraction there. Due to a Burmese invasion that flattened the rest of the area aside from a single stupa (a mound-like structure), little else was left around in that vicinity.

Unlike many of the other temples in Ayutthaya, our next stop, Wat Yai Chai Mongkhon temple, continues to be an active temple where Monks reside. It is one of the most important temples in the area. The main bell-shaped 'Chedi' (alternative name for a stupa, used for meditation) at this temple is a prominent landmark. There are dozens of Buddha statues gazing over the landscape, temple and us tourists as we climb up steps to gain their same views.

We were still going strong, unlike the unfortunate Wat Phra Si Sanphet, which had mainly been desecrated during a Burmese Invasion. Before that, it had been the holiest and grandest of the temples in Ayutthaya. It was a Return to the Chedi, for three of these bells still stand. They are a reminder of where the temple had initially been positioned on the grounds of the Royal Palace built by King U Thong way back in 1491.

Wat Mahathat temple, our last one, was renowned for being the centre of Buddhism. It enshrined Buddha relics and had been the seat of the Supreme Patriarch of Buddhism. However, it was the famous Buddha head entwined amongst the roots of a tree that drew us (and many others) to this place. Nobody knows for sure how the head managed to be set within the tree. I, for one, was fascinated by this enigma. I proceeded to take numerous photos, at varying angles, and some with Dinky Doo to give a scale of the statue's height. By the end of our tour, we were well and truly templed out (even Dinky Doo showed signs of beardom!). It was time to take our opulent 3rd class train journey back to the hostel. Once there, we had a burning of the sandals ritual, saying goodbye to my broken footwear.

My final day did not get off to the most promising start. I had placed my brand new android tablet up on top of the coat rack where bizarrely, the only plug socket in my room was strategically placed. Why on earth it was so high up, I have no idea. There is a difference between having a socket too low that it could be dangerous to toddlers, and having it so high you need to be a basketball player to reach it easily! And so it was of little surprise to me the tablet slipped off the coat rack through my hands crashing to the floor! I had no time to deal with it, as I had a plane to catch, so it was hurled into the bin. I left Thailand with a broken item left behind; but I took with me increased confidence in my backpacking and feeling of contentment. Here was an example of feeling comfortable in a country after making a second trip there and venturing out, absorbing the surroundings in a more relaxed manner.

Arriving at the airport, my flight details were not on display. I questioned if I was at the correct airport and, if not, how would I get to the right one. Fortunately, it transpired my flight was from this airport; it was delayed, just not yet showing on the board. Panic over, until I realised that my shuttle was booked at the other end and I would be late for it. With the airline unwilling to make a call, I gave in and found a bar for a glass of red wine. This would help me on the next leg of my journey, heading to Malaysia for the first time.

~ ~ ~

Top Tip: We all tend to have some form of electronics when we travel, so you will need to check out the voltage for that country and preferably carry a multi-adapter plug that can be used in most countries. USB chargers are also useful nowadays, e.g. for phones/tablets, so one wire can serve several purposes.

Dinky Doo in Bangkok

MALAYSIA 2012

Hitchcock's Birds in a Bird Park!

Malaysia consists of two geographical regions: Peninsular Malaysia, which lies between Thailand and Singapore, and East Malaysia, which lies on the island of Borneo. Peninsula Malaysia has a long coastline with several popular beaches and low lying plains that span either side of forested mountain ranges from north to south of the country. Intertwined between the landscape is some 40,934 miles of highway that is longer than the Earth's circumference and connects major cities.

Kuala Lumpur, the capital city (referred to as KL), is home to the Petronas Towers, the tallest twin tower building in the world at 88 storeys high. Just under halfway up on the 41st floor, there is the Skybridge, where you have approximately 10 minutes to take photos of the views over KL. You will probably be drier up there as in the monsoon season flooding is expected. Watch out for any KLites, residents of KL, wearing a lot of lipstick. There was a ban on excessive lipstick from 1996, which originated due to Government concern it would lead to illicit sex problems in the city. Pucker up Buttercup and minimise your make-up!

George Town was named after King George III of Great Britain and is a UNESCO World Heritage Site. Of particular beauty are the various murals, which express the daily life of residents of Penang. One of the best activities is to follow the various mural trails and get unusual photos where in some, there are physical objects so you can interact and look like you are part of the scene. See if you can find the "101 Lost Kittens" by Ernest, consisting of 12 murals, especially poignant as they promote the protection of and raise awareness of stray animals. Want a new pair of high heels? Where better to find them than George Town, the birthplace of Jimmy Choo, the famous shoemaker.

Having noted that my flight to Penang was delayed, my thoughtful shuttle driver had returned to the airport to collect and drive me to George Town. He transported me to the entrance of the Chew jetty, where I was met by the young lady from reception at my homestay. It was just as well, as I had not realised my homestay was situated in the middle of a UNESCO World Heritage site. More to the point, it was known for its many wooden walkways built like a maze out over the water - I would never have found my way on my own. As we walked, my receptionist explained that this settlement of wooden bungalows on stilts developed in the late 19th century, homing Chinese clans. Originally there was no electricity or water, and to this day, residents do not pay tax as they are not on dry land. Several of the wooden houses have street art murals adorning them; I was to discover my homestay was one of them. Each day at sunset, I would sit out on the back veranda on a rocking chair overlooking the water, reading. Occasionally I would look up from my book and spot tourists taking photos of me; well, actually, it was of the famous mural located just behind me!

I liked George Town, and I filled my few days there following the Heritage trail (my thinking was that it would be unlikely that I would get lost). I viewed the majestic historical façades of various buildings: the World Heritage Inc building, the Islam Museum, Armenian Street (said to be the location for the filming of Anna and the King), the Chinese Yap Clan Temple, Customs Building; and the Victoria Clock Tower (built to commemorate Queen Victoria's Diamond jubilee, standing at 60 feet high - one foot for each year of her reign). I must have clocked up a fair few miles and photos of facades already, interspersed with pictures of murals I came across.

Still, I carried on, and I crossed the small drawbridge to enter Fort Cornwallis, where I was promptly subjected to the 1812 Overture over a speaker system! How random. Set close to the esplanade, Fort Cornwallis is the largest standing fort in Malaysia and was named after Lieutenant-General The 2nd Earl Cornwallis (1738-1805). Interestingly, one of the cannons there, the 'Seri Rambai', is popularly regarded as a fertility symbol.

Back on the trail of the grandiose buildings, I found: the Cathedral of the Assumption, Kapitan Keling Mosque, and Kuan Yin Temple or the 'Goddess of Mercy' Temple. I was very tempted to dip my well-trodden sore feet into one of the two wells in the temple grounds, mind you, at least I still had both sandals!

As you can imagine, after all that walking, I was ready for a treat, and so it was I ended my day in the plush Eastern & Oriental Hotel for a tea and cake treat at $7. I worked it out that this was the same as the cost of some of my hostel rooms. Still, it is not often I dine in a luxury hotel (except as in Istanbul), and I had dressed Dinky Doo up in his best suit for the occasion; he at least did not look out of place. This hotel was built by the Sarkie brothers, who also established the famous Raffles Hotel in Singapore, anyone for a Singapore Sling?

My other jaunts took me out of Georgetown to Penang Hill, Kek Lok Si Temple, and Hindu Temple, all just an easy bus ride away from Georgetown. Sightseeing became a case of playing dodgems, working out when to be inside a temple, and venture out to the external sites. The weather was similar to England, being sunny and then raining, just on steroids as the sun was hotter and the rain more torrential.

On my final day on Penang Island, I set out on another bus heading to the Penang National Park. I got chatting with a few tourists on there, which worked out well as we all chipped into a tour boat ride inside the park. We had a couple of hours spare before the boat trip. So we hiked up and down through a jungle trail, incredible scenery and exercise before relaxing on the boat. Our guide had met us at our allocated spot, and we now drifted past various beaches. We were advised they were too dangerous to swim in for multiple reasons, including jellyfish. I believed the guide when I spied a lovely beach where I would have liked to have sunbathed. Except then I spotted what initially looked like a crocodile strolling along where my sunbed would have been! (it was, in fact, a monitor lizard).

Early (very early) the following morning, I was packed up and ready to go by 06:00. I was booked onto the ferry which would take me to Butterworth, where I would subsequently board a train to Kuala Lumpur.

This time I was travelling in luxury, no 3rd class seat for me, I was in 1st class with air-con. However, thirty minutes into the journey, I was beginning to regret this decision, as I was freezing cold. I asked the attendant to set the air con to a reasonable temperature, not for one minute believing this would happen. However, after I had scurried through six carriages to the toilet and mooched back, I returned to the warmest carriage on the whole train!

In Kuala Lumpur, I threw my bags into my small single room at the Pods Hostel and walked out to a small café no more than thirty seconds away. I liked this hostel and was to return several times over the years. It was friendly, had a kitchen to cook your meals, and was very well located (near the bus and train station and amid shops).

I had been tipped off there was a massive electronics mall in Kuala Lumpur where I could buy a new tablet or electronic notebook. The electronics mall in Low Yat Plaza is indeed huge - six storeys of gadget heaven. I was like a child in a sweet shop parading up and down the floors whilst trying to decide what to buy. Four hours later, I was the proud owner of a new electronic notebook, which I was guaranteed was of the best Malaysian quality. The next day I was back at the Low Yat mall as the new laptop was not working. I took it to the booth where I had bought it, and two hours later, it was fixed. It seems the person who had set it up for me the day before had missed off part of the procedure, seriously! As I was in the area, I took the opportunity to eat out at one of the street cafés. I was a bit wary seeing the menus with a plethora of meat and fish dishes of all kinds of species. Their menus announced the like of 'Meat, Frogs and Noodles', I was just pleased there was not a Dinky Doo on the menu. I thought it best to stick with what I knew, and so vegetable stir fry it was, with rice- definitely not noodles!

The following day I was accompanied to the famous Batu caves by a young lady from the hostel. She had been travelling with a female companion, but they had parted ways after two months on the road. She, too, had taken to the solo travelling and had found much more of a sense of independence. Like myself, she enjoyed hooking up with other travellers for the odd day out, and so we did just that. Another advantage on this day trip was working out the train journey between us and not getting lost; we would need our energy for the forthcoming stairway at Batu. The Batu caves are set in a large limestone mountain, and you climb 272 steps to reach them. They are guarded by a monumental statue of the Hindu deity Lord Murugan. These Hindu temples are the most popular outside of India. I had almost transformed into a Hindu Deity by the time I got to the top of the stairs; it was indeed a long climb!

My final day in Kuala Lumpur was spent in the Lake Gardens and the bird park. I like to find somewhere with nature amongst all the skyscrapers and the density of buildings in a city. Although it was only a 15-minute walk from my hostel, it was a very dangerous one across six lanes of the motorway. Something was telling me that I should not have been on foot around there (after all, nobody else was). There was probably a safer but longer route, I just couldn't find it.

The Lake Gardens were very ornate and seemed to be a popular backdrop for numerous brides and grooms having their wedding photographs taken. Yes, they had lakes, lawns, oriental flower beds, fountains and even a miniature Stonehenge. I mooched around and stumbled across the small deer park. Thankfully it was not too vast as I was hungry; it was time to eat my packed lunch. It was just as well I ate it then, as I spent my next four hours excitedly negotiating my way around the best bird park I have ever visited.

After the trauma of paying, what I considered an excessive fee to gain entry to the Perdana Bird Park (around $14), I found myself amazed at the variety of birds and their freedom. Most of them were not in any kind of cage, and you could walk amongst the birds. Well, I loved this and was in my element. I went to see the bird show, which I was not so keen on because the birds were trained to do tricks. The best bit was when Mike the Eagle flew off as part of the act but then refused to come back, and they had to finish the show without him. Mike was happily sitting in a tall tree watching the rest of the performance.

I was just posing for a picture by a waterfall where the storks perch on the bridge behind you, when the weather turned. What was supposed to look like a photo in the perfect setting, in nature with the birds and me smiling in the forefront, turned out to be something more like a scene from Alfred Hitchcock's film 'The Birds'. In the few split seconds when a passer-by was preparing to take my photo for me, there was a loud clap of thunder, and a noisy flash of lightning lit up the sky. It frightened me, making me jump, but also scared the storks around me who had merrily been nibbling on their quota of fish. In fear, they all ran and flew towards me. I had storks coming at and past me from all angles, which frightened me more. They were just trying to get to cover under the rocks behind the waterfall. I, in the meantime, was frozen to the spot looking like a frantic scared rabbit, great photo!

After recuperating from the trauma with a cup of green tea, I decided to take cover in the parrot enclosure where it would be feeding time. I was engrossed with the feeding routine when an attendant asked me if I would like a photo feeding a few parrots. This could be quite tame, I thought, whilst he proceeded to place bird after bird on my arms and hands. All was fine until two of them starting fighting. I must have flinched as another parrot greedily feeding off my hand, bit one of my fingers, and drew blood. The attendant ignored my displeasure and carried on, placing a large white bird on my arm and taking more photos! My look of disapproval was pretty evident during his photo shoot, and so he eventually relented. Maybe he felt a little repentent and tended to me, washing my hand and placing a plaster on my gnawed finger. I was travelling to Australia the next day and was hoping I would be accepted into the country, albeit I might be harbouring rabies!

~ ~ ~

Top Tip: Prepare for the weather in the countries you are travelling to; this may seem basic and easy to pack if you just think layers. However, in some countries, the weather can be more than what the name portrays. For example, you may be aware you are travelling to a country renowned for its hot sunny days. Still, it may also be subject to high humidity, and the heat does not seem to diminish through the night.

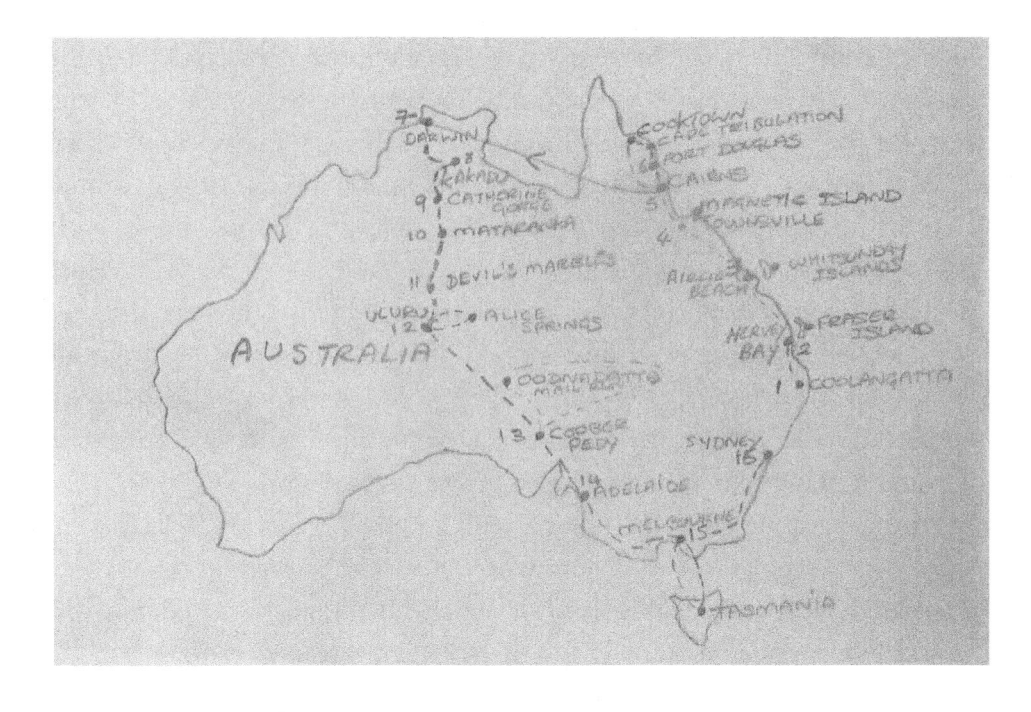

AUSTRALIA ROUTE

1. COOLANGATTA
2. HERVEY BAY & FRASER ISLAND
3. AIRLIE BEACH & WHITSUNDAY ISLANDS
4. TOWNSVILLE & MAGNETIC ISLAND
5. CAIRNS & COOKTOWN/CAPE TRIBULATION
6. PORT DOUGLAS *TOTAL SOLAR ECLIPSE*
7. DARWIN
8. KAKADU NATIONAL PARK
9. CATHERINE GORGE
10. MATARANKA
11. DEVIL'S MARBLES
12. ALICE SPRINGS & ULURU (AYERS ROCK)
13. COOBER PEDY & OODNADATTA MAIL RUN
14. ADELAIDE
15. MELBOURNE & TASMANIA
16. SYDNEY

AUSTRALIA 2012

Goldilocks the Winging POM

Eclipse Path: Australia - Pacific
I viewed at: Port Douglas
Date/Time of Maximum Totality: 13.11.2012 at Local Time
Length of Totality: 04m 02secs.

Australia is the sixth-largest country globally yet is one of the least densely populated. The indigenous Aboriginal people make up only 1.5% of the total population. You are more likely to come across a sheep in Oz than a person, as there are 3 times as many of them as humans. In the desert, you are also unexpectedly more likely to find some of the 1 million wild camels roaming, the largest herd in the world. The introduction of these camels by the Europeans back in the 19th century has turned out to be a long-term disastrous choice by them. This is due to their negative impact on the environment. Also imported were convicts, sent in by the British, initially in Botany Bay (Sydney) and then to other areas of the East Coast, West Coast and Tasmania. Today, 49% of Australians were born overseas or have a least one parent that was, with 20% of them descended from the imported convicts. Not sure, ask a Police Officer; they should know as the very first police force was made up of 12 convicts believed to be the best well-behaved!

Sydney may claim fame as the first city to host convicts; however, surprisingly, it is not the capital. It is more commonly thought either Sydney or Melbourne are the capital city. After a lengthy debate in the early 1900s as to which of these should be the capital, a compromise was reached by building a whole new city at the mid-way point between them, and hence the capital Canberra was born.

Mainly due to the interior of Australia being desert, 90% of Australians live on the coast, but why wouldn't they with such famous landmarks such as the Great Barrier Reef. It is the largest eco-system globally and is one of the Seven Wonders of the Natural World. It stretches halfway along the East Coast and can even be seen from space. Then there is Fraser Island, the largest sand island globally, and the Great Ocean Road, the world's largest war memorial. This coastal highway was built by returning soldiers after WW1 and was dedicated to those who died fighting.

Many animals in Oz are unique to their country (around 80%), such as kangaroos, koalas and wombats. But beware of the varying dangerous animals that live on land and in the sea. Avoid the Tasmanian Devil, or the several varieties of the world's most poisonous snakes, and numerous species of deadliest spiders (such as Funnel Web), the Box Jellyfish, the Platypus and the Blue-ringed Octopus. You have been forewarned!

At last, I had landed in the Land of Oz, the land of dangerous animal life, yet also stunning contrasting landscapes. I was arriving at the comparatively small airport and the coastal town of Coolangatta. I believed that it was very tightly controlled entering Australia, so I was interested in how this would pan out for me. Before any of us alighted the flight, a medical officer from Quarantine boarded the plane as a passenger had been ill. It transpired that it had been food poisoning, which was fine for the rest of us, as we had been advised that if it was a virus, we would all be quarantined. Passport control was a breeze after that, and at customs, even though there was a lengthy queue, I got picked out to go through Lane 1. This meant I could walk through and not be stopped for a search (this made a refreshing change from previous customs experiences). And there I was, near the golden sands and colossal surfing waves on the Gold Coast. I felt slightly nervous but excited too; I was here at long last, after everything I had given up back in England. This was my time.

I was easing myself gradually into the Australia jaunt, as I knew I would be up to all sorts over the next two months, and so it was lovely to relax for the first couple of days. The best part was meeting up with my climbing Everest compadres Rada and Don. We chatted away the whole time, catching up on the past four years since our hiking up and down together. It was nice to see familiar faces in a land so far away and where I would be heading off alone up the East Coast the very next day.

I tend to get jet-lagged in whichever direction in the world I am going. It does not need to be east to west, just anywhere that involves a flight - in fact, I have been known to suffer jetlag after emerging from a car! So a couple of days after my flight to Oz, when I reached Brisbane and having just alighted from the Greyhound bus without my handbag, I blamed it on jetlag. The driver had clearly announced on the microphone to make sure we had taken all our belongings. The driver, by now, being in the distance along the highway. I rushed to the Greyhound counter, and they managed to contact the driver, whereby a system was set up to retrieve my handbag. Greyhound would organise for a passing bus coming into the bus station to bring my bag, and my bus to Hervey Bay would have to wait for it. I never did admit to the other passengers why we left late that day and took to wearing my handbag strapped across my body thereafter.

I stayed in a great hostel in Hervey Bay, the Flashpackers. What stood out for me with this place was that the guy who owned and managed it organised events like free cheese and wine evenings. This was to encourage backpackers to spend time chatting together rather than sitting all evening on their various devices. Anything with 'free wine' in the title had me there for a start off. In fact, I had not realised the purpose of the event and seeing the cheese and wine sitting there looking at me, I had already tucked in before our 18:00 start.

I was not in Hervey Bay for long as I was going off onto the 2-day tour to Fraser Island. We bumped around in the 4 x 4 truck for the two days across the world's 120km long largest sand island; it was relentless. We did not venture out of the vehicle unless instructed that it was safe to do so. We had been warned of shark-infested waters and dingo dogs (and let's face it, if anyone was going to get bitten in the group, it would be me). The guide had a boomerang; I hoped he would throw it for one of the dingo dogs to catch.

Having escaped being bitten by a shark or dingo, my hand became the object of desire of another form of Australian sea life. We were at the Champagne Pools beach, one of the few safe places to swim along the whole of the Australian coast, and we had been wallowing in the lovely warm sandy rock pools. As we were departing, I spotted a shell I liked. I made sure it did not have any sea life in it, showed a couple of friends and took a photo as I had no intentions of keeping it. I like to leave nature as nature should be. I placed the shell under a large rock containing a small amount of water, so it had a new happy home, but I noticed the sand moved as my hand went in. I crouched down and looked, and there was an octopus!

My finding seemed to draw quite a crowd, and it got to the point where a heated argument started between some guys because one had been prodding the octopus with a stick. I was mortified and ran to get a ranger telling him to take the offending stick away. On the way back down, the ranger was asking me questions about the colour of the octopus (was it blue or orange?). I was wondering why he kept questioning and did not hurry up to save the octopus. It transpired that if it had been a Blue Ringed Octopus, I would not be telling this tale now, for it is a deadly, highly venomous creature.

~ ~ ~

I slept soundly that night on the overnight bus. I dreamed of dingos, sharks, orange and blue octopi, champagne rock pools, soft coloured sands, and deep blue tranquil seas. I woke up having arrived at Airlie Beach, which was to be my base for a trip to the Whitsunday Islands. These beauty spots are up there on the list of must-sees, or to be precise, most 'must-seas!' Close your eyes and imagine the most beautiful white sand shores and turquoise blue seas. You will find them here amongst the many tranquil beaches of the Whitsundays.

Donning my sailing cap and swimsuit, anchors aweigh, and it was out onto the tranquil waters. Onward Ho! to Whitehaven Island, Blue Pearl Bay and Langford Island. It was a heavenly two days of snorkelling (well, my attempt at snorkelling where I looked like a demented mermaid) and swimming in these idyllic waters. Our overnight stop was on board the boat, and looking at the cramped quarters, I decided that sleeping out on deck seemed more favourable. After a few beers, there were four of us braving it up on the deck for the night; after all, who would not want to sleep under the shimmering bright stars and rocking away gently on the lapping waves? Ironically, even though I was the oldest by far on the boat, it was I who survived the night out on the deck; the others had gradually abandoned deck. It was touch and go as to whether I stayed out there, only because at one point when I woke in the night, there was a black mouse-sized creature, I don't know what it was as we both jumped, and the critter scuttled away.

Land ahoy! Yes, the following evening, we were back at Airlie Beach. I had just enough time to pack up and catch up on emails before getting a good night's sleep ready for my bus the next day to Townsville. By now, I was two-thirds of the way to my destination, Port Douglas, my total eclipse viewing point. I hadn't yet met anyone heading that way to watch the eclipse but kept an eye out for weather reports and general eclipse news. There tends to be a build-up in the local and national media as the eclipse date approaches. This offers the chance to watch it to thousands of people who may not otherwise have known about it.

I would not be spending much time in Townsville, as I was heading off to Magnetic Island the following day. However, what stood out for me during my short time there was the sheer amount of dogs being walked and the number of people exercising. It was a shame I was not hanging around for long, as I found out later that Townsville was also home to an Army base. I might have got arrested, though, for lurking around outside with intent!

It was a short 20-minute ferry ride to Magnetic Island and a short bus ride to Horseshoe Bay, where I stayed for the next two days. This turned out to be my favourite island on the East Coast. It may not have the scenery of the Whitsundays or the natural rock pools of Fraser Island, but it had koalas, birds and wallabies. I had definitely picked the right place to stay to indulge in meeting these faunas, the Bungalow Bay cabins, as it had its own animal sanctuary.

Later that afternoon, a few of us took the bus to play with the Rock Wallabies. I loved it; they came very close and took seeds that could conveniently be bought from the store across the road. I wanted to take two of these Wallabies home so that I could start my own animal sanctuary. As I continued my travels, the list of pairs of animals grew; this would be a big campsite/petting sanctuary. I guess it would be a kind of 'Mandie's Ark' as I wanted at least two of each creature so that they would not be lonely!

Back at base, we had a BBQ, and to my surprise, Tim and Sarah (from the Netherlands) had arrived. We had met back on Fraser Island and had not mentioned where we would be further along the coast. We had a few beers together until the bar shut, laughing, chatting and catching up on each other's travels. Tim joked that I was on safari here after telling them about my excitement at engaging with the Wallabies and my proposed ark.

"Many a true word is spoken in jest" is the saying, and the following day, Tim's words came true. We all set off with the Bungalow Bay's owner on a walk (safari) around their eco-accredited Koala Park. We were allowed photos with the different animals as we walked around, including a baby crocodile, a turtle, and varying sized lizards. It cost extra to hold a baby koala, but there was no way I was going to miss out on that. I diligently listened as they explained exactly what I had to do and how to hold the little koala to not upset or hurt her. I did as was instructed, but I can tell you, they had a hard job prising her back out of my arms! By now, you would think that I would err on the side of caution due to my past experiences of being bitten by animals and parrots. However, I was fearless that morning. And so it was that I was kissed by a large black Red-Tailed Cockatoo called Shadow, emerging in one piece without a trace of blood. The trick was to place a sunflower seed between your lips, and Shadow would dive in and peck the seed out. This required the person taking the photo to be quick, my photographer was clearly not fast enough, and so a few takes were needed. Dinky Doo, watching from the window, found it hilarious.

As I felt so brave, I finally gave in at the last enclosure to allow Sam the Snake onto my shoulders. This took some coaxing from the others, as I have never wanted to be embraced by a slithering reptile. I gave strict instructions that Sam must not be on my shoulder for any more than five seconds. During that time, as many photographs as possible should be taken. This instruction was ignored, yes the photos were taken, but Sam was left lazing on my shoulders. That was until after what seemed an eternity but could have been only about a minute or two. He was finally removed to my cries of 'get him off, get him off," ringing out. I declared this would be the one and only time I would allow such a creature on or near me. But hey, I had been brave and left my comfort zone again. I do this so much on my travels!

~ ~ ~

By the following evening, I had encountered a scary creature of a different kind - the woman in the bed across from me in the hostel female dorm. I had reached Cairns, and a couple of older guys sat on the train across from me gave me a lift to my hostel as they were concerned for my safety late at night. They were probably concerned about my hostel, too, I was. This hostel was to be one of the worst I have ever stayed in. It was nowhere near clean, was above all the nightlife on the promenade, and seemed to accommodate some dodgy characters.
I laid down on my bed only to realise I had no sheets. When I asked the other females if they knew where my top sheet was, it went quiet until a scary woman across from me sat up in her bed. She pulled across what I thought was a curtain, but what turned out to be my sheet. To be fair, she admitted she had it and offered it back, but her tone and wafflings were scary enough for me to tell her she could keep it! I think I was hygienically safer in my sleeping bag.
The next morning for once, I got up early through choice, and I was out of there. I got the first shuttle van that I could to Port Douglas, out of harm's way, and yes, I was at my Eclipse destination at last. And guess who else had turned up, yes Sarah and Tim! I spent the evening with

them having a bbq and beers outside their cabin, along with a guy they had met on their camp, an Australian called Jerry. I was surprised/shocked at how openly he (and some others) made racist views. The explanation came at museums I later visited during this trip.

I made friends with one of my roommates Kate, also here for the total eclipse. We discussed an eclipse action plan. It was decided that the following morning we would go out very early. Our mission was to carry out a reconnaissance mission of where we would station ourselves for eclipse viewing. This expedition would be crucial for finding space due to the expected 50-60,000 crowds of people, and we were hearing weather reports of cloud cover. It seemed that it would be hit and miss as to where the right place would be to escape the cloud. Although only a few miles away, Cairns was predicted to be shrouded in some areas, and the same was the case for our 4- Mile Beach.

As this was to be a crucial expedition, Kate and I set out at 04:00, readying ourselves as much as possible in advance so as not to disturb the other females in our dorm. Our search extended along the narrow band of beach that stretched for around four miles. We found it difficult the further on we walked as the strip of beach got narrower, and we entered tree-lined swamps. We were standing in a shallow pool of water with trees behind us on one side and incoming sea on the other. We looked at one another, said nothing, and turned to return along the beach. Back at base later, we confessed to each other that we had both been concerned there could have been crocodiles in or near the shallow pools of water, which is why we had both made a hasty retreat!

About one kilometre from where we had started, we found our perfect spot. As it transpired, this was also the preferred spot for Grady and Shelley, a lovely couple from the USA. We agreed on a plan with them; whoever got to this spot first the following day would save enough space for the four of us and the photographic equipment belonging to Grady and Kate. Satisfied we had covered all bases, we ended our military operation for the morning and relaxed by the pool.

~ ~ ~

ECLIPSE DAY - 14th November 2012

Kate and I had prepared our bags and equipment the night before and were suitably set at 04:00 for our venture down to the beach for the main event, the total eclipse. We saved enough space for Grady and Shelley, although they were not far behind us anyway. We had a great system in place; Kate and Grady would set up their tripods and photographic equipment while Shelley and I chatted. I settled Dinky Doo into his viewing spot and marked our territory with a semi-circle of coconut shells that no one was to cross. To be fair, nobody tried; I think my artistry had worked, or perhaps they had noticed Shelley and I being told off each time we walked in front of or near the cameras.

Sunrise occurred around 05.30, and so way before the eclipse began, we were treated to a spectacular scene in the sky that reflected onto sea and sand. The oranges and yellows of the changing face of the sun merged into the shoreline, whilst there were differing hues of the greys and pinks of the sky infiltrating the sea and the sand. A big ball of glowing sun rose out of the sea on the horizon, up into the sky with clouds occasionally drifting past.

It seemed like the partial phase of the eclipse just morphed out of the sunrise. The moon began to bite chunks out of the sun, making the sky gradually grow darker over the space of the next hour or so. The sun started to take its crescent shape as the bites got larger. We were in a kind of twilight, and the birds began to fly home to roost for the night. We were close to totality. There was just a thin slip of the sun left; the blues and greys of the sky disappeared. The clouds parted, and the eclipsed sun rose majestically above them. Totality was here; the sky had darkened. A bright white rim encased the blackness of the moon crossed sun, and all went quiet. The bright white corona glowed out around the perimeter of the sun; we were all mesmerised.

Of course, my favourite part was yet to come, and it did not let me down - the magnificent Diamond Ring effect beaming down at us on the beach! It meant totality was finishing, unfortunately. But at the same time, the bright white diamond ring shape around the blackness of the sun/moon, glowing for those few moments, can take your breath away.

At times like that, you feel like you are only a tiny ant in the scheme of the whole bigger wide world and nature. I was my own world, trying to capture the moment and reflect on how my life was indeed changing. I felt ecstatic and peaceful; this is the magic of the eclipse!

At the end of totality, when the sun began beaming through again, the whole beach erupted. The cheers must have been heard far along the coast in Cairns! A news helicopter was hovering above us with a large camera pointing out - we were all waving and cheering up to it. I was shouting out 'Engerland, Engerland' (like a football supporter at the World Cup) in the hope that my friends and family back home would spot me. I cracked open my bottles of bubbly and shared them with everyone in the immediate vicinity. We were all ecstatic and realised how fortunate we had been to see such a spectacular eclipse. We already heard that those in Cairns and at the other end of the beach had not been so fortunate. Our research and early mornings had paid off; as it transpired, we had picked the only unclouded spot along that stretch of coast at the time of the totality.

I did miss my Honu friends (whom I met on Easter Island); most of them were at a festival out in the countryside near Cairns. I wondered how they had experienced the eclipse. Another event I had missed at the festival site was the marriage of Mary and Brian. I wished I could have been there for that, but I would meet with them later in my Australia trip.

We could not linger too long on the beach, as what none of us had accounted for was the effects of the sun and the moon causing a high tide, and the narrow beach was becoming more and more sea than sand. It was ironic that when I wanted the eclipse to affect the water and cause a tidal bore in China in 2009, it did not want to play the game. It was of no matter; we would retreat to the hostel and join the Eclipse After Party.

~ ~ ~

I decided to make the most of my geographical position on two of my last three days on the East coast by going as far north as possible and venturing out to the Great Barrier Reefs. The Cooktown tour was way too expensive and too far for a day trip, so I went out on a Cape Tribulation tour. It was fascinating and refreshing out in the depths of everything Daintree; the rainforest, tea, ice cream, beach and Daintree River. My favourite part was at the Mossman Gorge Centre where we participated in a 'smoke ceremony' to protect us in the rainforest. We also had an inspirational talk by a local indigenous guide. He spoke about getting to know your landscape for survival and getting to know your spiritual self (he must have known of my new spiritual quest).

Second on my bucket list of day trips out from here was the Great Barrier Reef. The Wavedancer catamaran was definitely dancing the waves on the way to the Great Barrier Reef, Low Isles, resulting in many people being seasick - but not me. I was making the most of the free coffee and cake! I seem fortunate when out on the rough seas; I seem to have a hardened stomach. I wish my sea skills would extend to my snorkelling technique; the harder I try, the worse I become. I had by then given up on ever becoming a super snorkeller. I discovered my own method by wearing eye goggles, plunging under the water, and seeing as much as possible. All this whilst holding my breath before emerging out of the water like a deranged fish!

The coral reefs were amazing to see, but I can only report back on that as a viewer from the glass-bottomed boat that I spent the rest of the day on. I did not have a 'snorkel buddy' (strangely, nobody wanted to pair up with me), so I was not allowed to go very far. It was deep enough for me that I did not wish to. Perhaps subconsciously, I had not got over the near-drowning experience back in Venezuela. So I cheated, sat on the glass-bottom boat and had a nice lunch and more coffee before our time to return to terra firma in Port Douglas.

It was helpful having one last day to catch up on emails, do laundry, and pack up, as my throat had gradually swollen up to the point that it was hard to swallow or breathe at night. I could squeeze in some time to get some medication from the pharmacy and chill out at the end of the evening. My guess is that the nearer I got to returning to Cairns, the more my throat had swollen up.

Fortunately, I had the foresight to change the hostel I would be staying at in Cairns. So I arrived at one far superior to the previous hostel with use of the kitchen, free wi-fi, and breakfast included. To be fair, I didn't care too much; it was clean, and there was nobody who it seemed would steal my sheets. I was tip-tapping away on my computer, updating my spreadsheets. When travelling, I like to track my itinerary, accommodation, all costs and expenses, and ATM withdrawals (see Appendix ll). Suddenly, I pushed a button and lost all my data! I seemed to have deleted everything I had on the USB pen drive. I was mortified, and a young lad tried to help me recover my documents, but to no avail. I decided ice cream would solve the problem; it would undoubtedly soothe my throat.

From Cairns, I took two days out on tours, both of which were thoroughly enjoyable in their own right. The first was to Kuranda, which involved going out through the Atherton Tableland and up in three cable cars to the touristy town of Kuranda. The nice part of the cable car rides was the views over the rainforests; the not-nice part of the ride was being in a cable car, especially on my own. A few people were surprised by a random female jumping into their carriage.

The Rainforest Nature Park would be the day's highlight due to getting close to various animals, including feeding kangaroos and the fun escapade on the 'Duck Tour. I really have not been on anything like it; this is mainly down to the vehicle itself. The DUCW, more commonly known as the 'DUCK', is a 6-wheel drive amphibious modification of the CCKW trucks used in World War ll by the US Military. Nowadays, we tourists get to traverse both land and water in this 2-ton monster. Quite aptly, I was with a group of 22 Americans in our DUCK; we loved it and had a great laugh together.

Sadly, around 14:00, it was time to say DUCK off and goodbye to my new friends. I headed to the train station for the Kuranda Scenic train to Cairns. The train itself is scenic, powered by a colourful 1720 Class Diesel-Electric Locomotive, with vintage style carriages. Opened in 1891, this famous railway descends from Kuranda through the dense rainforest and into the wide-open rolling plains leading to Cairns.

It turned out to be more of an 'au revoir' with my American friends as they had descended upon the vintage train carriage I was in. They had numerous debates about who was sitting where, although we were supposed to be sitting in our allocated seat numbers. The train made its regular stop at the Barron Falls, the largest waterfalls near Cairns, falling 250 metres down through the Barron Gorge. Anymore seating debates by my carriage compadres, and I could see a fall out between them, perhaps over the lookout railings!

If this day to Kuranda was mildly tranquil, the next day tour would be the complete opposite. I had booked onto the Barefoot Adventure tour into the Atherton Tablelands, the keyword there being 'adventure'. We had been to numerous water-based places by the end of the day, including Lake Eacham, a gorge with a deep pond, Millaa falls and Josephine Falls. At said places, I had been on a water slide, jumped off a small cliff into the water, been swimming, and copied the hair shampoo advert where the woman bends her head down into the water and flicks it back swiftly, so it creates a spray of water. This took several attempts to get it right as I was clearly not so graceful! At the natural rock waterslide, I sat on a large rock at the top, waiting my turn. Without warning, the guide got hold of both my feet and somehow swung me round into a contorted position, lying upside down, causing me to go down the waterslide backwards. I must have been subject to his party piece, rolling down the slide to a symphony of chuckles!

Over the past few days, all of that fun was interspersed with reuniting with various friends I had made at the eclipse on Easter Island in 2010. I met up with Sean and Alice on her birthday, so we just had to celebrate! I also met with a couple of the Danes I had visited at New Year in Copenhagen after our meeting on Easter Island. And then there was my endearing friend Nacho, who was happy to see me as he had missed me at the Cairns Festival, and who was impressed with my quest for spirituality. We sat chatting that evening in Cairns in the park whilst the thousands of bats in the trees flitted above our heads.

~ ~ ~

It was time now to head to mid-Australia and move off the East Coast; I was flying to Darwin and making my way straight down the middle of Australia. It sounds straightforward enough, but trust me, it was one big fun adventure all the way.

My first escapade was on the Kakadu tour, which involved driving from Darwin to the Kakadu National park. We stopped off for breakfast at the 'Humpty Doo' Roadhouse, famous for its drinking competitions out of the Darwin Stubby (a 2-litre vessel) and for exhibiting the world's largest water buffalo horns above the bar. I wondered if Humpty was distantly related to my Dinky Doo; I made sure he was still in my daypack when I left.

Onwards and upwards it was, as we touched into the Australian outback. We headed straight out onto the Corroboree Billabong Cruise; next, it was the wetlands of Kakadu National Park, and finally, the Barramundi Gorge, where we partook in a refreshing swim by the Maguk Waterfall. We were treated to a wealth of wildlife viewing in the Wetlands, namely Eagles, Saltwater Crocodiles, Peccelo and Jabberoo (it's actually a Jabiru, a breed of stork). I was in my element amongst all this nature.

Although plenty was included in our tour to see and experience, two things stood out for me most on that trip. The first was dropping my expensive camera and breaking it. That occurred just after I had photos taken of me licking the bum of a Lime Ant (to see if it did indeed taste of lime, I can confirm it did). The second was a strange thing I did; I spotted a brown cap with the word 'CAT' on the peak, lying on the floor near a CAT Lift Truck (forklift truck). It seemed significant, so I took the cap, washed it back at the hostel and wore it for the rest of the trip. I still have it to this day.

I was now heading deeper into the outback in a truck with seven other adventurers and our guide Ollie. There was never a dull moment on that trip. Aside from our activities, Ollie kept us entertained the whole time, even when driving through the relentless heat and orange desert sands. I loved the roadhouse choices Ollie made, as this time, we stopped off at the Adelaide River Inn. Here, prominently overlooking the whole bar, is 'Charlie', the water buffalo made famous in his starring role in the film

Crocodile Dundee. After his film debut, Charlie wallowed in his watering hole at the Adelaide River Inn until his death. The owner did not want to part with him and so had him stuffed and positioned in pride of place on the bar.

We stopped off at the stunning Nitmiluk (Katherine) Gorge for a swim; why we did that, I do not know, as the river is home to crocodiles. Apparently, the freshwater crocodiles spend their time sunning themselves on the river banks and are not a threat to humans; oh well, that makes it alright then! Except occasionally, the more enormous saltwater crocodiles immigrate there; they have evidence of that as they have found them in the traps they set up.

We turned from crocodiles to Flying Fox Bats the next day at the Mataranka Thermal Pools. It was relaxing floating around in the thermal pools. Yet, it was also fun, diving under the water and taking photos of each other with our eyes open and smiling (another new experience for me). It was not so much fun looking at thousands of the Flying Fox creatures swirling around our heads and pooping in the water around us. Leaving schitt creek behind us, Ollie drove us along the Stuart Highway (a major Australian highway). He stopped off for a photo opportunity at a sign saying 'No Fuel for 500kms'; Ollie thought that was funny, along with the jokes he would make about our lack of fuel. However, he redeemed himself at our next roadhouse, where the owners bought out a little baby Joey (baby kangaroo), all swaddled up in a blanket. The poor little mite was now an orphan as his mother had been hit by a vehicle and died. Thankfully, the vehicle drivers thought to check the mother's pouch and found the little Joey. I was elated when they placed the swaddled little Joey in my arms; I was honoured as I was the only one allowed to hold him. I honestly did not want to give him back (another addition to my animal sanctuary).

We had more fun photo opportunities at the Tropic of Capricorn sign, and the Devil's Marbles rocks back out on the road. Here, the idea was that you would look powerful holding up all kinds of sizes and shapes of boulders. I tried several poses and managed one where it looked like Dinky Doo was holding up a large rock; he's strong for his size!

The fun continued at our camp that night whilst waiting out on the field for dinner to be served. It started with one of the guys playing the bongo, to which I started belly dancing, then one of the girls joined in with tribal dance, another with Indian Bollywood style dance until there was a large circle of us just dancing doing our own thing. Those are the kinds of travel moments to treasure (along with holding baby Joeys).

On the final leg of this tour, we reached the centre of Australia; it was so marked by the presence of the Erldunda Roadhouse, allegedly, it is in the 'centre of the centre'. Again, it had its unique touch, and here you could visit their Emu enclosure, and if you so wished, you could feed them. I declined to not tempt fate; I chose to keep my fingers and hands in one piece.

We visited the Valley of Winds of imposing steep sandstone Kata Tjuta domes dotted in a rugged landscape. It was a strenuous 3-kilometre hike, but the breathtaking views over the desert and large red rock formations were well worth the effort. And yet, the main event of the day was still to come.... sunset at Uluru. It truly doesn't get much better than sunset and champagne at Uluru. If you ever have that idyllic image in your mind of the glowing red sandstone rock formation, backed by a bright cloudless blue sky turning all shades of red and orange as the sun sinks downwards behind it, with a glass of champagne in your hand, here it was. I was suitably overwhelmed by this stunning setting, as was everyone else, to be fair.

Sunsets I like, sunrises I am not so good with as it usually involves an early start. However, the next day at Uluru, I would make an effort as I did not want to miss out on this spectacle. I was not let down in the vastness of the half-lit desert landscape, with the grasses gently swaying in the early morning breeze and the ever-changing rock texture and colours. It is very well thought out at Uluru with dedicated sunrise and sunset viewing areas located, so the rock formations appear to change colour when the sun's rays hit them.

Besides being a UNESCO world heritage site, Uluru is Australia's most recognisable natural landmark. Some are more familiar with the name Ayers Rock. Uluru is the traditional aboriginal name for this landmark.

The name Ayers Rock was introduced in 1873 by a surveyor, William Goss, after the then Chief Secretary of South Australia, Sir Henry Ayers. A dual naming policy is now in place to address the indigenous and the often more commonly known (or colonial) names.

After the spectacle was over, we took a walk of just over four kilometres around the base of Uluru. We were encouraged not to climb up there (none of us did) due to respecting the wishes of the indigenous Anangu people, the traditional owners of the land. The Anangu people see Uluru as a sacred site, a resting place for their ancestors and past spirits. While using the land for their traditional ceremonies, they take care of Uluru and its surroundings. Inside their cultural centre, I found it fascinating reading the 'Sorry Book', containing apologies by people from all over the world who have taken pieces of Uluru. The apologies are most often accompanied by 'Sorry Rocks' sent back by those wishing to return the articles they felt guilty having taken. Some also included stories of how they believed they had been riddled by bad luck after taking the sacred rocks.

I was sorry to leave, but we were now on the final stretch of our trip, driving through the desert landscape via the McDonnell ranges, Kings Canyon, Mount Conner (also known as 'Atila' or 'Artila') and the Salt Lake Amadeus. Sometimes there is only so much stunning scenery the eye can take, but we soaked it all up as we would be leaving it behind to stay in a town that night; it was back to urban life.

That evening we went out for a post-tour drink and meal, we had had great fun as a group, and we're now having to say our goodbyes. We were being entertained by the owner of the bar, who had brought out his pet snake. He offered it round, no, I would not be doing that a second time, no snake on the shoulders for me. But then, who should walk in, again, but Tim and Sarah! We were thousands of miles from where I last saw them in Port Douglas; how random. We had some catching up to do, and sharing of stories washed down with a few beers, as was our usual.

~ ~ ~

I spent my time in Alice Springs catching up with laundry, emails and so on. Most importantly, I needed to buy a new camera and opted for a bright pink one that I could use underwater (it was the only one in my price range). Suitably reinvigorated, the next day, I was to start my next leg of the journey through the red centre of Australia, heading to Coober Pedy- the 'opal capital of the world'. Every now and again, I like to stay somewhere unusual, and Coober Pedy accommodated my wishes in that respect. Most of the town's inhabitants live underground due to the scorching 40-degree heat, so why would I choose to do differently from the locals? I opted for a female dorm bed in an underground budget motel; it wasn't claustrophobic but was a strange feeling staying in the depths of an old opal mine.

The owner was really helpful and arranged for me to go out with the postman to deliver letters and parcels the next day. On the face of it, you would think nothing was exciting or unique about that. However, I can assure you that it was one of my best experiences around Australia and one of my most memorable experiences ever from my travels. We would be spending the day driving deep into the outback, where relatively few people have ventured.

I was picked up by Pat, the postman, at 08:45 the next day outside the Coober Pedy post office. We hit it off immediately, which is just as well with the number of miles to cover and the hours we would spend together in the mail truck. It was definitely a unique experience, seeing the original 'Dingo Fence' (instead of parts on display for tourists). The dingo fence was originally erected in the 1880s to keep the dingos off of farmer's fertile lands and to protect sheep. It is purported to be the longest fence in the world (even longer than the Great Wall of China), stretching over 3,000 miles. That day, Pat and I were to cover 600 miles .of the outback, a fifth of the length of the dingo fence.

We visited various cattle stations, with an average of four permanent residents. Some ranches would have seasonal workers to build up their population. The most extensive homestead we visited was the Anna Creek Cattle Station, which is the largest in the world at almost 24,000 square kilometres (reputedly the size of Belgium). So we would be spending a fair chunk of our day driving through its land. It was interesting to see how life was on the ranches and talk to the few people living on them living in such heat and isolation. In particular, I was pleased I got to see a real-life 'school of the air' (a unique type of correspondence school). I had previously only seen these on television. The school of the air is for children living in remote outback areas. They have a combination of home-schooling by their parents and a radio transmitter on the air to their teacher and classmates.

Considering how far out we were in the middle of nowhere, I was surprised to meet a young English female when we stopped for a late lunch; I mean, what would be the odds? I was in the small town of Oodnadatta with a population of only 200 people and was eating in the Pink Roadhouse. You would never miss this place; it is by default, as the name suggests bright pink, and dominates the landscape. I just had to ask how this young English girl came to be here, and her story was that she had travelled through a few months before and liked it so much she had decided to come back and live there. I suppose if she had no visa, the Government would have a long way to go to track her down!

After my lunch, whilst Pat was chatting with the owner and her sister, I decided to visit the museum along the road. I got up to leave, and the owner called out, 'you'll need this", and there in her hand was the key to the museum! Yes, I had to open it up and then lock it again when I finished visiting and report what condition the museum was in, as nobody had been over there for a few months.

Pat drove slowly on the way back so that I could enjoy the dark night sky with the plethora of stars. I had heard about the desert stars, not polluted by urban lighting and smog, and I was not let down. It was the perfect finish to the day of delivering mail.

Feeling jetlagged the next day, I got up late and visited everything underground and local: the Catacomb underground Church, Desert Cave Motel Museum, and Old Timer's Mine & Museum. The only exception to my underground ventures were the Big Winch Lookout (a structure sitting on a hill overlooking Coober Pedy) and Josephine's Gallery and Kangaroo Sanctuary. The art was amazing, but it was the little baby

Joeys that drew me there, all orphaned but cared for by the sanctuary owners.

~ ~ ~

It was time to pack up and board the overnight bus to Adelaide. It was a strange feeling being back in a city, but if I was going to be in a city, Adelaide was a pleasant one to be in. I arrived at my hostel around 08:00 and promptly went out to explore. I didn't have much time in Adelaide, only two days, and in hindsight, I wished I had at least one more day there; I could have taken that off my next city Melbourne.

I saw tree trunks, traffic lights, street signs, post boxes, and even the Queen Victoria statue on my way to the Adelaide Gaol. There was nothing unusual about that, except they had been yarn-bombed (street art that employs colourful displays of knitted or crocheted yarn). Reaching the Gaol, I discovered it was operated as a prison from 1841 to 1988 and was the first established prison in South Australia. During its period of operation, 45 people had been hanged there (the last one in 1964). Their bodies are reputed to be buried in the prison grounds, which may explain why the Gaol Ghost Tours are popular!

I found the Migration Museum quite harrowing, and for me, the visit was a true eye-opener. The original building itself was a 'Destitute Institution' opened in 1851 (similar to a British Workhouse), which housed the sick, elderly, pregnant women, and orphaned or neglected children. After its closure in 1922, it was used as a centre for immigrating boys from Britain. There was, unfortunately, a lot of abuse on the women and children, much of which would not come to light until decades later. A graphic timeline displayed stories inside the Migration Museum highlighting how the changing government policies affected the lives of many immigrants/Australians. The timeline commences from people living as 'aliens under a White Australia' policy. Moving along with a gradual shift of attitude and policy of rejection and enforced conformation, to integration. There had been an inherent racism, but the signs were that Australia was moving towards multiculturalism.

Outside on the museum walls were multiple plaques with apologies made to indigenous children and child immigrants from various countries. It was the first place I saw the apology from the Government made in 2009 to the indigenous people and the 'Stolen Generation' of aboriginal children.

I had a potent mix of feelings at the previous injustices; sadness, anger, disgust etc. Was I just a 'whinging POM'? That evening whilst waiting for my bus to Melbourne, I was engaged in light-hearted conversation with an 87-year-old man and his son. He jokingly called me a 'POME' and would not tell me what it meant. Of course, I had to look it up and found Prisoner of Mother England as a likely explanation. Those initials or POHM (Prisoner of Her Majesty) were stamped on the clothing of prisoners arriving from England back in the day, and the whinging comes into play due to their complaints of life down under.

~ ~ ~

I had two of those 'small world' encounters within two days in Melbourne. The first one being at my hostel in where I met a young Irish girl, and we were chatting away. I told her about my day out into the outback delivering mail and how random it was that I met an English girl in the middle of nowhere. The next moment, she had her phone out, showing me a picture of herself and that very same girl. It transpired that she had known her well as she had worked with that girl at the Pink Roadhouse! Is this place seriously in the middle of nowhere? The second encounter was down at the train station, just a five minute walk away from the hostel. I was looking around to get my bearings for when I moved on to my next destination by train, but more immediately to find free wi-fi. A Police Officer approached me and asked if I was alright, as I looked lost- oh if only he knew how many times he could have come in useful elsewhere! I explained I was fine, just looking for free wi-fi. We got chatting, and it turns out his mother in law lives in Hockley, Essex (very near to where I live). I really had been fine before he approached me, but to reassure me further, he proceeded to inform me that there would be hundreds of officers on duty after 20:00. I briskly walked back to my hostel, wondering why there would be the need for so many police.

The following day, I took the free city tram ride to get my bearings and then visited the Immigration Museum. Although informative, for me, it did not have the character of the Migration Museum building back in Adelaide. I squeezed in a visit to St Paul's Cathedral before heading to the Old Melbourne Gaol, now that was an experience.

The staff really do immerse you into prison life at the Old Melbourne Gaol. Before entering, we were made to line up against the wall. During being booked in, we were lined up again whilst a Prison Officer shouted at us. I made the mistake of making a noise, I am not sure if it was a whimper or a chuckle, but the officer turned her attention to me. The officer called me Goldilocks (my blond hair was in plaits) and fired questions at me. I was supposed to have remembered my short script, but she was so quick and making me so perplexed that I ended up giving my answers whilst nervously laughing. I was not laughing when they locked us in a cell and proceeded to turn the lights off.

By my second day, I had discovered that I was not staying in the most salubrious area of Melbourne. My hostel was on a road well known for gentlemen's clubs, and the train station was a known area for crime. When my friend Kat found out where I was, she came to pick me up to stay with her and her partner for a few days. Kat had been a housemate of mine for a while back in England. I spent a few days chilling out with Kat, her partner and friends; it was good to be a part of local life, even if it was for a short time. We drove out to the Twelve Apostles, and on the way, we saw a wild Koala by the side of the road. It stared at us for a while, and I was still too slow to get my camera out. As soon as the camera was out, the koala was off into the trees!

The Twelve Apostles is a stunning site, situated off the shore by the Great Ocean Road (which runs between Adelaide and Melbourne). The limestone pillars rise majestically out of the Southern Ocean at the height of 45- 65 metres. They are thought to be more than 20 million years old, about the same age I felt lugging my backpack around from place to place for the past two months. And yet still, I was off again, jetting off to Tasmania....

If you can picture the Tasmanian Devil that swirls like a whirlwind, that is what I looked like as I took in the sights of Tasmania. And, of course, the Tasmania Devil was at the top of my list to see there. I cannot say I had an affinity with them; they looked like vicious little critters! They couldn't even seem to play together nicely. For once, I was not keen to fuss or feed an animal; I am pretty sure I would have lost a hand or an arm. I still managed to get bitten, though, this time by an emu who I was feeding; he thought there was more food in my hand and tried to get at it! It hurt, but at least he did not draw blood as the parrot did back in Malaysia.

My whirlwind Tasmania 3-day itinerary included: Richmond town and historic bridge; Tasmin Devil Conservation Park; Port Arthur Historic Site; Arch & Devil's Kitchen; Tessalated Paving Stones; Great Oyster Bay; Cole's Bay; trek up to a lookout for views of Wineglass Bay; Honeymoon Bay; Cape Townville Lighthouse; New Norfolk; Mount Field Park with its many waterfalls; Bonorong Wildlife Park; Mount Wellington, and Cascades Female Factory. I found the Female Factory particularly harrowing, yet understood the purpose of the tour to denote the triumphs as well as the tragic. The factory had housed female immigrants from England and local women from the Hobart area who had committed offences. Their behaviour and trustworthiness determined their life after prison; for example, good conduct and credibility could result in being sent on into service of respected families. Either way, all suffered long hours of labour each day and a geographically inhospitable environment. Remind of triumphs again.

Doo Town was a highlight for me out of the stop-off places due to my teddy being named Dinky Doo, and so this was the perfect photo opportunity for him. Each house or shack in Doo Town has the word 'Doo' in its name. The fun was started back in 1935 by an architect called Eric Round, who named his own shack "Doo I 99". The neighbours cottoned on and came up with names like "Make Doo", "Doo Me", "Doo Drop-In", you get the gist, "This Will Doo"!

I was glad to get back to Kat's home in Melbourne for a night of rest after my whirlwind tour. The next day, was back in Melbourne centre in the same bed in the same female dorm. My two roommates that night in Melbourne were a stripper and a madam, both coming to work in separate 'gentlemens' clubs across the road. They were very amicable, not leaving me out of the conversation. I did not have much to offer to it, but it was certainly an eye-opener. It got me thinking about a career change, though, when they mentioned the money they could earn!

I had one more jaunt across the water before heading off along the coast towards Sydney in a couple of days. I was on the Philip Island tour, mainly as it offered up a variety of animals. I was not let down at the Maru Animal Park, where I saw Koalas, emus, kangaroos, wallabies, alpacas, and a donkey. Even though he did not bite, the donkey seemed to have the whole of my hand between his lips. The park's highlight was paying to go into the dingo enclosure to have my photo taken with two dingos. I didn't realise I was going right in, I thought I was going in the section near them, and they would be in the background- but no, I was sat on a rock while I tentatively stroked them, and they licked my face!

No trip to Phillip Island would be complete without visiting Nobbie's Rock in the protected area to spot seals and the Nature Park to watch the Penguin Parade. Once there, we settled into our seats just as the heavens opened, and it poured with rain. The torrent did nothing to deter us tourists while the penguins nonchalantly waddled along the boardwalk to their nesting spots, past what resembled a group of drenched rats.

I was packed up, ready to get the overnight Melbourne to Sydney train the following evening, but preceded it by going out on another train. I was taking an excursion on the famous Puffing Billy. After the stress of rushing to get to the Belgrave Puffing Billy Station, I was rewarded with getting the last ticket on the 10.20 train. Off we went on the heritage 2ft 6-inch narrow gauge railway track.

There were some pleasant views on the way to the lakeside. We were traversing through the Dandenong Ranges, lush rainforest with giant Mountain Ash trees towering above us. After a couple of hours, we reached our destination. Gembrook Station is the final stop and has the

Lakeside and park adjacent to it. After an hours pleasant stroll, it was homeward bound. I decided to sit in a different carriage near the guard's carriage and was on my own in there. The next thing I knew, I was whisked away up into the driver's bunker carriage. I spent the rest of the return journey there, enjoying a cup of tea and a bar of chocolate while learning the workings and the history of Puffing Billy. I even got to turn the lever handle that controlled the steam/water. Now that is the kind of day out for me!

~ ~ ~

My experience on the overnight train from Melbourne to Sydney proved to be a somewhat different experience. To say I was disappointed, and distraught not getting any sleep is probably an understatement. It had not crossed my mind how many miles it was from Melbourne to Sydney, but it did during the journey. The train was going so slow that I began to wonder if I should get out and help by pushing it! It was not too bad during the first hour or two during the last of the daylight. However, it was getting monotonous in the dark, plodding along at around 45pmh.

It was bad enough that it was freezing cold with the air-con, and a hysterical child was screaming a few seats behind me. Yet my night was worsened when a rather large hipped lady got on a few stops later and sat next to me, or on me. I had half of my seat left, which I was squashed into, which would probably not have been so bad if it had not been the space I was supposed to sleep in that night. I gave up after a few hours due to having a numb bum and stood in the back of the carriage near the toilet area. I vaguely remember a man who had been sitting in front of me talking to me and said he had noticed my predicament. He reported it to the train guard, but the night was gone, and so was any chance of snoozing. I don't know if I was dreaming or not, but I thought I heard him say his son had bought a wolverine from Siberia for the Taronga Zoo in Sydney. Mental note to visit the zoo. Somehow I slept walked to the connecting train to Bondi junction near my hostel, where I checked in and promptly caught up on some well-deserved sleep.

I would be spending this week over Christmas near Bondi Beach. Way before I made this trip, I had the image of me in a red and white bikini/swimsuit sunbathing on a hot Bondi Beach on Christmas Day. The reality was very different. On Christmas Eve, I went down to the beach, and it was indeed hot and sunny, but on Christmas Day- no, not so much. It was windy and rainy. So to that end, I found the only way to get my desired photos was to skip down to Bondi Beach, strip off down to my bikini, get the pictures hastily taken and skip back to the hostel. That plan worked, but to be fair, the images reflected that it was overcast and would do little to make people back home jealous of a hot sunny Christmas! All was not lost on Christmas Day, though, as I had a lot of fun in the small hostel kitchen with other backpackers. We got out bubbly, and nibbles which we shared, and generally had a good laugh, with blaring music and dancing in the tiniest of spaces.

Christmas Eve had been fun too, as I visited Mary and Brian. They had recently got married at the total eclipse festival near Cairns (I had met them on Easter Island). It was great seeing them again, and I enjoyed meeting their friends; I was made to feel so welcome. We exchanged gifts and danced and laughed from Christmas Eve into the morning.

I spent the rest of the week relaxing, chatting with backpackers, going to the beach, and venturing along the cliff coastal path as far as Coogee beach (a 10 km round trip). The views were stunning, and it was nice to experience the different beaches on the way (Tamarama, Bronte, Clovelly Bay, and Gordon Bay). I strolled, sunbathed and even ventured into the sea - possibly the only mistake of the day. The waves were crashing around. Suddenly a child appeared from nowhere, kind of in front of but below me. At the same time, a huge wave came crashing towards us- I had nowhere to go, and the best I could do was try and dive over him. I was fuming at him getting in my way and even more furious with his parents, that wave was at least five times bigger than the child, and he could have got crushed by me too.

As much as I love to be by the seaside, my time was up, and I had to return to the centre of Sydney ready for the New Year's Eve fireworks. I would say that Sydney was one of my favourite cities; it had a good vibe and feel for me. I ventured out to look around the city, visiting the Contemporary Art gallery (in the free sections), the Chinese Gardens, and the Botanical Gardens. I scoured Macquaire Point on a mission to find the perfect viewing spot for the fireworks on New Year's Eve.

I also went to the Taronga Zoo; I looked for the wolverine. However, it must have still been in quarantine (or I had dreamt that conversation). So I took pleasure in seeing other unusual animals such as komodo dragon, platypus, gorillas, tree kangaroos, snow leopard and Himalayan Tahir. I can't make up my mind about zoos, I am much happier seeing animals in the wild, and I am sure they are much more comfortable living there. But I am starting to wonder if some of these endangered species are, in fact, safer in the zoo, and I feel much more assured if I know there are conservation projects in place.

I don't know what to make of the New Year's Eve experience; it was slightly chaotic, to say the least, but this event had been on my bucket list too, and here was another tick. The theme for this year's fireworks was Kylie Minogue, and another 16,999 people must have had this event on their bucket list; it was rammed. I had grouped up with some of the others from the hostel, and we all got up early to make our way to the NYE celebrations. We got there at 08:00, and altogether there was nine of us. We were amongst the thousands of others, at that point, just sitting chilling and eating our picnic breakfasts.

Officials put us all in lines for a queue. It was chilled out until the front of the queue started moving. Bizarrely, the back of the queue people started running forward - so we ran with them. Once we got into the botanical gardens, we selected a spot for the day and mooched around, eagerly awaiting an exciting night of entertainment and fireworks. I thoroughly enjoyed the company and spectacular firework display. However, I was just as happy back at the hostel some 10 hours later watching the London firework display on television. Especially as I could relax while watching them in the warm, with a bottle of bubbly.

I toasted to the New Year, but also to my trip around Australia, to the total eclipse, to the people I had met, and many adventures. It was so much to take in, from the varying landscapes of cities to beaches to vast wild desert. I felt so grateful to have been able to experience all of this but was aware that I had worked hard and saved for this trip and should be proud of myself for going through with it all. I was slowly undergoing a transformation, moving away from the old me. I loved this backpacking lifestyle, meeting travellers with whom you could share tips and stories, and teaming up when mutually desired to see new places together. We looked out for each other too. For example, when a New Zealander genuinely had difficulties getting funds from his bank for a couple of days, I loaned him my phone to call his bank and made sure he had meals, whilst another guy provided him with beers. There was a true sense of camaraderie in the hostels, I liked being in the female dorms, and it was interesting to see the different facilities available. Some hostels offered more than others, such as plug sockets and/or lights next to bunks and privacy curtains. I felt that in myself, I was indeed developing my character; I was becoming more patient, tolerant and understanding. I was practising gratitude daily and knew I had so much to feel grateful for. I took this with me on the next leg of my journey; I was heading to one of my favourite places in the world, New Zealand.

~ ~ ~

Top Tip: Locals don't usually eat out every night, and even though in some countries it is cheap enough to eat out regularly, it is okay for you to not eat out every night either. Where you have the facilities (many hostels have kitchens), have a go at cooking your own version of the local cuisine. Markets are a great source of cheap nutritious vegetables, fruit, fish etc. When travelling a country like Australia, catering for yourself can significantly cut your trip cost, especially if you get used to which supermarkets have the best offers. Check out the free food shelves in the cupboards and fridges at most hostels.

Total Eclipse, Port Douglas

Holding a Baby Joey, Red Centre

Australia, Holding Sam the Snake

New Zealand, Dinky Doo near Mt Cook

Christchurch, Restart Centre

Ben Lomond Hike to the Saddle

Dunedin, Baldwin Street (steep!)

Cathedral Cove, North Island, NZ

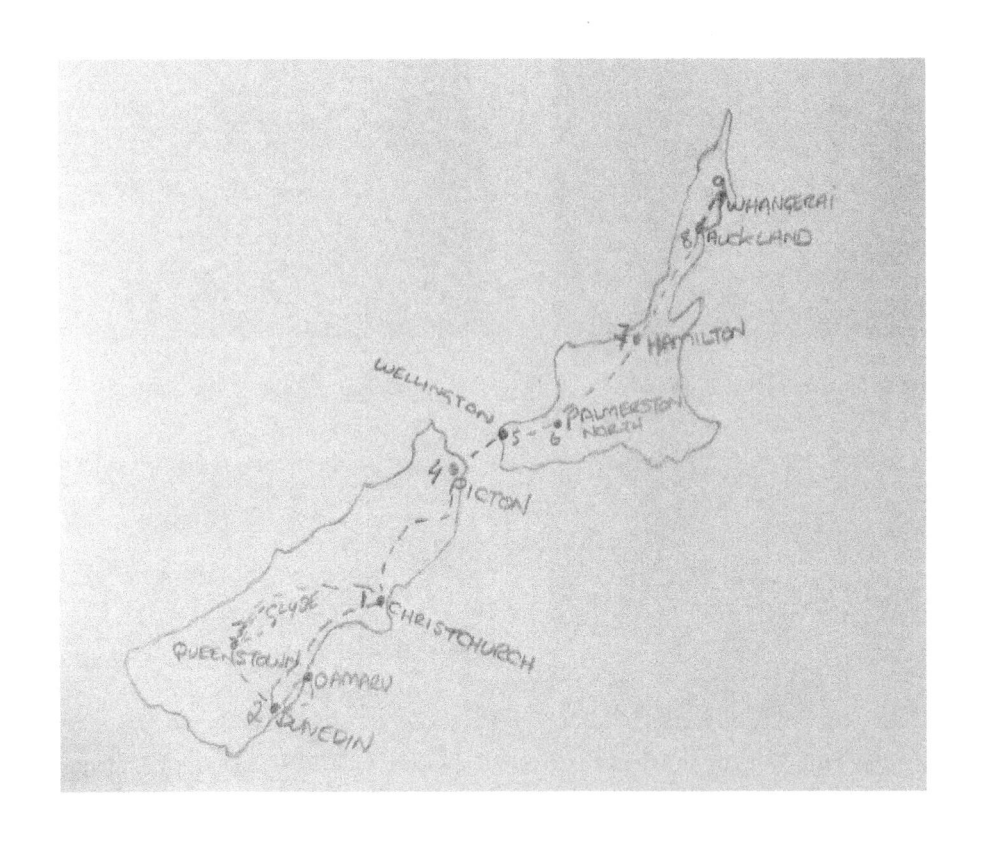

NEW ZEALAND ROUTE

1. CHRISTCHURCH
2. DUNEDIN
3. QUEENSTOWN
4. PICTON
5. WELLINGTON
6. PALMERSTON NORTH
7. HAMILTON
8. AUCKLAND
9. WHANGAREI

NEW ZEALAND 2013

Round NZ on $1 Bus Fares!

New Zealand's history dates back just a few hundred years as it was the last country in the world to become inhabited by humans. That is also when you include the indigenous Maoris who were living there before European immigrants settled. Today, there is still only a small-scale population of 4.4 million people spanning the North and South Islands. Most of them live on the North Island, with a third of their total population living in their largest city, Auckland. It is widely assumed that Auckland is the capital city; however, Wellington heralds that title due to its favourable geography and central location.

Although there are ten sheep to every one human in New Zealand, unlike Australia, it does not have an abundance of dangerous animals or sea life. However, it has some of the largest insects in the world, such as the Weta species, which have ears on their knees, and weigh up to 70 gms (they can be as big as gerbils). New Zealand is home to the flightless Kiwi bird endemic only to their country and gives New Zealanders their nickname (Kiwis).

The start of a new year and the beginning of the next adventure into kiwi land. It was the 2nd January 2013, and I was going to New Zealand. I had been there once before, some twenty years prior, and I thoroughly loved it there; I was excited to be going back. I was not so excited on the morning of departure from the hostel in Sydney. They insisted I owed $12, and I insisted I didn't as I had fully paid back in England. We agreed we would sort it out on my way back from NZ. With that problem solved, for the time being, I was off to the airport.

As advised, I arrived at the International terminal, only to discover that I should be at the Domestic. I jumped into a taxi and made it just in time for check-in. Great, except the girl at the departure desk, was new, did not understand my paperwork, and questioned me. I could not figure out why you would be interrogating someone when they were departing the country. Surely if you didn't want them in the country, you would do the questioning during entry? I played along with her, and after her supervisor had corrected her, I trotted off to get through security. But no, there she was behind me again. This time, she had my paperwork in her hand, which she had accidentally retained, but blamed me for leaving there. In her defence, she felt bad and got me through security quicker to not miss my flight.

I have never been so glad to be in a prison cell. I was at the Jailhouse Hostel in Christchurch, where they really immerse you in the experience of being in prison. The building was previously the Addington Jail, and I was to be sleeping in a cell that night, fine as long as it was not haunted! Interestingly, the prison had only finished operating in 1999, which may account for its authenticity. The structure looked pretty much how you would imagine a prison with its grey concrete walkways and iron railings. There were artefacts on display and the opportunity to have your photo taken in an outfit to portray an incoming prisoner - of course, I was not going to miss out on that.

I spent the day walking around the pleasant botanical gardens in Christchurch, which are among the best I have seen anywhere. It was definitely the right place to de-stress and get out in the air. The next day I would be on a train all day, on one of the world's most scenic train journeys, the Trans-Alpine express route from Christchurch to Greymouth. Well, that was the original plan; it did not quite work out that way. I had forgotten there was a time difference and so had not changed my clock, and my mobile had not changed time zone either. I woke up at what I thought was 06.45 and rushed to get ready for my 07.15 shuttle pick up; however, it was actually 08.45. I was gutted; that was a very expensive £90 oversleep! However, luck went my way for once. The train company advised of flooding on the track, and the service had been cancelled; I was given a full refund.

Due to the expense of the Jailhouse hostel, I had to move to a different hostel that day. Having accomplished that task, I now had some more time to get re-acquainted with Christchurch. It was a very different city centre than I had visited previously, twenty years earlier. A colossal earthquake had struck the year before, and the after-effects were still apparent. It was pretty heart-rending to see some of the buildings in tatters and the piles of rubble. I can only imagine how my friend Michelle must have felt when we were in Poland the year before, finding out the news of this disaster. This was her home city; her daughter was living here during the earthquake, and we had been informed of the tragedy after being in a car crash. In the true style of NZ resilience, the city had built the 'Re-Start Centre' where shops and cafés were housed in colourful shipping containers. Due to being robust and easily relocatable, they were used as a temporary measure whilst rebuilding the city shops.

~ ~ ~

After reminiscing in Christchurch, I made my way by bus to the city of Dunedin. If you ever fancy walking up the steepest residential street in the world at a gradient of 35%, then you can do so here, namely Baldwin Street. My legs would definitely confirm to you the steepness of the street, as they certainly felt it by the time I reached the top.

I usually like to get out of a city as soon as I have arrived, even just for a day or few hours, and so it was the next day I ended up on a bus trip out to Oamaru. Another factor in this decision was that I was only paying NZ $1 for each way (the equivalent of 50 pence for each journey). I was paying that for pretty much all of my bus journeys around New Zealand. I had found the online offers of two leading bus companies before I left England and booked in advance.

Although it is the largest town in North Otago of the South Island, Oamaru seemed very olde-worlde with its Victorian architecture. I took an instant liking to this place and roamed the streets and the botanical gardens. However, I missed out on the penguins who come out at sunset, and I also missed out on the Steampunk Museum as it was closed. It looked very intriguing, though, and I took to climbing up the fence and looking over to where I could see skeletons, one of which was sitting on a tractor. Yes, a visit to Oamaru was warranted for a future visit.

I would say my favourite town in the whole world (that I have travelled to so far) is Queenstown. A couple of days later, I was there - it felt like home (actually better than home, if we are talking about Southend on Sea). To me, it has everything - beauty, hiking, adventure, nightlife, shopping, and a blue lake. Southend really does not compare.

I decided to walk up Mount Everest - well, it wasn't actually that mountain, but it was so similar that I thought I was back there. The young guy on reception at my hostel advised a 'stroll' around Ben Lomond. At no point did he mention it was at least a 2-hour hike up to what is called 'The Saddle', with the operative word being 'up'! And that is after you have got off the cable car, which takes you up to the skyline, cutting off a portion of this steep ascent. Thinking I was going for a gentle stroll, I had not taken my usual essential water and food provisions or my first aid kit. I met an English couple at the Ben Lomond saddle, and we got chatting. They said I was courageous doing such a hike on my own; I assured them that it had not been my plan. I felt very under-prepared and certainly not dressed for such a hike. And of course, this was confirmed whilst we were looking out over the lovely scenery of the distant mountain ranges in the foreground when a snowy rain started coming down. Well, that was just the icing on the cake. The visibility was lessening, and the distant mountains began fading; it was time to retreat. I vowed to come back and reach the summit of Ben Lomond; I would be in the appropriate attire and well prepared. It was not going to beat me.

There had been a problem with my bus bookings, and the company had emailed me to see if I wanted to use up a couple of NZ dollars worth of vouchers. I took their recommendation to take a day out from Queenstown to Clyde. It took me all of twenty minutes to see the small town of Clyde, and I still had a few hours left there. I decided to take a walk along the Clutha river along the Rail Trail, and it was such a peaceful stroll. The trail was tree-lined, and the river water was of turquoise and green hues. I was contemplating how much further to walk when I spotted a sign for a vineyard with complimentary wine tasting; now that was more like it.

Having guzzled a few complimentary red wines, I almost became engaged to the owner of the vineyard! He had been pouring out the wine, showed me around his home, and we had sat out on the porch, where he had been hinting at wanting to marry somebody to share this lovely place with. I, meanwhile, had a coach to catch. I had to get out of there, or after a few more wines, I could have been wed with a vineyard as a home! I must admit, there was some appeal to the prospect in terms of living in a vineyard.

As it turned out, I need not have rushed so much. Whilst standing at the bus stop, I heard a siren; it sounded pretty eerie as I had heard nothing like it except on documentaries about the air raid sirens during WW2. I was quite concerned as there was nobody around to ask. It transpired that it was a call for the Fire Service, who were at the fire station within minutes and out in the fire engines. At that point, I did not realise the impact of them being called on my journey.

My bus arrived, we drove approximately twenty minutes along the road, straight into a long line of traffic. Now I had never heard of or imagined a line of traffic ever occurring on the South Island; there were not enough people or vehicles to cause one. And yet, here it was. What I liked was the driver's reaction to the queue of traffic- he simply pulled out of the line, drove straight along past the motionless cars, and turned off into a parking site next to the river. Better still, he got out a beer and cracked it open for me. The delight and surprise were evident in my big bulging eyes. This was definitely the way to not waste time sitting in traffic!

~ ~ ~

The next day I was heading back to Christchurch with a NZ $1 bus fare. It was not too far from the bus station, but lugging my backpack made the route feel that bit longer. As I neared the bus stop, a horrible image came into my head - it was my laptop sitting on top of the fridge back at the hostel charging up. I ran with my backpack to the bus stop, blurted out to the driver my predicament, threw my pack on the ground near the bus, and ran back to my hostel to retrieve my laptop. Reaching there, the horrible realisation hit me that I had handed back my key, the electronic type operated on a keypad. Even worse, the receptionist would not be due to start work for another half hour. I was panic-stricken, and then miraculously, a roommate came out of the door - I dived in, retrieved my laptop and charger, and ran back down to the bus stop, red-faced and out of breath. The driver, not having had too much of a choice, had waited for me, and so it was I stumbled into my seat to get my breath back and enjoy the upcoming scenery.

The scenery on the way back to Christchurch was indeed spectacular; we went via Oamaru, Lake Pukaki, Lake Tekapo, Mount Cook, Mackenzie Basin, Mount Michael, Geraldine Forest, Southern Alps and the Canterbury Plains. Now, this confirms my theory that the journey through New Zealand on the bus was a vital part of the trip for me, not just the destinations I was heading to. Aside from the scenery, I love the New Zealand bus drivers. In the most part, they are a refreshing change from a lot of the grumpy/jobsworth England drivers (in their defence, they have every reason to be cranky over here - but let's not get political). They were friendly yet professional, knowledgeable about their country, giving a thorough commentary as we drove from one destination to another. The driver's this day were no exception to that rule.

I arrived in Christchurch with a head full of new information and some funny jokes! I had only one evening in Christchurch, and I made a night of it with some other backpackers in my hostel, out on the town drinking and dancing. We got on well with each other and had a great laugh. I was not laughing the following morning when I had to catch a bus at 07:00. I wanted to sleep, but the scenery was no less spectacular than yesterday (or on the whole trip), and so I somehow kept my eyes propped open to soak in the passing sights. We stopped in Kaikoura for lunch, and what a lovely place to stop on such a stunning stretch of coastline. I had a drink and snack looking out over the beach and the crashing blue waves, being slightly disappointed I had not included Kaikoura on my itinerary. I had passed through here twenty years before and had not stopped off here on that trip either. I had enough time for an afternoon whale watching, but after having booked the boat trip, it had unfortunately been cancelled due to the bad weather conditions. Here was another place to add to my growing sites of must-visit more thoroughly.

~ ~ ~

It was on through the mountains towards Picton, where I would catch the ferry across the Cook Straight into Wellington. Upon reaching my hostel in Wellington, I simply dumped my bags down on my dorm bed and hopped over to the Te Papa Museum. Now, this museum is not only the NZ National Museum, but it is also a national treasure, and quite rightly too. It would be difficult to describe this fantastic place, due to the changing exhibitions. Still, there is something about it stands that out. Even if you do not usually find museums interesting, this one could be the exception to the rule.

The next day was just one of those days that was not that bad, but not that good either. I woke up bleary-eyed in my dorm bed to see someone standing there, then they backed out. I noticed that my purse was on the floor, and my debit card was not where it usually was, but nothing was missing. I decided to be extra careful after that and warned my roommates (and reported to reception). All in all, I have heard very few stories of theft or wrongdoings in hostels and certainly have not experienced such myself.

I went up to the botanical gardens and to the Zealandier Wildlife park. The wildlife seemed somewhat elusive that day, except for a few rare birds when I got my packed lunch out. The botanical gardens did not seem overly inspiring that day either; perhaps I was just not tuned in properly.

Back down on the Wellington waterfront, I was strolling along minding my own business when I was hurled abuse at by a young Maori lad. I carried on walking, not so much scared as incensed. I am pleased I mentioned him to a lurking Police Officer as it transpired that the officer had just released him, having suspected him of being disorderly and throwing a knife out into the rocks by the sea. The Police Officer took him away again, much to the protestation of the young lad.

If I am honest, the next day, I was pleased to be leaving 'Windy Wellington' (the 'windy' bit comes from its nickname due to the usual blowy weather). I was heading to Palmerston North to stay with 'friends'. I shall use this term loosely, for they were purely an elderly couple I had become penfriends with. I had served them tickets during my days of working at Victoria Coach Station in London. It had been ten years since they had been at my counter asking for bus tickets to take them around the best spots in England. We had laughed and chatted, and I spent time recommending the best places for them to visit. They walked away pleased with their new itinerary and the promise of the most spectacular sights in the UK. They were clearly not disappointed, as they wrote a thank you letter to my management (I still didn't get a promotion or pay rise!), and that was how I came to be in Palmerston North.

There was a slight issue when neither of them initially recognised me at the bus station where they were waiting for me. To make matters worse, the wife had lost her memory and really had no idea who I was and why I was visiting her house! To be fair, they were very accommodating hosts taking me out and about. However, some of the driving around hair raising bends left me wondering if I would make it to my next destination. But no, you could not fault them as hosts, even if they were not sure who I was.

~ ~ ~

This would not be an issue at my next destination Hamilton, where my esteemed friend Sonya would be waiting to meet me at the bus station. I had first met Sonya twenty years ago in Hawaii. Sonya was on her honeymoon with her new husband, and I was just about to get married to my fiance. We all clicked straight away; we laughed, joked, and were honoured to have Sonya and Chris as our only wedding ceremony witnesses in a small chapel on the island of Kauai.

Rolling on forward twenty years and I was greeted by the smiling face of Sonya at Hamilton bus station. I, too, had a big smile on my face for I had been sat next to a Swedish male model who had been showing me his modelling portfolio! The windows were steamed by the time I left that bus. I swear that it was not down to me, it was due to the air con not working and the whole bus being overheated.

This was definitely a reconnecting trip, as I also got to see Annette, who I had climbed with up to Mount Everest Base Camp. We had a great time going back through the photos, and we laughed as we both confessed that we still had our red thermal pyjama bottoms. Annette remembered Dinky Doo, and so out he came to prove he was still wandering with me on my travels. It had been five years since we had first met, and it was as if not a year had passed. That sometimes happens with people you share special moments in life with.

We were to have one big gathering up in Whitianga, in the North of the North Island. Along with Sonya, Chris and their two children, we would meet with her sister in law Lynette, her husband Warren and their three children. I had already met Lynnette and Warren on my first trip to New Zealand, and they had since come to visit me in Southend; what a reunion. The whole big group of us had a whale of a time by the beach in Whitianga. The adults would have a few beers and wine in the evenings while the children scampered around nearby. This made my time in NZ feel like a more authentic and chilled-out experience. That did not detract them from being great hosts and taking me to scenic sites like Cathedral Cove and Cooks Beach. You can walk to and through the gigantic Cathedral Cove arched cavern from the sandy Hahei beach, which joins two coves. It was a veritable photographic feast to the eyes, the grandeur of the rock set against the white sandy beaches and the blue sea. Being a popular place, I did, of course, have to get Dinky Doo out to block unknown people out of my photos.

Sadly, it was time to say goodbye to my friends and to New Zealand. Sonya, her husband and her children, drove me back down to Auckland Airport, and as we said our fond farewells, I vowed to come back. I felt that two weeks was not enough time to see New Zealand; I had barely scratched the surface, there was so much more to explore. This is all part of the learning process, you can pick up on all the smaller/practical tips while travelling, but there are also the lessons gained to make up the bigger picture. I came away from NZ with newfound knowledge and thinking gained over the past few months. Would I use any of this at my next destination? I was on my way to India, which I believed could be a country bringing its own challenges. It would be my first time there, and I had been filled with preconceptions of poverty, filth, chaos, and scammers letching onto tourists. Would I be able to see past all this fed to me by books, films and the media? Would I discover a dual or multi-faceted India?

I broke up my journey there, going via Australia. I returned to the same hostel in Sydney and flopped down on my dorm bed. Well, I believed it to be my dorm bed, but then so did a young South Korean girl. I explained to her that it could not be hers, as she had not followed the process of using the hostel labelling system for it, and the bed was not made up - therefore, it was mine. She was not happy, but it may have been because she did not understand a word I had said.

The following day I needed to catch the train and knew that I needed the correct change for the ticket machine at the train station. I was 10 cents short, so I turned to the nearest person, my friend, the South Korean girl, who had some money in her hand. She did not want to give it to me and said she did not have the money. I could clearly see it in her hand and snatched my required 10 cents. Now I did not feel too good about that, but I was on a time limit and had a train to catch - I left her sitting there bewildered; I am sure she never understood a word I said. Of course, this would bite me on the bum at the train station as the ticket machine would not accept so many coins. This was unbelievable, after all the trouble I had gone to get the right amount! After several attempts, I was beginning to get stressed, and at the same time, I was causing a queue. A kind woman behind me gave me a dollar, not just to help me but to get the line moving.

One train, one plane and one bus later, I was back in Kuala Lumpur and back in the Pods Hostel. The best thing about going back there was that I knew my way from the bus station to the hostel, so I easily navigated through the shops and streets for the short 5-minute walk. This was only a quick overnight stop. My intention was to relax, as I was flying the next day to India, and I felt I would need all the energy I could muster for this next adventure.

~ ~ ~

Top Tip: Sometimes, it really does pay off to book transport in advance in the country you are travelling to. Booking my bus trips for New Zealand in advance kept most of my fares down to $1 (50p at the time). The same concept applies to other forms of transport such as flights, train travel etc. If you don't want to be tied to booking everything in advance, you may save money in other ways for activities. There are phone apps now that give discounts on travel and activities where there are last-minute spaces available. Even if you book in advance and change your mind once at your destination, you might consider that you have not lost much if you do not use your seat. It is polite to let the company know, though, if you do not intend to travel.

Jailhouse Hostel, Christchurch   Queenstown Lake View

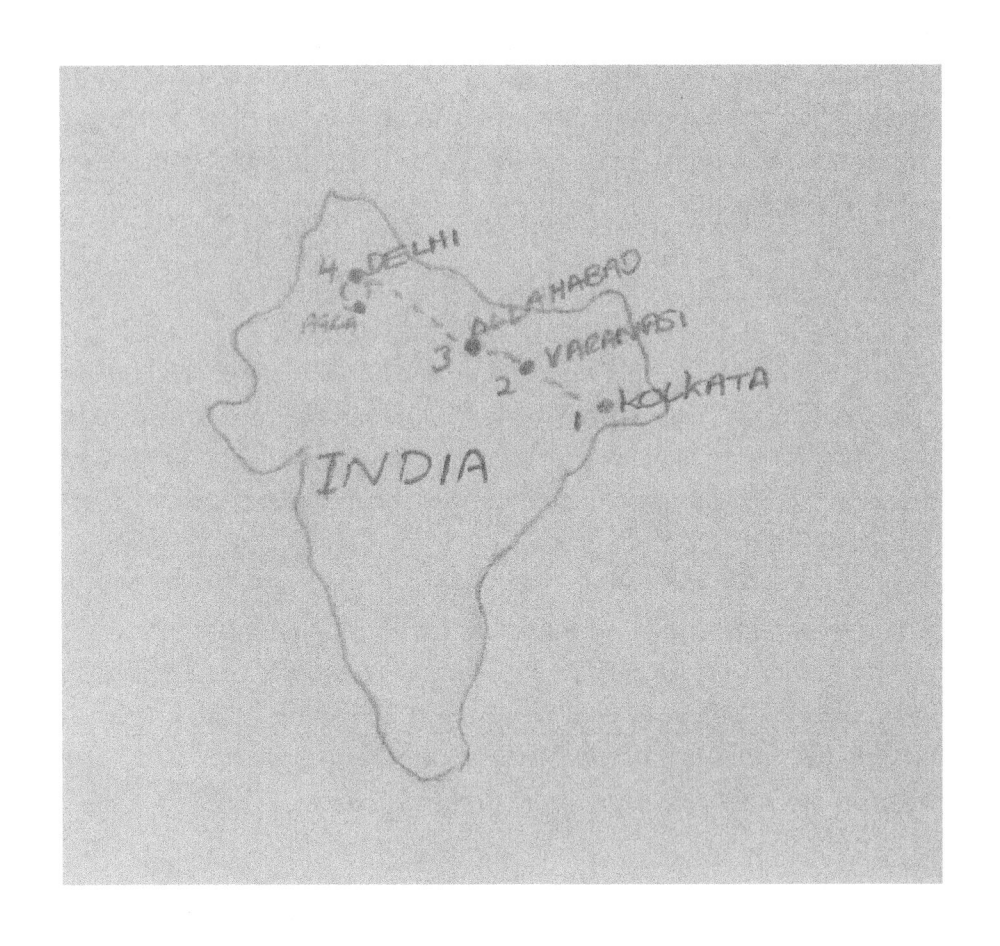

INDIA ROUTE

1. KOLKATA
2. VARANASI
3. ALLAHABAD
4. DELHI

INDIA 2013

A Naked Saddhu Wielding a Spear by the River

India is seventh in the stakes of being one of the largest countries in the world, but is also listed as the second-most populated country in the world. Many of these people will not be eating meat, as it is estimated that around 30% of the population are vegetarian. Maybe there is something in the food as India has one of the lowest divorce rates globally, citing only 1 out of 100 marriages ending with divorce. A more plausible explanation is the cultural customs and arranged marriages. And where else other than India would you find married frogs? In the holy city of Varanasi, traditional beliefs lead to an unusual ritual when the rains are delayed, and so to please the rain gods to bring rain, the frogs are caught and married off! I wonder what their divorce rate is? Hopping through Varanasi, you will discover that this city is believed to be one of the most ancient living cities globally and is even purported to have been home to Lord Shiva and the Goddess Parvati.

Another ancient site is the Taj Mahal in the district of Agra, some 220 miles from Delhi. Unfortunately, this magnificent mausoleum of white marble is changing its colour, turning yellow, and beginning to show reddish-green and brown spots. The causes are said to be pollution, construction and insect faeces.

Visible from space is the pilgrimage festival of the Kumbh Mela, Earth's largest gathering. Millions of pilgrims descend on this auspicious 12-yearly celebration to one of the four sacred sites located on riverbanks of either Haridwar, Nashik, Ujjain or Allahabad. You won't find typical snake charming, but you will likely find the well-known game of snakes & ladders, which originated in India. It was first created to teach young children to understand and remember morals and lessons in karma. Morals must be ingrained from their ancient populations as India has not invaded any country in her last 100,000 years of history. If only the same could be said for other countries.

My application for an entry visa to India should have indicated the strife I would have getting into the country. Naively, I had waltzed up to London to the visa centre with what I thought would be every document humanly required and all the evidence I could muster. But no, that was not enough! I was called up several times after gathering each new piece of paperwork requested until the point of near tears and stressed into almost giving up. This could explain my sour face on the visa photograph, which I ironically had to purchase from them. However, finally, all was in order, and I was set to go.

And here we were, Dinky Doo and I had arrived at Kolkata airport, and I was instantly reminded of the concept to expect the unexpected in India. I got through passport control effortlessly. Considering my experience in London at the visa centre, this was a surprise. However, it was all too good to be true that it would go so smoothly, and yes, of course, it went downhill from there.

Whilst waiting for my backpack to come through on the carousel, I went to the toilet. An older Indian lady appeared who seemed friendly enough until she started asking me questions like "Was I travelling alone?" "Was I married?" "How old was I?" etc. I noticed she had a badge on and thought she was maybe a toilet attendant. It became unnerving at the point where I was trying to put my waist wallet on, and she started to ask how much money I had. I began to think that she was a black market moneychanger or mugger. Surely this old lady was not going to try and rob me in the toilets, especially if she worked here! We walked out of the toilets together, her repeatedly asking me how much money I had and me gesturing that I needed to fetch my baggage! I collected my backpack quickly and went to walk through customs . . . . and there she was, my suspected toilet attendant was, in fact, a Customs Officer! She was standing with her colleagues (who were, I might add, in uniform whilst she was wearing a sari), well, who knew?

And so, the questioning began by her colleagues. Was this my first time in India? Why had I travelled to so many countries? How much money did I have? How long was I going to be in India? Why did I only have a small amount of US dollars (something to do with the fact that they are no use to me in England and would be no use in India)? I explained I had plenty of dollars and then was questioned why I had lied to his colleague. How could I get out of that one? I could hardly tell him I thought his colleague was a money launderer, thief or drug pusher! I mustered every last ounce of politeness that I could, putting an end to this barrage of questioning, and replied that I worked for the Local Government back in England - that worked! I was allowed on my way.

~ ~ ~

Patiently waiting outside Arrivals was the driver I had arranged, holding a placard with my name on it. I survived my first taxi ride in India purely because I hadn't got over the trauma of going through customs at the airport. I didn't flinch once on the 40-minute journey to my hotel in Kolkata city centre, not even when a bus shrieked to a stop sideways on in front of us. Nor when we were dodging people/horses pulling carts with loads that defied gravity, cows, tuk-tuks, and pedestrians.

At the hotel reception, I realised that I would not use my US dollars. Hence, the reception arranged for a hotel porter to assist me across the road to a bank to obtain some rupees. I am not sure what was more stressful on my first attempt to use the ATM - crossing the road to get to it or using it correctly! Being my first attempt to cross a street in India, I was relieved to reach the other side alive, considering I had trams, tuk-tuks and all kinds of vehicles coming at me. My relief was short-lived as my initial encounter with the ATM was only marginally successful. After pressing several buttons, not necessarily in the correct order and an error message flashing up. I finally managed to obtain the grand sum of 500 Rupees (appx £4.50)! Naturally, I did not realise this until I had ducked and dived back across the road. Having gotten back to the hotel to pay for my room and needing somewhere nearer to 5000 Rupees, I trotted back across the street to top up my funds. To accomplish this, I realised it was better to keep moving; hesitating increased the likelihood of being hit by something mobile.

Later, after a revitalising shower, I ventured out along the road to the

Howrah Bridge, located over the Hooghly River. I enjoyed the experience of walking along past the market stalls. The stallholders would call out 'Hello' and smile, and the children would stare with big wide eyes. Some would call out their goods for sale, but none hassled me to stay and look or try their wares.

Globally, the Howrah bridge is believed to be the longest and busiest Cantilever Bridge. Scarily, it is constructed without nuts and bolts. Hundreds of thousands of vehicles and pedestrians cross every day between Kolkata and Howrah, and it somehow magically holds all that weight and movement. Alongside the Howrah Bridge at the Kolkata end was the Mallick Ghat flower market, one of India's busiest and most historic markets- and what a stunning colourful spectacle it was! It took my breath away when I first looked down from the top of the Ghat steps. It was an incredibly dazzling array of colours - reds, oranges, yellows, smells wafting upwards, and sounds of bustling activity.

I was making my way back to my hotel when I met Peter, an Australian solo traveller. I didn't so much meet him as trail along behind him for about 1km before he realised I was there. In my mind, I thought I would be safe as it would appear that we were together. I was appropriately walking behind, he would therefore get pestered, not me! We were looking on his Ipad at a street map of Kolkata. Initially, one young Indian doctor was helping us get to where we knew we were going. Then several others joined in, pointing us in several directions or just staring. Through my travels in India, this became something I admired in locals who always seemed to want to help by asking your destination and trying to show you the right way to get there. This was in stark contrast to the warnings I had been given that people would try and take you to places you did not want to go if they knew you were lost. Peter and I decided to have lunch, and so it was Thalis all around. Thali is a traditional platter made up of several small dishes of vegetables, dahl, chapati etc., and is tastier (in our opinion) eaten by hand, as locals do. I was converted! Intrigued that the restaurant manager did not seem overly bothered about collecting our payment for our meals, I discovered that in India, the hosts are not purely driven by money/tips/promotion. As a respected guest in their establishments, you are fed copious amounts of food in their wholehearted desire to please. This was definitely evident with our Thalis.

My confidence now in full flow, the next day I decided to visit the Victoria Memorial. It is a stunning building constructed in marble between 1906 and 1921 in dedication to Queen Victoria (Empress of India at the time). The memorial is set in gardens covering 64 acres. It has pristine lawns, noble statues and a large lake (where you can see the marble building reflected - photography tip there, you're welcome).

It was about a 10-minute walk to the Central metro station from my hotel, where I bought my ticket and skipped down to the platform heading towards Maidan. This, I was told, was the nearest station to the Victoria monument. The metro trains themselves were old and crowded, although no more crowded than those I have been on in London or Paris. Once at the Maidan station, it was only a 10-minute walk to the monument, and I noted I could get some good photographs from outside the gardens of the building.

After perusing the various galleries in the Victoria Memorial, I noted that I could not find any public toilets. I wondered if it was to do with no food or drink permitted within the premises (including the gardens). I meandered back through the gardens towards the north gate where I had entered, on a mission to find a toilet. I noticed many young couples sitting together on the benches or the grass on the way. I had heard that public kissing was taboo and witnessed how this was adhered to and handled. The couple would cradle in one or other arms or would be nuzzling into the neck of their partner, close your eyes Dinky Doo! Toilet trip completed, it was time to hotfoot it back to my hotel restaurant for last orders of Thali!

~ ~ ~

My time in Kolkata was over, and I moved to my next destination, Varanasi. I had quite liked Kolkata, it seemed for me, to be a suitable introductory city in India, except for my airport arrival experience.

Having experienced two taxi journeys already to and from the previous airport in Kolkata, where the drivers seemed to be rally drivers, I wasn't quite prepared for what followed when I arrived in Varanasi. The taxi driver sat upright, holding the wheel at 2 o'clock and drove slowly. This seemed to outrage all other drivers on the road, and we moved along to a continuous symphony of hooting! Everyone else seemed to be driving somewhere urgently, prehistoric cars were bibbing in a mission to reach their destination. The only time there was respite was when a sacred cow held up the traffic.

The driver's companion upfront was unfazed by all this and chatted to him and played music. When we finally arrived in Varanasi old town, after dodging tuk-tuks, people and cows, we stopped briefly to check our destination. A guy in a brown leather jacket stepped forward and gave me a card for the Suraj Guest House. Okay, I thought, at least I am on track, I had already booked this hostel. We drove on a little further, in what seemed to be a circle, and then stopped. The two guys up front got out, and I just sat there as I could not see the guest house. I thought I was in a scam. The drivers explained that the alleys were too small for the car to go any further. They pointed across the street - and there was the guy in the brown leather jacket again! Where did he spring from? I hauled my luggage down the maze of lanes, dodging past cows, and cow dung to the haven that was the Suraj Guest House. It was to be my home for the next eight days, a retreat I initially vowed not to leave. That was until I met my new friend Allie from Canada.

My vow was broken the very next day when Allie asked me if I wanted to go out to lunch. It was a simple route to take, and the only one in which I did not get lost over the coming days: turn left, walk down through the alley to the Lilita Ghats, down the steps halfway to the river, turn right, follow the river for few minutes and turn right up the steps to the Ganpati restaurant. Every long step up was worth it in the end for the views over the Ganges River and the gastronomic delights awaiting. Each day after that, I would take my familiar route to the Ganpati and choose something different but flavoursome.

Of course, no meal would be complete without a visit to the Blue Lassi, famous for its delicious Lassis of all types of flavours you can think of. They are so filling; they can be considered a meal in themselves! For all you Blue Lassi virgins out there, the base of the lassi is yoghurt, which then becomes infused with a choice from mango, pineapple, saffron, coffee, and over 70 other flavourings. All mixed to your palette. After Allie showed me the way, I noted where this haven was, and it became another of my regular haunts. Where better to sit with Dinky Doo whilst supping a fruity concoction watching the world go by? It was situated at the corner of two alleys with all the comings and goings of another regular Varanasi day Varanasi. It was somewhat surreal and quite sobering to see the numerous bodies on stretchers being taken down to the Ghats at the Ganges River for cremation.

Another reason, in defence of my initial non-adventurous misgivings for going out, was that my right eye had been bitten during the first night here. It had puffed up so that I could barely see. I took to wearing my dark sunglasses on my trips out. They didn't help me spot a cow that reversed towards me in a small alley and would have head-butted me had I not been pulled into a shop doorway for safety!

~ ~ ~

It was a chilly morning at 05:30. However, Allie and I were okay because we were wrapped up in several layers and had blankets over our knees. We were the only two on our sunrise boat tour down on the Ganges River. Not only would we witness the sunrise above the river, but we would also see the ancient city spring into life and Hindus practising their early morning rituals. This is the kind of experience you do not have every day. It was one that I would be content to see only once, not because it wasn't visually or culturally stimulating, but because I do not function well in the early hours.

Thankfully there was a 2-hour break with the opportunity to thaw out, have breakfast, shower and generally recuperate. Allie and I were then guided around the old town, visiting a few temples and learning about Shiva and Varanasi history. This city of pilgrim-drawing spiritual significance where Hinduism originated is one of the holiest of seven sacred cities for Hindus and Jains. It is one of the world's longest continually inhabited cities.

Down at the Manikarnika 'Burning Ghats', we learned about the cycle of life and death. The Hindus believe that if the deceased's ashes are laid in the Ganges river, their soul will attain Moksha meaning an ending to the cycle of rebirth. Varanasi being one of the holier places, with one of the most sacred rivers, minimises the chance of returning as a even a sacred cow or a monkey (although ironically, there seemed to be plenty of those in Varanasi). The Burning Ghats themselves are a surreal place, and one where you question as to whether you should be there. After all, who wants to say farewell to their loved ones with a bunch of gaping mouthed tourists in attendance. Feeling uncomfortable, Allie and I did not linger long amongst the heat of the fires - the smoke - the ashes - and bodies swathed in cloth and flames. We listened to our guide explain the process and then retreated to the Blue Lassi for a reassuring coffee, pear and apple Lassi.

After Allie left the next day, the realisation hit me that I would have to find my way around on my own, and so it was I came up with a new plan. I drew a map as I walked along, marking various landmarks that I would recognise. With my knowledge of where the Blue Lassi was and the Ganpati Restaurant, what could possibly go wrong? However, I was not so distraught being on my own after Allie left. Because who should walk into my hostel that evening, but Peter, who I had met back in Kolkata. He greeted me with "of all the guest houses, in all the world"! Of course, it was only appropriate to introduce Peter to the culinary delights of the Blue Lassi. We were accompanied the next day by a lovely couple of Varanasi newbies, Brett and Anna. They were all enthralled at the goings-on in the bustling alleys around us whilst I sipped on a chocolate, banana and saffron lassi.

We could not linger too long, though, as we had some sights to see, and off we went to the Bharat Mata Temple. This temple is unique because it had not been built for a deity but is considered a shrine to 'Mother India' (Bharat Mata). Also noteworthy was the massive marble topographical map of India without any man-made boundaries or lines. To finish the day off, the four of us (Peter, Brett, Anna and I) were back down on the sacred Ganges river, this time for a sunset boat tour. Aside from the beauty of the sun lowering down with hues of reds, oranges and golds on the buildings lining the ghats and the river, we sat in awe as we watched the 'Ganga Aarti' (River Worship). This elaborate ceremony is staged nightly at the Dasaswamedh Ghat. It comprises conch shell blowing, waving of incense sticks and large flaming lamps, and young 'Pandits' (Priests). We witnessed a magnificent spectacle and thought our boat tour well worthwhile (ours was booked through our hostel).

We celebrated our visual delight afterwards in a restaurant, listening to a sitar player, with a teapot of lager, yes you read that right! Alcohol is frowned upon and banned within a specific range of temples. Therefore, local establishments come up with creative ways to sate the tourist palette. Being one to follow the pack on occasion, I joined in with the celebratory teapot of beer. Still, I was mindful of respecting the local cultural beliefs after that. It was easy in the case of meat which is also banned in certain areas in Varanasi, being a vegetarian.

~ ~ ~

The next day Brett, Anna and I were to take the longest 10 kilometres of my life, with a rally driving tuk-tuk driver! How we ever got to Sarnath alive or without accident, I will never know. To give him his due, the driver's reactions must have been very quick with the speed and the weaving in and out. Even Dinky Doo looked a little bit nauseous after the journey. We found it much easier and safer to walk between the various historical sites in Sarnath.

Our "to see" list was the Sarnath Museum, the Archaeological gardens, Buddha Temple, Thai Temple, and the Digambar Jain Temple. The Jain Temple stood out the most for me, not so much due to this place's deep historical and spiritual significance, but mainly because we got chatting with a Jainist monk. Until this point, I had decided that if I were to adopt a religion, it could well be Jainism. This was due to having seen a programme about Jainism on television a few years back. It explained that the welfare of all creatures is at the essence of their beliefs. They even filmed a Jainist monk sweep tiny ants away from the temple entrance, so they could live to see another day.

Unlike the Jainist monk who stood before us, the tv programme had not explained that women are lower in the order of Jainism. Simply put, to achieve the Jainist principle of 'aparigraha', you need to absolve of all worldly goods, including clothing. It is acceptable for the male to be naked whilst on the path to asceticism, but not so for the female, where nudity is deemed inappropriate. Therefore, by wearing clothing, the woman cannot obtain true 'asceticism ' and cannot be as complete a Jainist as the male. I am not saying this is the view of all Jainists; however, that is what I was told that day. So for me, being a Jainist was now out - either I would have to go about life naked or be an underdog, and neither seemed appealing. I can vouch for the nudity of the male Jainists, as the monk took great delight in showing us photos of himself naked!

After being templed out for the day and surviving a crazy arsed drive back to Varanasi, we took a walk to the Blue Lassi as it was Brett and Anna's last day. I was sad to see them go but did not mind so much whilst guzzling my banana, kiwi and pear Lassi.

~ ~ ~

Whether it was because I was now on my own to go sightseeing, after such great company, or because it was another temple, the next day, I was not so delighted by the Golden Temple as I thought I could have been. The "Kashi Vishwanath" (or Golden Temple) is one of the most famous and divine temples dedicated to Lord Shiva. This is a temple that devoted Hindus would try to visit at least once in their lifetime. I felt like it was the least serene temple I had ever come across as it was noisy and crowded. I must have been there the day that all pilgrims also decided to visit. I hoped for their sakes they found or experienced what they were seeking amongst the mayhem.

To set the scene, imagine yourself walking through numerous small alleyways rammed with people, cows and monkeys peeing from above. You get near your destination (the temple). As you do so, the alleyways become smaller and more tightly packed, and the heat is unbearable. You have to go through police and soldier checks in a queue with hundreds of other people. You are then required to go through passport control with the police, where you are packed into an office with eighty other people and space for only twenty! On top of that, your passport is taken from you, and you wonder will you get it back, or will you get the right one back? You pass through one more security check. At this point, you are still not in the temple, but cannot fault them for their scrutiny.

I did not initially go straight into the main temple area, as I could not cope with the heat, the crowds and the chaos. I miraculously found a quiet spot in a small temple and attempted to get some peace and my head back in order. It was not long before I was approached by a man who asked what I was doing. He could have been plain-clothed police (perhaps a customs officer from the airport!), I could have been somewhere I shouldn't be, or he could have been genuinely concerned for me. "I do not know" was my reply to him, and I honestly didn't, and that was enough for him.

I mustered up the energy to join the long queue to enter the main temple. I noticed that the line was heading towards a small statue sat at the end of the building. Nearing the figure, I was pulled from the queue by security - I asked myself, "what had I done now?" I had done nothing and was being given preference to view the statue. I usually do not like this kind of thing; I believe it is only fair to wait my turn. However, it transpired that the security/guide had wanted to give me information about the statue. I would have been in the way and held the queue up if I had stayed in line. I was grateful for the information given to me about the seated statue, the main deity of the temple known as 'Vishvanatha' or 'Vishveshvara', and the profoundly rooted importance of the temple to the visiting pilgrims. I felt honoured to be there and humbled, too, as I had been able to view something that many others wouldn't. I reflected on this later over a kiwi, mango and mint Lassi.

~ ~ ~

I don't know if I had overeaten, or had supped too many Lassis or whether I had caught a disease, but the next day I was ill, very ill. I was sick throughout the day, except for when I was sleeping. This cycle continued until around 04:00, and then the diarrhoea kicked in! All I could do was rest up and take tablets to calm my stomach, as I was supposed to be travelling the next day.

The following day, I woke up lying to myself that I was feeling okay and just about well enough to undertake the trek ahead of me. Lugging my backpack around was not too much of a problem as I was helped to the train, so I settled myself for the journey to Allahabad. Well, that is what was supposed to happen.

Some elderly Indian guys sat around me on the train took to protecting me. They protested when the ticket inspector charged me extra - apparently, the ticket price had gone up since I purchased my ticket. When the guy who sold me a newspaper did not give me my change, they shouted at him until he did. I, meanwhile, was nonchalant; I was still too ill to care. Their interference became overbearing when they decided that I had to get off the moving train! They told me that the train was not stopping at Allahabad due to the Kumbh Mela festival, and I must get off. The fun began when we reached Cheowky station, and the four men bundled me down the train corridor whilst one of them phoned my accommodation to tell my driver to meet me at Cheowky station as I was on the platform. Except I wasn't, and the train had already left that station. This didn't deter the men from opening the train door and trying to get me off! I was clinging on for dear life in the open train doorway until the train stopped at red lights.

One of the older men jumped down with his bag, caught my backpack thrown by the others, so I followed suit, jumping onto the trackside. The signalman and about eight curious onlookers came over to us; I could not understand what was occurring as I did not speak fluent Hindi. I just stood there with my backpack on the stony track, with a lot of shouting and gesturing going on whilst my stomach continued churning over. It was decided that a young guy on a motorcycle (and one helmet) would take me and my luggage and Dinky Doo to Cheowky station. Except he didn't! He decided he was taking me to my accommodation in Allahabad. Somehow we squashed onto his bike with my luggage, the latter taking up most of the space. I wished he had chosen a different route, but no, he decided to drive along next to the trains, along the rocky and stony train track. It resulted in my whole body vibrating as we rode over stone after stone and the sickness and diarrhoea wanting to resurface. I will never forget that experience; it is ingrained in my memory due to the pain of having to hold everything in!

There was some respite when we arrived in a small town where the driver stopped to ask a police officer directions to the Kumbh Mela Ashram. I took the opportunity to jump off the bike in case I was being abducted, but the police officer promptly shouted at me to get back on. I was flabbergasted but guessed I must at least be safe.

Amazingly I arrived safely at the Ashram. The motorbike driver and I sat at reception to get our breath back. He had not asked for any payment, and reception informed me he was a good man doing me a favour. Although they acknowledged it might have been a bit scary for me, that was an understatement! After rewarding the driver, the receptionist took me by the arm and led me to my room. I asked for the nearest one to the toilet! The rooms were more like square boxes joined in a block, one next to the other. The room contained just a double bed and a small table. I did not care; I just needed to sleep.

~ ~ ~

And that is pretty much what I mostly did for the next couple of days, sleep. I was still sick, could not eat, and was generally drowsy. At one point, I remember lying at the foot of the bed, lolling over the edge, too weak to move fully back onto the bed. The door was ajar as I needed air, and when the staff spotted me, they reported me to the company's owner.

It was not long before the owner came to the door and decided I must go to hospital. I recall two young ladies, one on either side of me, holding me up and walking me to a car to take me to the hospital. I could not argue as I was too weak. I soon perked up when the doctor told me she would admit me into the hospital, and I would be put onto an intravenous drip. Well, I was having none of that! To be able to leave, I had to promise to eat and to drink lots of water. I would have promised anything just to get out of there, and so I gave my oath.

Back at the Ashram, I laid on the bed with a supply of water. I had promised to eat, but what did they bring me, an entire Indian spicy meal with rice! It really was not the kind of thing you would eat to improve the welfare of your stomach. I waited until they had gone, set aside a bit of rice to eat, and threw the rest outside someone else's hut.

It was lucky that I had plenty of sleep the previous two nights, as there was a ferocious storm. The rain lashed down, the thunder roared, and the lightning crackled loudly. I heard a commotion and banging on my door. The roofs had collapsed on some of the dormitories, and mine could be next. That definitely woke me up as I dashed through the pouring rain to reception to spend the next few hours with others in the same predicament, waiting for the storm to pass.

~ ~ ~

With both myself and the roof intact the following day, I braved it out to the breakfast area. The Ashram was set out with many basic blocks of rooms but with an extensive buffet area where we could eat our meals. The buffet was the centre of the universe for us. It was very communal where people from all nationalities would meet and socialise. Whilst eating my breakfast (I managed some dry toast), I chatted with Penny, a photographer from the U.S.A. She offered to take me over to the Kumbh Mela. I decided it was time to get out.

I was with thirty million other people who had come here to Allahabad for the Maha Kumbh Mela. The festival of Kumbh Mela takes place once every twelve years. It rotates between religious locations:

Haridwar, Nashik, Ujjain and Allahabad. The Kumbh Mela is epitomised by its pilgrims, many of whom would have walked tens of miles to get there with their families. They come to enjoy gregarious entertainment, religious shrines, processions, food stalls, crowds, chaos, smiles, charity, and good nature.

Their ultimate goat at the festival for the pilgrim is to bathe in the sacred river. Allahabad is believed to be the most auspicious of the four religious sites for the Kumbh Mela. It is on the confluence of the "Triveni Sangam" (three rivers) - the Ganges, Yamuna and Sarasvati. It is believed that bathing at this Sangam is a means to 'prayascitta', which cleanses them of their sins, and atones them for past mistakes. I wouldn't be able to swim far or long enough to get rid of mine!

Penny and I spent hours walking around the festival site, taking photos of events, crowds, the general scene, the unusual, and families wanting their pictures taken with us. The whole area was enormous, and a lot was going on; it was mind-boggling trying to absorb it all. We watched the entertainment, stalls with throngs of crowds around them, food stalls with all kinds of local foods imaginable, monks and the poor being fed, boats taking people out onto the rivers, and women washing their saris hanging them to dry on the wooden poles. Dinky Doo took it all in his stride as usual, with his little head poking out of my daypack, watching the world go by.

At one point, Penny and I got called over by security, and they allowed us into an area by the water, which was closed off. We were encouraged to take photos of two men with an entourage enjoying their reverential dip into the water. We were informed they were famous, it meant nothing to us, but we obliged and took photos. Then darkness descended, and it was time for us to return to camp. We heartily shared stories around the buffet tables as we were all excited about what to expect over the next few days. They say it is a small world, and so it was, for at my table was a guy from Southend, my home town and he worked in an office just a 3-minute walk from my house!

I decided to mix things up the next day and walked to the right out of our Ashram camp, opposite everyone else going to the central Kumbh

Mela. I found an isolated Ashram, where a very famous guru stays. I was shown around by a monk, and then we sat and drank tea. I felt very relaxed, and my body was well on the way to recovering. I needed all the energy I could muster, for the following day would be the main event for processions and bathing in the Ganges. It would be a long but culturally exciting day.

Penny and I met at 01:00 the following morning and made our way to the Maha Kumbh Mela. We spent quite a bit of time finding the ideal spot to view the processions and were finally happy with our site behind a wooden barrier about two-thirds of the way along the procession route. We watched the Sadhus (holy people of Hinduism and Jainism who have renounced ordinary life) and the Babas (the religious fathers).

However, if we thought the procession of the Babas and Sadhus was impressive, unbeknownst to us, it was going to become even more so. It was already 07:00, and we thought the procession had finished as nothing more seemed to be going on. We made to leave our area but were advised to stop by three young Indian men, who told us the main event had not even started, and we were to join them as they were from the media. Now, Penny had a professional camera that would pass the grade, but I only had my little compact camera. With any stretch of the imagination, I could not see how the soldiers would believe we were with them- yet somehow they did. And so it was, we hopped behind the media barrier- to watch a procession of 5,000 Naked Sadhus! I can honestly say I have never seen anything like it in my life. There were thousands of men; bodies painted an ashen grey, most naked, and some with a few strategically placed ornate garments. Some Sadhus were dancing, or on horses, or waving their spears and tridents into the air. All were heading towards the Sangam.

Sometimes, maybe I should just say "No", but I didn't and followed the pack on this occasion. As the last of the naked Sadhus paraded by, the media carried on snapping away and ran alongside them, still taking photos. We followed. There were now thousands of people in a relatively small area down by the side of the river. During the parade, the Sadhus had not minded photos being taken. What occurred next clearly demonstrated they were no longer going to entertain being the subject of paparazzi. I can still clearly visualise what followed; it all seemed to happen in slow motion and yet was so quick. I spotted a wild-eyed Sadhu squatting on the ground, then suddenly he had leapt up roaring, which started off several other Sadhus. These men came running at us with their spears - in that split second we ran, we literally ran for our lives! At the same time, running and shouting at us were the soldiers with their guns; I was so scared until I realised they had run to us to protect us from being impaled. Penny and I and the media men became separated in the melee, and it took some time for the soldiers to help us find each other. Hidden in amongst the crowds, we just looked at each other unable to stop shaking. I burst into hysterical nervous laughter. Had I really just been attacked by a naked sadhu wielding his trident?

The soldiers wanted to keep us out of further trouble. They took us to the water's edge to watch and take photos of the people who were being allowed to take a brief dip in the Sangam. I didn't particularly want to take pictures of them but did not dare refuse. I snapped away while balanced against a small wooden pole they had positioned me against until my time was up and I was yanked away again. It was nothing different from what the pilgrims were experiencing. No matter how young or old, they were allocated a few brief seconds in their sacred water before being yanked straight back out again. But they did not mind; each one emerged from the water wet and with a big smile.

Ah, the Kumbh Mela, my final observations: bright colours, police and soldiers working hard to keep control, pilgrims walking miles barefoot, pilgrim devotion, the smell of urine/poo, dust, atmosphere, vastness, noise, chaos, calmness, smiles and millions of people in one place. Where else would you find so many foreigners, middle-class Indians, and lower classes (or castes) all mingled together? Where free food was distributed to the poor, locals gave rice and money to beggars, and everyone intermingled having the same purpose for being there? I guess, for me, the Kumbh Mela truly signified the India I had imagined, and I felt honoured and humbled to be part of the experience. I was sweeping away the negative preconceptions I had been fed back in England; I was seeing past them to a multi-faceted India.

~ ~ ~

Two days later, I was on my way to Delhi. I was apprehensive about going to the train station in Allahabad. A footbridge there had collapsed only a day earlier, and 36 people had died (with many more injured). Train stations can be busy at the best of times, but with 100 million people expected over the festival's 2-month period, it was inevitable that the train stations would be overwhelmed with pilgrims and tourists. There was never a shortage of kind locals ready to help me find my train and carriage as I wove my way through a sea of people sitting on the platforms. I found my 1st class sleeper carriage and settled in for the night. However, during the early morning hours, I became very unsettled by the train's speed and wobbling on the tracks. Please don't start my stomach off again! My concerns were confirmed the following morning by my carriage compadres. They, too, had been perturbed by the speed and the train's rocking on the track believing the train could very well de-rail. These two businessmen often travelled on trains, but this had been a worrying experience even for them.

I had prepared myself for Delhi as best I could. I had to balance between letting go of previous preconceptions, being more open-minded and being safe. I had been forewarned about train station scams where luggage could be stolen, and so my backpack was duly chained to my waist. I had purposely booked a hotel within a 5-minute walk of the train station. That way, I would not have to enlist the services of anyone that may employ any of the various scamming techniques. It did not stop them from trying, offering to take my luggage (was that literally?) and expensive tuk-tuk rides. I ignored them, I was on a mission to reach my hotel just a short distance away, and off I strode.

I naively braved it out the next day, heading to Connaught Place, but walking along the road alone was a fatal mistake. The sweltering heat was insufferable, but not as intolerable or frustrating as being approached by several men. I don't know their intentions, but I doubt by some questionable behaviours, they were all honourable. So I retreated to my hotel. I decided the way to go was to use the Couchsurfing meet and greet amenity, where locals would go out with you for the day to introduce you to their city. This worked well for the next two days, as I was escorted by locals, which gave me an insight into the places we visited and helped stave off unwanted advances.

I was, therefore, able to visit Connaught Place, where I mainly wanted to see the large white building and park, as opposed to the shopping experience. Photos taken, and it was onto the Red Fort with its 75 feet high red sandstone walls, the foundations of which were first laid back in 1638. My next port of call, the architectural delight of the red sandstone Humayun Tomb of the Mughal Emperor, goes back even further, having been built in 1570 and was considered to have inspired the design of the Taj Mahal.

No trip to Delhi would be complete without a visit to the Taj Mahal. And so it was, at 05:00 the next day, I was up and ready and on the bus heading to Agra, the home of the Taj Mahal. There were only two westerners on the bus, which was packed full, an American guy called Barry and me. As we neared Agra, the two of us were hauled off the bus and told we would be going ahead of the others. We could not understand why but did as we were told.

The Taj Mahal, one of the New Seven Wonders of the World, was built as a memorial by the Mughal emperor Shah Jahan who reigned from 1628-58 to his wife, Mumtaz Mahal. Husband and wife had been inseparable since their marriage in 1612. The emperor was inconsolable after his wife's death whilst she was giving birth in 1631, and hence this magnificent shrine to her was born. Little did he know back then how many millions of people would come to visit this unique architectural achievement. I was one of the 7- 8 million people to attend that year. I tried to get some artistic photos, and I managed to get a few where Dinky Doo's head blocked out the crowds behind. Naturally, I wanted the picture of me sitting on the bench where Princess Diana previously sat, trying to emulate the same serene pose.

It was after leaving the Taj Mahal that the tour took a strange turn of events. Barry had to depart early to get a train, so I was left on my own in the guide's hands. He took me to a jewellery shop where the owner showed me the silverware for sale and then came up with a too good to be true offer. If I took £600 worth of jewellery back to England, the owner would meet me in London a few weeks later, and I would earn £300 for handling them. I did not understand the plan and could not figure out why he didn't take them himself. Needless to say, the owner was pretty bereft when I left empty-handed.

Back on the bus returning to Delhi, I was placed at the rear of the bus with a large group of young Indian men, a few of whose wives were sitting halfway along the bus. These guys and their wives were so amiable, we chatted the whole journey, and when we had a couple of more tour stops, they accompanied me around the sites. I am indebted to them for their graciousness and insistence that the driver drop me at the top of the road for my hotel. The driver had previously ignored my requests. It was late; it was so late that it was the early hours of the morning. It had been a long day, and I slept well. Now, the excitement of India was over; I was to make my way back home via Amsterdam… the trip wasn't over just yet!

~ ~ ~

Top Tip: You just need to embrace some countries and take them for what they are, and India is one such place. Shrug off any negative preconceptions, and immerse yourself in all that the country has to offer. Be aware of the poverty, but also the guidelines on giving and charity.
*Please make yourself aware of child beggars; they can be subject to kidnapping and child trafficking. Unfortunately, the more that is given to them, the more the cycle of poverty continues.

A Quiet Street in Kolkata

Mallick Ghat Flower Market

Dinky Doo at the Ganpati

Varanasi Cow Wanting a Ride

Kumbh Mela Festival 2013

Pilgrims Going to Kumbh Mela

Taking a Dip in the Sangam

Naked Sadhus at Kumbh Mela

AMSTERDAM 2013

A Day Around & Around the River

The Netherlands translates as "the lower countries", as it is the lowest-lying country in Europe (approximately a quarter of the country lies below sea level), and is why it is built on eleven million poles. Who knew? Many people have known this country as Holland; however, it has not been proper to refer to The Netherlands as Holland, colloquially or officially, since 2020. It is a small country, but ironically is a nation of the tallest people in the world. This could be due to what they eat, for the Dutch are the healthiest population in the world. The Dutch are also the most active in Europe, which could be explained due to there being more bicycles than people! They may be healthy, yet it was here that gin was first invented in the 16th century before being exported to us Brits. Of course, there is also the Dutch beer, with The Netherlands being the second biggest beer exporter globally.

Amsterdam is both the capital and most populated city, primarily known for its world-class museums such as the Van Gogh Museum, the red light district, 'coffee shops' and 165 canals (of which there are 100 kilometres). Not so well known are the Torture Museum, Micropia (world's first zoo for microbes) and ' De Poezenboot' - a houseboat just for cats!

Having left the sticky heat of Delhi, I arrived in a cold, snowy Amsterdam with the hope that one of my friends from home had managed to find me a thick roll neck jumper. However, there seemed to be an international shortage of anything warm and wool-like. I could not find anything in India (well, to be fair, the average heat was 40 degrees, so why would there be anything?). Apparently, the girls could not find anything back in England either.

That was the least of my problems; I first had to get through Customs

Control at the airport. Of course, I got stopped; it was becoming par for the course. I was questioned whether I had been asked to carry any heroin or any other kind of drugs. I indignantly replied that I most certainly had not, and I would not entertain such behaviour. The officer apologised, and I was on my way. Well, I was almost on my way. I could not get the ticket machine to work at the train station, so a kind Irish couple gave me some Euros to put in. I was the proud owner of a new ticket which I clutched in my hands. I realised afterwards that I had been trying to put Turkish Lira into the ticket machine.

Talking of hands, I then became a hand model! Yes, I was approached by a young man who filmed my hand holding my paper ticket. Somewhat random, you might think (so did I), but it transpired that the train company were phasing out paper tickets by the end of the year. They would then replace them with plastic cards, and wanted a memento. I was famous already (well, my paw was), and I hadn't even been in the country one hour. With my newfound fame, I reached my hostel, and there were the girls- Michelle, Ann and Sharon, ready and waiting for me to spend the next few days celebrating my birthday. A question had crossed my mind about how I would feel meeting up with old friends after making so many new acquaintances and having been away so long. But one look at their grinning faces, and we launched into non-stop chatter over a few bottles of wine, my concern dissipated.

What a great end to my trip; this would be a blast, although I was a tad wary, due to my previous birthday experience in Amsterdam. It had been my 30th Birthday, and it was supposed to be a special occasion, but as you may have guessed by now, it was not going to be straightforward- it didn't even come close to that. It was just one mishap after another. It all started before we even left England. After putting a lot of effort in to get twelve of us free ferry and coach tickets to Amsterdam, the other person on their 30th Birthday and seven others failed to turn up at the coach station on our day of departure. They had all been celebrating the night before and overslept with hangovers. So only four of us merrily set off Amsterdam bound.

We were sitting on the coach going through Belgium, and I happened to look at our ticket. To my horror, the hotel we were booked in was in Paris! After some frantic phone calls, we managed to get the company to book us into their Amsterdam hotel. We got to the drop off point late at night and had no idea which way to go. We walked a long way around the city of Amsterdam- finally ending up back at our coach stop where we had been dropped off. We had lost an hour by then, and so we gave in and got in a taxi to the Hotel Hansa. The driver literally drove us two minutes round the corner, and there was our hotel! To really rub salt in the wound, all we kept seeing for the next three days were trams with big posters on the side advertising our hotel. I had never taken drugs. However, having heard of the famous cafés with coffee and 'spacecake', I wanted to celebrate my Birthday by trying this piece of culinary delight for the first time. It was not to be, but not for want of trying. I still cannot fathom how there seemed to be a city shortage of this allegedly common staple each time I asked.

~ ~ ~

I was more concerned with taking in the culture on this latest birthday trip (pardon the pun). The four of us trudged around in the snow visiting the markets; I was still on the hunt for a jumper. We sat on a heated canal boat tour to view the famous sites along the rivers' banks, and to thaw out. It was so lovely and warm inside the canal boats that we spent most of the day on them. Another reason we spent so much time on there was because we had not worked out the routes very well and seemed to go around in circles, viewing the same sites repeatedly! Aside from that merry-go-round, we went out drinking, visiting the sex museums, and wandering through the Red Light district in the evenings. Two of the group members who will not be named and shamed took it one step further to go and see a sex show. My birthday night was an exceptional affair and blurred in with all our other escapades. Perhaps I ended up posing in a red light shop window or a sex museum? I hope not!

On our last day, we split ways, with Michelle and I taking in one last day of culture. We ducked in and out of the falling snow by going into the Tulip Museum, the Cheese Museum, and the Magna shopping centre. By sheer chance, we spotted a large doorway in the corner of Dam Square. It turned out to be the Royal Palace, and it became one of the highlights of our trip. Michelle and I thoroughly enjoyed our walk around there; it was so amazingly spectacular. In particular, I loved the walkway with 3D effect with the mirrors where they seemed to go into infinity. We learnt that Queen Beatrix would be abdicating imminently. She was handing the throne over to her son, Willem-Alexander, who would be the first King since 1890.

In the meantime, the other two ladies had decided they wanted to try out the very same kind of cake that I had wanted to try some years before on my 30th Birthday. They had more success. I could tell this by their continual giggling that evening and the non-stop chatter. That was before the adverse effects kicked in, leaving two very drowsy, not feeling well ladies.

Our Amsterdam jaunt was over, and we were heading back to England, having had some eye-opening moments and giggles. Yet there was a part of me that was apprehensive about going home, I felt it would be strange back there after all I had been through in what seemed like a long time away. So there was something comforting about having my friends accompany me home on the last leg of my 4-month journey. It had seemed a lifetime ago that I had embarked on this trip, making accquaintances/friends along the way. I had learned many travel and life lessons and immersed myself in the wide range of cultures I passed through. I was carrying home a backpack of new experiences and insights, along with my faithful Dinky Doo. My friends had reunited with a newer me, but one I felt would fit back comfortably in our social circle back home. I had many memorable moments and mishaps to share with them from my travels over the years. I had been chased by a wild elephant in Africa, gone over the edge of a mountain on a bus in Venezuela, almost drowned there in a deceiving river and had been stranded on a remote jungle island! I had stayed in a treehouse in Turkey, been in a physical fight with a male in Brazil, and challenged myself by climbing a mountain for the first time; I had made it to Everest Base Camp.

I had been privileged to have a baby Panda sit on my knee in China. I crossed the Pacific Ocean to the remote Easter Island, where I met some of the most genuine people, the honu tribe. I had learned that life could be short, for I had almost been killed in a car crash in Poland. I soon cheered up when the hospital staff gave me an x-ray of my afflicted area for my birthday! It taught me to get over myself with the age thing; I was growing older (thankfully) and (hopefully) wiser. I should be grateful that I had reached 40 and was on the way to 50. Long may my travels continue, despite the fear of flying I had somehow developed.

I had subsequently taken the slow road to Australia, via Istanbul, where I had coffee and gold leaf topped cake in a posh hotel; experienced rally jeep driving over the desert dunes in Dubai; and been bitten by a parrot in Malaysia! All of this, and I hadn't yet reached Australia. I had traversed a large portion of Australia, starting along the East Coast where I struggled to snorkel in the Great Barrier Reef, but had held a baby koala and even a slithery snake! I then flew over to Darwin in the mid-North and into Kakadu, where I licked a Lime Ant's bum. Whilst driving deep through the middle of Oz to the South, I got to cuddle the cutest baby joey and deliver mail with the postman far out into the outback desert. And the icing on the cake - I had been on the beach in Port Douglas witnessing a spectacular sunrise followed immediately by the very purpose of my journey - the total solar eclipse.

It had been a quick hop skip and a jump over to New Zealand where I travelled from the South Island to the North Island all on $1 fares, visiting friends (some who remembered me and others who didn't), and hiked a mountain unprepared, thinking I was going for a stroll. And finally, there was frustrating yet lovable India. The sticky heat, the incredible people, the noise, the calm, the tastes of exotic foods, the bright colours - all invading your senses. I had arrived in Kolkata, where the Customs Officers had tried to dupe me. I had immersed myself in the spirituality of Varanasi (with a few Blue Lassis). I experienced Allahabad where the pilgrims came to dip in the holy river

- whilst a naked Sadhu chased me with a spear! I felt I had experienced a journey of learning and seeing, both physically and spiritually. Would I do this kind of journey again? Yes, of course, I would, and I have. That's a whole new book! Could I possibly learn and experience more in future travels? Would there be more challenging situations and adventures? I hoped so! I would say I am a living example of someone who travelled solo (but not feeling alone), facing challenges and mishaps along the way but proved that these things could be overcome. With true grit and determination, if it is a genuine calling for you, then you can go out there and do this too.

~ ~ ~

Top Tip: Some element of planning/research is preferable for a lengthy trip. This will help save time as you make your way around your chosen countries. It doesn't have to be thoroughly planned; I have met many travellers who prefer to make it up as they go along. This needs to be balanced with not losing time when you are away. For example, searching for accommodation upon arrival in a city and everything is booked up, perhaps due to a significant event in that area. I prefer to be out seeing and doing things rather than wasting time doing something I could have done back on a cold winter's evening back in England. Be open-minded in how you travel and where you travel - you will get a long way.

My Birthday in Amsterdam   Dinky Doo Cruising on the River

THE END?

No, not at all. It was the beginning of a new chapter, one where I would not go back to my old life of a stressful job and being just another cog in the wheel. I had fought for a career break before I left England to go on my epic 4-month trip, but I knew deep down I didn't want to work for that organisation by the time I returned. I needed to sit down and work on my life plan (something I would recommend, it can always be revisited/adapted). The basis of my future life plan to aspire to and achieve had been the same for many years: I wanted to live in England for a portion of the year and travel the world in the remainder. I now had to be strong, confident and work out exactly how I would carry out this plan. I had a few properties under my belt, and with a few more, I worked out that I could travel on a budget, as long as I cut luxuries back in England. With my passion for chasing total solar eclipses, I now had an excuse to go to many places I would not have otherwise, and all in the company of my faithful companion Dinky Doo.

And what of the elusive total solar eclipse? I had travelled from England where I met the Professor and then experienced a 'first love' eclipse; to Africa where I only saw a partial eclipse whilst drunk on a houseboat and talking to a monkey! Then there was the amphitheatre in Turkey, where I saw a spectacular eclipse in the company of a local family, and China, a clouded eclipse and no tidal river bore. I was subjected to the festival of hell on Easter Island but rewarded by a stunning total eclipse on the beach, all whilst making lifelong friends. And finally, Australia, the most well researched in the early morning hours total eclipse, a sudden surprise out of the clouds, on a 4-month trip that would change my life. My affinity with eclipses evolved each time I had one more under my belt. I believe the eclipses had both a direct and indirect impact on me and my spiritual development. Yes, I was drawn in by the magic of the total solar eclipse! And there was more to come...

APPENDIX I

Sample for a Useful Information Template

Passport number: Passport Expiry date:
NI No: NHS number:
Insurance Company: Policy number:
Start Date: Exp:
Ins Claim Tel:
Driving Licence No: Expiry:

DOCTOR:
Tel:
Vaccinations: Blood Group:

British Embassy in Country of Travel-   British Consulate -
Address:
Telephone:

Santander Tel No. If card Lost/Stolen:
Barclays Visa Card Telephone number to ring if card is Lost/Stolen:
Barclays Visa Card No:
Nationwide Visa Card No:
Santander Visa Card No:

Card Pin Numbers:

Next of Kin:
Name:
Relationship to You:
Address: Telephone:

My Email Address:

APPENDIX II

TRIP COSTS SPREADSHEET

Destination	Food/ Drink	Transport / Sights	Sights	Tips	Accom	Total
Day 1 -Date						
Day 2						
Day 3						
Day 4						
Day 5						
Day 6						
Day 7						
Day 8						
Day 9						
Day 10						
Day 11						
Day 12						
Day 13						
Day 14						
Day 15						
Day 16						
Day 17						
Day 18						
Day 19						
Day 20						
Day 21						
Day 22						
Day 23						
Day 24						

Printed in Great Britain
by Amazon